# Cheating

# Cheating

## *Ethics in Everyday Life*

DEBORAH L. RHODE

Oxford University Press is a department of the University of Oxford. It furthers the University's objective of excellence in research, scholarship, and education by publishing worldwide. Oxford is a registered trade mark of Oxford University Press in the UK and certain other countries.

Published in the United States of America by Oxford University Press
198 Madison Avenue, New York, NY 10016, United States of America.



Library of Congress Cataloging-in-Publication Data
Names: Rhode, Deborah L., author.
Title: Cheating : ethics in everyday life / Deborah L. Rhode.
Description: Oxford [UK] ; New York : Oxford University Press, 2018. |
Includes bibliographical references and index.
Identifiers: LCCN 2017030282 | ISBN 9780190672423 (hardback) |
ISBN 9780190672447 (epub)
Subjects: LCSH: Law and ethics. | Cheating. |
BISAC: LAW / Ethics & Professional Responsibility. |
LAW / Jurisprudence. | SOCIAL SCIENCE / General.
Classification: LCC K247.6 .R46 2017 |
DDC 174/.3—dc23
LC record available at https://lccn.loc.gov/2017030282

1 3 5 7 9 8 6 4 2

Printed by Sheridan Books, Inc., United States of America

*For Eun Sze*

# CONTENTS

*Acknowledgments* ix

1. Introduction 1
2. Cheating in Sports 19
3. Cheating in Organizations 37
4. Cheating on Taxes 61
5. Cheating in Academia and Plagiarism in Professional Settings 75
6. Copyright Infringement 93
7. Cheating in Insurance and Mortgages 101
8. Cheating in Marriage 113
9. Conclusion 133

*Notes* 141
*Index* 197

# ACKNOWLEDGMENTS

This book owes many debts. I am deeply grateful to David McBride at Oxford University Press, who supported and improved this project from the outset. I am also indebted to Joseph Bankman, John Coffee, Mark Lemley, David Luban, Daniel Luban, Robert MacCoun, and Bradley Wendel, who offered insightful comments and suggestions. The staff of the Stanford Law Library made superb reference assistance constantly available. Special thanks go to Leizel Ching, Sean Kaneshiro, Marion Miller, Sonia Moss, Rich Porter, Sarah Reis, Sergio Stone, Beth Williams, George Wilson, and Alex Zhang. The book is dedicated to Eun Sze, who provided invaluable research and manuscript assistance on this and countless other projects. Finally, I owe my greatest debt to my husband, Ralph Cavanagh, whose support and editorial guidance has made this book and so much else possible.

# Cheating

1

# Introduction

Cheating is deeply embedded in everyday life. Costs attributable to its most common forms total close to a trillion dollars annually in the United States alone.[1] Part of the problem is that many individuals fail to see such behavior as a problem. "Everyone does it" is a common rationalization and one that comes uncomfortably close to the truth. That perception is also self-perpetuating. The more that individuals believe that cheating is widespread, the easier it becomes to justify. That is how cultures of dishonesty take root.

The recent election of Donald Trump is a case study in Americans' indifference to cheating. A steady drumbeat of disclosures about fraud, illegal self-dealing, and stiffing contractors by Trump organizations did little to dislodge his support.[2] After his election, Trump paid $25 million to settle some of the most notorious claims that Trump University had cheated its students and misled them about his own involvement in its instruction.[3] Only a third of Americans thought he was honest and trustworthy.[4] Close to 63 million voted for him anyway.

Whether or not Americans are cheating more, they appear to be worrying about it less. As researchers note, what is most notable about analysis of the problem is "how little there is of it."[5] Few efforts have been made to "connect the dots" between different forms of cheating and "see them for what they represent."[6]

This book aims to fill that gap. It offers the only recent comprehensive account of cheating in everyday life and the strategies necessary to address it. This introductory chapter offers a brief overview of the definition and scope of cheating, its most common causes, and the most promising responses. Because cheating is highly situational, subsequent chapters drill down on its most common forms: sports (Chapter 2), organizations (Chapter 3), taxes (Chapter 4), academia (Chapter 5), copyright infringement (Chapter 6), insurance and mortgages (Chapter 7), and marriage (Chapter 8). A final chapter (Chapter 9) offers concluding thoughts about common themes and reform efforts.

## What Constitutes Cheating

The *Oxford English Dictionary* defines cheating as "fraud, deceit, and swindling;" other dictionary definitions include acting dishonestly, unfairly, or in violation of a rule in order to gain an advantage.[7] Although straightforward in theory, the concept blurs in practice. Cheating is what theorists consider a "fuzzy set," with degrees of resemblance among various forms of misconduct. Because notions of unfairness are baked into the concept, that raises the question of whether acts that can be morally justified constitute cheating as commonly understood.

Moral philosophy has given surprisingly little attention to that issue. As Bernard Gert notes, "Cheating is often taken as a paradigm of an immoral act; thus it is somewhat surprising that the concept of cheating has been almost completely neglected by philosophers."[8] There is, however, a rich literature on dishonesty, which is a core element in cheating. Contemporary philosophers generally reject Immanuel Kant's position that honesty is a moral absolute demanding strict adherence regardless of the circumstances.[9] Some lies, such as "It's lovely to see you," "fool no one and are not intended to."[10] These "white lies" involve small stakes and are generally viewed as "social virtue[s]," not actual deceptions.[11] They typically foster more trust than brutal candor.[12] Other misrepresentations, what philosophers term "benevolent lies" or "prosocial lies," seek to benefit the target and occur under exceptional circumstances that provide moral justification for the deception.[13] Plato called these "noble lies."[14] A traditional example, which has appeared in various forms since biblical times, involves a would-be murderer who inquires where his intended victim is hiding.

However, few lies in everyday life fall into these categories.[15] In one representative study in which participants recorded the lies they told daily, only one out of four served primarily to benefit others.[16] To identify situations under which lies are justifiable, Sissela Bok suggests a principle of veracity. It holds that "in any situation where a lie is being considered, one must first seek truthful alternatives." A lie should be a last resort.[17] She also advocates a principle of publicity, similar to one John Rawls articulates. A justification for lying should be capable of public exposure and defense.[18]

Cheating should also be subject to these principles. There are no obvious analogues to the white lie, where good manners or social conventions call for cheating. But there may be circumstances where a disinterested observer would find cheating morally justified. My first legal case was a case in point. I was a Yale law student working in a New Haven legal aid clinic. Our client was on welfare and had a small amount of unreported income that disqualified her from coverage. That income was, however, what enabled her and her child to survive while she competed a dental hygiene training program that promised self-sufficiency. Then as now, welfare payments fell far short of what would pay for food, rent, and utilities; the additional income was essential. But signing documents that misrepresented her income would have constituted welfare fraud. I had made the mistake of asking one too many questions about her situation—a mistake that seasoned poverty attorneys avoided. Fortunately I had to sign no documents and my supervising lawyer was careful not to replicate my mistake. But I was troubled by the issue, and when I raised it with the professor teaching the legal aid clinic, he responded with what I already knew: "That's a hard case." What makes the case hard is the unfairness of the underlying system, a problem that persists. Today benefits available through welfare fall below 50 percent of the poverty line in all states.[19] Survival needs force many families to rely on unreported income, and the system seems to assume that they will do so.

Doubts about the fairness of underlying rules drive cheating in other contexts as well. Take, for example, the struggling single mother who works as a waitress and under-reports her tip income on tax forms because that is the only way to make a living wage. Or consider a doctor who misreports the probable cause of a low-income patient's injury so that the treatment will be reimbursable. These examples are, however, atypical cases. The vast majority of everyday cheating lacks plausible moral justifications. The conduct persists because so many individuals see the benefits as much more tangible, immediate, and compelling than the costs.

Yet as Bernard Gert notes, "if everyone knows that they are allowed to cheat when their particular act of cheating causes no harm, that knowledge may have serious harmful consequences."[20] These consequences are substantial when impartially assessed. They cluster in three categories: harms to the person cheated or other third parties, harms to the cheater, and harms to the general level of social trust.[21] These injuries are cumulative, and hard to reverse. The harms to those cheated are self-evident. By exempting themselves from rules that are generally observed, cheaters gain unfair advantages and third parties pay the cost. The harms to the cheater include the loss in self-respect from the inroads on integrity, and if the cheating is discovered, the damage to reputation and credibility. Cheating also distorts individuals' perceptions of their own abilities; cheaters believe they are smarter than they are and overestimate their performance on future tests.[22] Moreover, with each act of cheating, the next comes more easily. As with lying, the "ability to make moral distinctions can coarsen, and the . . . perceptions of the chances of being caught may warp."[23] The costs to society are of equal concern, however difficult to quantify. Trust and cooperation depend on a general level of truthfulness. As Samuel Johnson once claimed, even devils do not lie to one another; the society of hell is no less dependent on truth than any other.[24]

Given individuals' natural instinct to skew the cost-benefit calculations of cheating in self-serving directions, society needs a general presumption against such misconduct. To justify an exception, a disinterested decision-maker should be able to conclude that the benefits outweigh the harms, that no alternatives to cheating are available, and that if everyone in similar circumstances acted similarly, society would be no worse off. That is a difficult test to meet, and deservedly so. Yet as subsequent chapters make clear, little of Americans' everyday cheating satisfies that standard.

## The Scope of Cheating

Whether measured by dollar costs or by the number of individuals involved, cheating is staggering in scope. The Internal Revenue Service (IRS) estimates the annual losses attributable to income tax evasion at around $450 billion, and other estimates are higher.[25] Those figures do not include state income tax losses, which add many billions more. The U.S. government estimates the cost of illegal downloading of music and videos to total as much as $250 billion per year.[26] Insurance fraud costs somewhere between $120 and $350 billion annually.[27] Estimates of employee theft range from $50 to $200 billion per year.[28] Ordinary Americans are the victims as well as perpetrators of such cheating. Taxpayers who are honest pay thousands more because of taxpayers who are not. Musicians lose millions because of illegal downloads. Consumers pay for business and insurance fraud in the form of increased prices and premiums.

Whether Americans are cheating more than in previous generations is impossible to say; we lack adequate data.[29] But as subsequent chapters indicate, some forms of cheating are on the rise and the aggregate amount of cheating, whether growing or not, is of major concern. Tens of millions of Americans routinely cheat in forms that constitute crimes, such as tax evasion, insurance fraud, piracy of music and videos, workplace pilfering, and in 21 states, adultery.[30] One IRS-sponsored survey concluded that 42 percent of all returns had some understatement of taxable income.[31] In another study, 46 percent of taxpayers reported definitely or probably overdeducting or omitting taxable income on their returns.[32] Research by the American Assembly at Columbia University found that 70 percent of young adults between 18 and 29 had illegally copied or downloaded music or videos, and that almost 30 percent got most of their collections that way.[33] In surveys over the last 15 years, between a third to a half of workers reported observing unethical conduct on the job.[34] A KPMG study found that 21 percent of employees had witnessed a colleague falsifying time or expense reports, and 18 percent had seen a colleague stealing or misappropriating company property.[35] A compilation of various studies found that the average number of students who report cheating in college was 70 percent.[36] In other large-scale research, two-thirds to four-fifths of high school students acknowledge exam misconduct or plagiarism off the Internet, although over 90 percent are satisfied with their ethical conduct.[37] In experimental studies, 30 to 50 percent of participants will cheat for rewards as small as $5 or less.[38] Surveys of cheating in marriage find that between 19 and 23 percent of men and 13 to 19 percent of women report extramarital affairs.[39]

## The Causes and Dynamics of Cheating

Most people assume that unethical behavior such as cheating is attributable to fixed character traits. That assumption is consistent with a widely documented cognitive bias that psychologists label "the fundamental attribution error:" the tendency to overvalue the importance of individual character and undervalue the role of situational factors in shaping behavior.[40] Behavioral ethics research makes clear that this view of consistent, stable traits is to some extent a "figment of our aspirations."[41] Moral conduct is heavily influenced by the social norms, peer behavior, and rewards and penalties applicable in particular contexts. In Hugh Hartshorn and Mark May's classic experiments involving cheating by children, only about 10 percent were always honest or always dishonest when a chance to cheat was presented to them. Most of the children cheated between 20 and 70 percent of the time.[42] Much turned on situational variables, including the amount of surveillance and where the opportunities occurred, whether in homes, schools, or Sunday school. Although subsequent re-evaluation of the data suggested some generality in moral behavior, strong situational influences remained.[43] Among adults, psychologists devising honesty tests to screen prospective employees find that people can be placed in one of three categories. Totally honest, incorruptible people constitute about 10 percent of the population. Totally dishonest people who will cheat in a wide variety of situations account for about 5 percent. The other 85 percent appear basically honest, but will succumb to temptation depending on the situation.[44]

Individuals can be exemplary in some aspects of their lives, and cheat in others. Bernard Ebbers, while head of WorldCom, started each board meeting with a prayer. He led a weekly Bible study class and was a deacon at his church. He also orchestrated one of the largest frauds in American history.[45] Ken Lay, the CEO who oversaw the collapse of Enron due to fraudulent accounting practices, also started business meetings with a prayer. He considered himself highly religious, and spoke often about the importance of considering moral issues when making business decisions.[46] Gary Fairchild, a Chicago lawyer, had a reputation for being ethically fastidious and for even questioning his partners' expense accounts. He also bilked them out of $784,000, using the firm's funds to pay for everything from home repairs to children's dental bills.[47] Oral Suer, the former

CEO of Washington, DC's United Way, labored ceaselessly over 30 years to raise more than a billion dollars for local charities, but also diverted hundreds of thousands of dollars to enrich himself.[48] Although major personality traits are somewhat stable over time, the behaviors such as cheating that we often attribute to character are not.[49] In *Out of Character*, psychologists David De Steno and Piercarlo Valdesolo put the point succinctly: "character is a fluctuating state . . . not a stable attribute."[50]

How, then, can we explain variations in the way that different individuals respond to similar temptations to cheat, as well as variations in the way that any single individual responds to different cheating opportunities? A vast literature on ethical behavior bears on these questions, and underscores the role both of cognitive limitations and situational influences.

## Decision-Making Processes

In explaining cognitive limitations on ethical decision-making, two approaches have been dominant. One stresses the role of conscious deliberation; the other stresses the importance of intuitive and tacit processes. The first approach is reflected in an influential framework of psychologist James Rest. It identified four dimensions of ethical conduct:

- Moral awareness: recognizing that a situation raises ethical issues;
- Moral reasoning: determining what course of action is ethically sound;
- Moral intent: identifying which values should take priority in the decision; and
- Moral behavior: acting on ethical decisions.[51]

Rest was a student of Harvard psychologist Lawrence Kohlberg, and the moral reasoning dimension of Rest's four-part framework relied heavily on Kohlberg's research on cognitive moral development.[52] According to that research, moral judgment is the most critical contributor to moral behavior, and people advance through stages in their reasoning about ethical decisions. At the lowest two levels, the "preconventional" levels, individuals base their decisions on what is right either on obedience to authority and fear of punishment (Stage 1) or self-interest (Stage 2). At the middle two levels, the "conventional levels," people judge what is right based on the expectations of others (Stage 3) or on rules, laws, and policies (Stage 4). At the highest levels of development, the "principled" levels, individuals rely on principles of justice and rights, and consider the common good (Stages 5 and 6). Most individuals function at the conventional level.[53] Although Kohlberg's work has been subject to considerable criticism, a large body of research has found some correlation between unethical behavior and lower cognitive moral development.[54]

However, that correlation is only modest.[55] And recent research, guided by neuroscience, suggests that most of what constitutes "everyday morality" is tacit. automatic, and intuitive, rather than the product of deliberative reasoning.[56] This school of thought, popularized by psychologist Daniel Kahnemann, explains moral behavior in terms of a dual process: "automatic intuitive responses with respect to familiar situations and conscious reasoning in response to situations for which no repetitive intuitive response has developed."[57] System 1 thinking is intuitive, "fast, automatic, effortless, and emotional." System 2 thinking is " slower, conscious, explicit and logical."[58] As a general matter, our intuitive System 1 responses are more likely to be immoral than our reflective System 2 responses.[59] Decisions with ethical importance generally call for System 2 thinking but individuals do not always put in the effort that it requires.[60] In characterizing this dual process of decision-making, Max Bazerman, Ann Tenbrunsel, Kristina A. Diekmann, and Kimberly Wade-Benzoni have drawn from well-established psychological theory to describe a conflict between people's "want self" and their "should self." [61] The "should self" and normative considerations predominate before and after an ethical decision is translated into action. The "want self" and concerns about potential rewards and punishment predominate at the point of action.[62]

Even when individuals make the effort to step back and engage in ethical reflection, they are subject to cognitive limitations that can undermine moral analysis and encourage rationalization of behavior that their initial instincts suggest is wrong.[63] In effect, people are subject to "bounded ethicality."[64] They find it particularly hard to acquire and process information necessary for sound ethical decision in the face of complexity or uncertainty, time constraints, or conflicts of interest. Physical or mental fatigue can also deplete individuals' resources for self-control, and impair their ethical awareness, all of which makes cheating more likely.[65] Self-interest further skews the reasoning process. The more tempted we are to behave unethically, the more common—and thus acceptable—we perceive the unethical action to be.[66] People find cheating less problematic after they have engaged in it.[67] In a famous experiment documenting the role of self-interest, researchers asked Dartmouth and Princeton students to view the film of a highly contentious football game between their schools and to count the number of rule violations. Students from Princeton reported twice as many violations by Dartmouth players as by Princeton players; students from Dartmouth found exactly the reverse.[68] Their self-interest encouraged what psychologists term "willful ignorance" or "motivated blindness"[69]

Psychologists Ann Tenbrunsel and David Messick similarly document the role of what they call "ethical fading," in which ethical consequences recede from consciousness.[70] This process preempts not only moral awareness but also "moral attentiveness:" the extent to which individuals proactively consider moral issues.[71] Euphemisms often aid this ethical fading process. So, for example, individuals speak of "aggressive" accounting practices, not evading taxes, and "sharing" music files, not stealing musicians' work.[72] During a "payola scandal" in which radio disc jockeys accepted bribes by music companies to air specific records, they referred to the kickbacks as "consultant" or "auditioning" fees, rather than payoffs.[73] Siemens executives similarly referred to some $1.4 billion in bribes to foreign officials as "consulting" payments.[74] Embezzlers have also engaged in rationalizations that enabled them to view their theft of funds as a form of "borrowing."[75] Studies of white-collar offenders find that they rarely saw themselves as "the kind of people who would create fraudulent enterprises . . . The individuals perpetrating these schemes were also victims of a sort—victims of their own self deception."[76]

Repeated exposure to ethical misconduct can also produce a form of "ethical numbing."[77] This is how cultures of cheating take root. The more that people see others cheat, the less they regard it as cheating. And the more that they follow suit, the more habituated they become to their misconduct and the less ethical discomfort they feel.[78] For example, factory workers have often managed to define pilfering as something other than stealing; in one study, two-thirds did not even experience guilt.[79] As one employee explained, "everybody is doing it so why should anyone feel guilty."[80]

Through habituation and desensitization, individuals become accustomed to misconduct and engage in it without significant reflection.[81] Small acts of cheating often go unnoticed.[82] Because they seem not to activate people's internal reward mechanism for honesty, they then pave the way for greater misconduct, which, over time, can become almost mindless.[83] One commentator describes lawyers' fraudulent billing practices this way:

> One day, not too long after you start practicing law, you will sit down at the end of a long, tiring day and you just won't have much to show for your efforts in terms of billable hours. It will be near the end of the month. You will know that all of the partners will be looking at your monthly time report in a few days, so what you'll do is pad your time sheet just a bit. Maybe you will bill a client for ninety minutes for a task that really took you only sixty minutes to perform. However, you will promise yourself that you will repay the client at the first opportunity by doing thirty minutes of work for the client for "free." In this way, you will be "borrowing," not "stealing."
>
> And then what will happen is that it will become easier and easier to take these little loans against future work. And then, after a while, you will stop paying back these little loans. You will convince yourself, that although you billed for ninety minutes and spent only sixty minutes on

> the project, you did such good work that your client should pay a bit more for it. After all, our billing rate is awfully low, and your client is awfully rich.
>
> And then you will pad more and more,—every two minute telephone conversation will go down on the sheet as ten minutes, every three hour research project will go down with an extra quarter hour or so. You will continue to rationalize your dishonesty to yourself in various ways until one day you stop doing even that. And, before long—it won't take much more than three or four years—you will be stealing from your clients almost every day, and you won't even notice it.[84]

The normalization of cheating is often so gradual that it is imperceptible.[85] People cross the line through a series of decisions without the benefit of thorough deliberation, and these decisions then shape future options in unanticipated ways. And because each decision may lead to only small deviations from prior behavior, the escalating misconduct does not raise moral alarms.[86] Mark Drier, who ran his law firm as a Ponzi scheme and misrepresented its financial conditions to investors, noted that "I didn't set out to steal hundreds of millions of dollars, but ended up doing so incrementally after crossing a line I could not retreat from . . . Once I started there seemed to be no way out other than to continue."[87] This is what psychologists sometimes term "escalation of commitment," or the "boiled frog problem."[88] Legend has it that a frog will jump out of boiling water, but when placed in a pot of tepid water that is gradually heated, the frog will calmly boil to death. The folk wisdom is wrong about frogs but right about humans. Small incremental acts of cheating enable people to fall victim to bounded ethicality and engage in behavior contrary to their own values without awareness that they are doing so.[89]

## Social Influences

Ethical awareness is also affected by both social norms and social consequences concerning the acts in question.[90] People respond to cues from peers and leaders, and observing moral or immoral behavior by others promotes similar conduct.[91] A key factor is social consensus concerning the morality of the behavior.[92] When people think "everybody does it," the risks of moral myopia escalate. As one employee explained his stealing of office supplies: "When you see other people do it, it seems to be no big deal. You think it's okay. As dumb as that sounds." Another employee agreed: "Everyone did it so why should I be different . . . ?"[93] Behavioral ethics research has found that when people witness dishonesty by even just one other person who is like them in important respects, they are more likely to behave dishonestly themselves.[94]

Bernie Madoff, who ran the nation's largest Ponzi scheme that cheated investors out of $20 billion, rationalized his conduct as typical of the business world. He believed that 80 percent of his clients also "were involved in cheating in one form or another."[95]

> Find me an owner in the manufacturing field that didn't cheat on his inventory counts or his taxes. Find me an individual who has not written off personal expense on his tax returns as business expenses. Find me a person that has not padded or filed false insurance claims. I acknowledge that there are different degrees of these activities and I am not suggesting that all are acceptable. My point is simply to state that I believe that this is the reality of life . . . [96]

A similar example involved conflicts of interest among Merrill Lynch's investment, advising, and banking businesses, which resulted in a $100 million settlement against the firm. Employees cheated customers by pushing stock that they privately ridiculed as a "piece of junk."[97] As one analyst put it, "The system was sordid . . . But because everyone knew it was sordid, it no longer seemed sordid anymore."[98]

## Rationalizations

"Ethical dissonance" also skews the reasoning process. Borrowing from Leon Festinger's theory of cognitive dissonance, psychologists note that when a person's behavior is inconsistent with his or her values, an uncomfortable state of tension results.[99] Individuals generally care about being and appearing ethical.[100] When that desire clashes with incentives to cheat, people often attempt to reduce the dissonance by rationalizing misconduct. In *The (Honest) Truth about Dishonesty,* psychologist Dan Ariely puts it this way:

> [O]ur behavior is driven by two opposing motivations. On the one hand, we want to view ourselves as honest, honorable people . . . . On the other hand, we want to benefit from cheating . . . . This is where our amazing cognitive flexibility comes into play. Thanks to this human skill, as long as we cheat by only a little bit, we can benefit from cheating and still view ourselves as marvelous human beings. This balancing act is the process of rationalization, and it is the basis of what we'll call the "fudge factor theory."[101]

In one representative study in which participants received payments dependent on their self-reports of performance, they inflated their reports by an average of 10 percent. Most people fudged, but by just a little.[102] A wide variety of research suggests that individuals are often "moral hypocrites:" they want to seem moral without the cost of actually acting morally.[103] In some cases, as with speeding, people see the value of bright-line rules even as they justify minor breaches.

To reduce ethical dissonance, individuals may also recharacterize the nature or harms of their behavior. The further removed cheating is from cash, the easier it is to rationalize. For example, participants in laboratory experiments cheated more in reporting their performance on a problem-solving task when the rewards that they received were not dollar bills but tokens from a jar, later redeemable for money. Their conduct felt somehow less dishonest when it was one step removed from cash.[104] For similar reasons, people are more likely to steal soft drinks than money left in a communal refrigerator.[105] They are also are more comfortable with cheating when they can do it through an intermediary. Individuals slip in more false receipts for business expenses when they give them to their administrative assistants to process than when they submit the receipts themselves.[106] Even the architects of large Ponzi schemes manage to rationalize their conduct because intermediaries are the ones who actually cook the books. As one CEO convicted of fraud put it, "I had nothing to do with selling the Ponzi and didn't do the accounting."[107] In his view, he was just running a business with "income recognition" problems.[108]

People also tend to overestimate the likelihood that they will behave ethically in the future and underestimate the extent to which they behaved unethically in the past.[109] In effect, most of us are "revisionist historians."[110] We selectively recall our own conduct or applicable rules in ways that minimize culpability.[111] In one typical study, participants had an opportunity to earn undeserved money by overreporting their performance on a problem-solving task. Before performing the task, they were exposed to moral rules. Those who cheated on their reports were more likely than non-cheaters to forget those rules, even though they were given a financial incentive to recall them and they were equally likely to remember morally irrelevant information.[112]

Other situational factors can similarly bias ethical reasoning. A sense of envy, unfairness, or inequity can trigger cheating in retaliation.[113] These instincts are deeply rooted. Even monkeys who see other monkeys getting better treats for completing a task will throw their inferior treats back at the experimenter.[114] Humans get even by cheating. Employees who believe that they are underpaid find it easier to rationalize pilfering workplace supplies or fudging on hours and expenses.[115] Even slight annoyances can trigger retaliatory cheating. A Philadelphia hotel guest, furious at being kept in line for an unreasonable period, stuffed the bed's comforter in her duffel bag. "I figured they owed it to me," she explained.[116] In one of Ariely's experiments, coffee shop patrons were offered $5 for completing a five-minute task. The experimenter gave them a small stack of bills and told them, "Here is your $5. Please count the money, sign the receipt, and leave it on the table. I'll be back later to collect it." He then left, ostensibly in search of another participant. He had given them $9 rather than $5. Forty-five percent of the participants returned the extra cash. In a second variation of the experiment, the experimenter's cell phone vibrated while he was explaining the task. He took the call and arranged a pizza dinner. Although the call took only 12 seconds, many participants were clearly annoyed. Only 14 percent returned the extra cash. As Ariely summarized the reasoning process: "Our dishonesty becomes retribution . . . . We tell ourselves that we're not doing anything wrong, we are only getting even."[117]

As that example suggests, individuals' ethical reasoning process is affected by their capacity to "neutralize" the relevance of social norms. In their landmark work on delinquency, sociologists Gresham Sykes and David Matza developed a typology of neutralizing techniques that has been frequently confirmed and is readily applicable to cheating.[118] Among the most common strategies are:

- Denial of injury; I didn't really hurt anybody;
- Denial of responsibility; it's not my fault;
- Denial of victimization; he or she had it coming;
- Condemning the condemners; they are moral hypocrites, they do it too, everybody does it;
- Appeal to higher loyalty; I did it for my friends or my family.

Such rationalizations were common in a survey of young adults. Many took the view that when it came to cheaging, "everyone does it," or that "if it's not hurting an individual, it's not really wrong." Big corporations "have funds that cover them."[119]

These views are especially prevalent among white-collar offenders. In one study, 84 percent blamed someone else.[120] Denials of injury and victimization were also common. Marc Drier emphasized that his law firm Ponzi scheme benefited the people who worked for him, and recalled that he had "tried to rationalize that the potential harm [to investors] was offset by the current good [to employees] and just hoped that it would somehow all work out."[121] Bernie Madoff told fellow prison inmates after his conviction that he "took money off people who were rich and greedy and wanted more." "Fuck my victims," he said. "People just kept throwing money at me."[122]

Other researchers have documented two additional techniques of rationalization. One is necessity: the claim that cheating is necessary to survive in a competitive business climate.[123] A participant in a survey of ethics among young adults expressed a widespread view that cheating is "how a lot of people have gotten ahead in life expecially in this country. It's like a cutthroat world out there. I will do what I can to get ahead.[124] A second strategy is "balancing the ledger:" people use their good works to license misconduct.[125] As one individual who engaged in "cyberloafing" put it, "It's all right for me to use the Internet for personal reasons at work. After all, I do work overtime without receiving extra pay from my employer."[126] Dennis Kozlowski, Tyco's former CEO who was convicted of fraud and misappropriation, saw nothing wrong in using corporate funds to furnish his apartment with expensive art, a $6,000 shower curtain, and a $15,000 umbrella stand. "People think that I'm a greedy guy," he explained. But "I worked my butt off" and his rewards reflected his performance in "Tyco's long established pay for performance culture."[127]

Such excuses function as mechanisms of "moral disengagement," which suspend the normal inhibitions to unethical conduct.[128] They also help people maintain a positive image for both an internal audience (themselves) and an external audience (everyone else).[129] As one researcher on white-collar criminals put it, "nobody is ever the villain in their own narrative." Faced with actions that "threaten to paint them as a bad person, they are more likely to change their opinion of what's right and wrong, rather than change their opinion of themselves."[130]

The chapters that follow provide frequent examples of moral disengagement and denial of moral responsibility achieved by distancing or devaluing victims.[131] One reason illegal downloading of music is so pervasive is that consumers see the costs as falling on wealthy record companies rather than on starving musicians. As one individual put it, "I know artists need to get paid, but the record companies are so rich."[132] Similarly, many Americans who cheat on their taxes view the victim as a government that squanders revenue, rather than honest taxpayers who are shouldering more than their fair share of the nation's tax burden.

Neutralizing techniques figure prominently in lawyers' rationalizations for "creative" billing practices. Auditors find demonstrable fraud in 5–10 percent of lawyers' bills and questionable practices in another 25–35 percent. Such practices include inflating hours, overstaffing cases, performing unnecessary work, padding expenses, and double-billing two clients for the same task or time.[133] Lawyers often deny that these practices cause injury, on the theory that the work was "worth more" than the time it required. They deny responsibility on the ground that the fault lies with their firm's unreasonable billable hour quotas. They deny having a victim because the client was a "jerk" or had refused to reimburse reasonable expenses.[134] They claim that "everybody does it." Ninety-two percent of surveyed lawyers believe that other lawyers at least occasionally padded their bills.[135] Web Hubbell, one-time chief justice of the Arkansas Supreme Court, acknowledged some 400 instances of fraudulently padding bills and charging personal expenses as business expenses while in private practice, but characterized the matter as a "private financial dispute" within the firm.[136] In a tape recorded conversation with his wife, he conceded the overbilling. When she asked, "You didn't actually do that, did you, mark up time for the client, did you?," he responded, "Yes I did. So does every lawyer in the country."[137] On similar reasoning, lawyers have fudged expense accounts, for example, by representing a pair of jogging shoes as "ground transportation," and dry cleaning of a toupee as a "litigation expense."[138]

## Moral Intent and Capability

Flaws in individuals' moral reasoning processes, however, are only part of what explains cheating behavior. Another factor is what James Rest termed "moral intent." To resist temptation, individuals must intend to prioritize moral values.[139] And they must intend to act morally, not just *seem* to act morally.[140] Moral intent is, in turn, related to moral identity—the centrality of moral concerns to individuals' self-image and self-esteem. Much depends on how they weigh these concerns in relation to potential gains from cheating. Those gains include not only objective benefits, such as grades or financial advantages, but also subjective well-being. Cheating in circumstances without sympathetic victims and obvious harms prompts what researchers term the "cheater's high." Just as some wealthy individuals enjoy shoplifting or joyriders take pleasure in stealing cars, some cheaters take pleasure in having gotten away with something.[141]

Once again, various situational factors affect individuals' motivations. People are responsive to the potential profit, the degree of risk, the characteristics of the potential victim, and the presence of witnesses.[142] The moral intensity of the issue also matters: relevant factors include the magnitude of consequences, and the probability, immediacy, and proximity of their effect.[143] Cheating is more likely when opportunities are readily available, when the risk of punishment is low, when other means to achieve the same advantages are limited, and when victims are impersonal or remote.[144] Reward systems, particularly in circumstances of low transparency, can also increase cheating.[145] One case history in the effect of situational pressures on cheating behavior involves Sears, Roebuck. In the 1990s, it changed the company's compensation structure for auto service personnel. Under the new system, employees received a lower base salary, which was supplemented by a commission on services sold or amount of labor performed. The new system required mechanics to do 60 percent more work to earn an amount equal to their previous hourly wage. Previously honest employees began recommending unnecessary repairs, and massive fraud resulted. Defrauded consumers brought 18 class action lawsuits, and government officials filed misconduct charges in over 40 states. Jokes even appeared on national television. David Lettermen's Top Ten repair jobs recommended by the Sears automotive department included "grease the ashtrays," and "add a redwood deck."[146]

A final factor affecting cheating behavior is an individual's "ego strength:" the capacity to follow through on intentions and to translate moral decisions into moral behavior.[147] That ego strength, in turn, depends on the person's ability to cope with pressure, resist impulses, and remain focused on moral objectives. Such capacities for self-regulation help predict ethical outcomes.[148]

## Strategies

Cheating is a massive social problem that requires responses on multiple levels. Because cheating is heavily influenced by situational factors, effective remedial strategies will often need to be context-specific. Accordingly, the following chapters each conclude with detailed strategies addressed to that particular form of cheating. Taken together, they suggest several general points about the necessary interventions.

### Cultural Reinforcement of Ethical Conduct

Most obviously, much more reinforcement of ethical values is needed in homes, schools, workplaces, and the media.[149] Parents, teachers, coaches, and other youth leaders must consistently affirm ethical norms and set the right example in their own behavior. Cheating incidents should become teachable moments: occasions for reflection and dialogue about the corrosive effects of deception. In the home, authoritative parenting styles, which enforce moral standards with reasoning and fairness, can help reinforce children's sense of personal responsibility.[150] Parents also should consider the messages that their own actions may inadvertently send. A prevention loss consultant describes an example of unintended irony: a father who expressed concerns to a school principal that one of his six-year-old son's classmates was stealing his son's pencils. "You realize that it is the principle of the matter," the father explained. "The pencils themselves are unimportant. I can always get all the pencils I need from my office."[151] So too, leaders of athletic programs need to ensure that good sportsmanship receives more than a mention at annual banquets; it should be reinforced daily at all competitive levels. In the schools, the enforcement of rules against cheating should be opportunities to foster moral reasoning.[152] When imposing sanctions, teachers should engage students in helping to define the problem, devise a solution, and develop self-discipline.[153] Caring classrooms that model fairness, honesty, empathy, and mutual respect are a key strategy in fostering ethical development.[154]

Adults as well as children need strategies for managing conflicts between the "want" self and the "should" self, and for making the "should" self more salient. For example, it generally helps to take time to deliberate and to consider higher order ethical principles before acting.[155] At the same time, people should also pay attention to gut instincts that suggest that certain conduct is wrong, regardless of how readily it is accepted by others.[156] Educating individuals about the ethical misjudgments caused by self-interest and social influence can help keep their moral compass on course.

## Organizational Cultures

Organizations need to create ethical cultures and infrastructures, in which informal norms, formal policies, and reward structures work together to reinforce integrity.[157] Ethical considerations should be integrated into all workplace activities, including hiring, promotion, compensation, performance evaluation, auditing, and communications. Role modeling by leaders, appropriate incentive structures, and honest discourse are especially critical.[158] Ensuring fair treatment of employees can also reduce retaliatory cheating.[159]

## Ethical Codes

Ethical codes, if effectively enforced, can be helpful in clarifying ethical standards, reducing moral wiggle room, and removing rationalizations for misconduct.[160] As Chapter 5 indicates, academic honor codes serve that function. In both experimental and real-world settings, they significantly reduce cheating.[161] Asking Yale and MIT students to sign a statement reading "I understand that this experiment falls under the guidelines of the MIT/Yale honor code" prevented cheating even though neither university has an honor code.[162] In real-world settings, however, ethical codes are effective only if they are reinforced by organizational norms.[163] Before its collapse due to widespread fraud, Enron inscribed the governing principles in its ethics code—Respect, Integrity, Community, Excellence (RICE)—on everything from coffee mugs to T-shirts and workplace banners.[164] "Good optics" was how one manager described the code, and after the company's collapse, copies were marketed on eBay under the description "never been used."[165]

## Moral Reminders

People also need more moral reminders—triggers that make ethics salient and remind people of their own values.[166] In one experiment, virtually no participants cheated when asked to recall the Ten Commandments before self-reporting their performance on a task; in a control group, cheating was widespread.[167] Having individuals sign a statement on forms attesting to their truth before filling them out can serve as a similar moral trigger. Those who sign at the top of a form rather than at the bottom are less likely to cheat.[168] Even having people initial a statement of organizational ethics can help nudge them in appropriate directions.[169] Providing decision-making processes that slow individuals down and invite them to engage in less intuitive, more reflective "System 2" thinking can have a similar impact.[170]

## Ethical Enforcement Structures

More support for whistle-blowers is equally critical. As Chapter 3 notes, those who seek to expose cheating and corruption in organizations typically encounter harassment, ostracism, and retaliation.[171] All too often, disclosures produce no lasting change. In commenting on the odds of vindication, one whistle-blower noted, "If you have God, the law, the press, and the facts on your side, you have a 50-50 chance of [victory]."[172] That needs to change, and one step in the right direction is more statutory and contractual protection of whistle-blowers from retaliation.[173] Media coverage that celebrates those who challenge misconduct can also help, as when the cover of *Time* magazine featured whistle-blowers from Enron, WorldCom, and the FBI as "People of the Year."[174]

We should also increase penalties for cheating and invest more resources in enforcement. Because minor acts pave the way for more serious and repeated misconduct, they need to be taken more seriously.[175] The day after settling criminal tax evasion charges, Credit Suisse officers held a conference call to reassure analysts that the case would have no "material impact on our operational or business capabilities."[176] All too often, as subsequent discussion notes, the upper-level employees responsible for organizational misconduct have escaped without significant sanction. In the recent Wells Fargo scandal, described in Chapter 3, the embattled CEO departed with over $130 million in pension, stock, and deferred compensation until public outrage forced a substantial forfeiture.[177]

In many contexts, an obvious way to reduce cheating is to increase surveillance. Even the simulation of surveillance may help. A survey of a university coffee lounge found that the image of a pair of eyes appearing to observe behavior dramatically increased coffee drinkers' contributions to an "honesty box" that collected money for beverages.[178] However, the design of effective monitoring systems is complicated. Researchers find that in some circumstances, these systems signal mistrust, which can lead to resentment and can reduce individuals' intrinsic motivation to act ethically.[179] They become, as psychologist Robert Cialdini puts it, "less interested in the desirable conduct for its own sake."[180] The risk of counterproductive outcomes is particularly likely when the sanctioning system is weak. Combination of Ann Tenbrunsel and David Messick find that a system with low penalties and a low probability of detection can promote a focus on the business rather than ethical aspects of a decision.[181]

Corporations are often reluctant to report white-collar "suite crime;" they don't want to air their dirty laundry in public.[182] Even when companies do report fraud, understaffed agencies may lack resources to take appropriate action. One survey found that of 600 alleged offenders who were referred to the Justice Department by the Securities and Exchange Commission, only 84 ended up with any jail time.[183] Even those guilty of massive cheating can emerge with relatively few long-term consequences. Michael Milken was sentenced to 10 years in prison for racketeering and securities fraud but served less than two. Despite a large fine, he left prison with hundreds of millions of dollars in family assets. Although his sentence expressly prohibited his participation in future financial enterprises, he earned millions as a consultant and by 2015 had a net worth of $2 billion.[184] He also taught a class at the UCLA Business School with case studies based on his financial dealings. Garry Trudeau's *Doonesbury* cartoon strip parodied the first day of his course, where a student asked, "Professor Milken? Can we cheat in this class?"[185]

In 1990, the year of Milken's sentencing, his alma mater, the Wharton School, featured a parody of its graduation ceremony. The student playing the class valedictorian stepped away from the podium and sang about how she achieved that role. In lyrics set to the tune of Michael Jackson's hit song, "Beat it," she explained:

> I cheated, cheated,
> Cheated, cheated,
> And maybe I sound conceited,
> You're probably angry,
> I'm overjoyed,
> I work on Wall Street,
> You're unemployed.
> I want a good job
> Who cares if it's right?
> To hell with ethics
> I sleep at night.[186]

Our culture needs to send a different message. The chapters that follow suggest why and how.

2

# Cheating in Sports

Cheating in sports is as old as sports. The Olympic games began in 776 B.C., and from the outset, they established penalties of flogging and fines for those who cheated. The most common offenses involved bribing opponents. Such misconduct was memorialized on statues of Zeus, funded by fines, which flanked the way to the stadium.[1] Use of performance-enhancing substances was not, however, considered cheating, and early Greek athletes ate hallucinogenic mushrooms to acquire an edge.[2] Cheating in the modern Olympics has been common, and began in 1896, its first year. Then, a bronze medalist forfeited his prize when officials learned that he had gone part of the marathon course in a horse and carriage.[3] A century later, the winner of the Boston Marathon was similarly stripped of her title after an investigation revealed that she had taken the subway.[4]

Empirical evidence on the frequency of contemporary cheating in either professional or recreational sports is limited. But if survey data is any guide, many individuals succumb to temptation in at least some situations. Eighty-two percent of high-ranking corporate executives acknowledged cheating on the golf course.[5]

Some of the nation's most prominent leaders have been known for such conduct. President Dwight Eisenhower took "gimmes" on long putts, and if he landed a shot in the rough he would "look around and then kick the ball out."[6] President Bill Clinton was notorious for taking Mulligans, a second shot off the tee if the first one did not land in a good position, and for taking gimmes on putts as long as 50 feet. When he was playing with professional golfer Jack Nicklaus, Clinton bragged that he had shot 80 and Nicklaus added in a whisper, "eighty with fifty floating Mulligans."[7] Donald Trump's conduct is similarly notorious.[8] According to sports writer Rick Reilly, "when it comes to cheating, he's an 11 on a scale of one to 10."[9] In one afternoon, Reilly watched Trump write down phony scores and take three Mulligans, as well as a gimme when his ball was yards away from the hole. Yet Trump told Reilly to "make sure you write that I play my first ball. You don't get a second chance in life."[10] Mark Mulvoy, the managing editor of *Sports*

*Illustrated,* recalls that when he once challenged Trump for moving a ball onto the green, Trump responded, "Ahh, the guys I play with cheat all the time. I have to cheat just to keep up with them."[11] Unsurprisingly, Trump denies such accounts. "I don't move balls," he told a *Washington Post* reporter. "I don't need to."[12]

To test attitudes toward such conduct, psychologist Dan Ariely asked survey participants to imagine circumstances in which an average golfer realized that it would be highly advantageous if his ball were lying 4 inches away from its current location. Ariely asked, "How comfortable do you think the average golfer would be about moving the ball 4 inches?" Participants thought that the average golfer would pick the ball up about 10 percent of the time, move the ball with his club 23 percent of the time, and move it with his shoe 14 percent of the time.[13] Participants also guessed that 40 percent of players would cheat by taking Mulligans on the first hole, and that 15 percent would do so on the ninth hole. The assumption apparently was that golfers would find it easier to rationalize that they hadn't really started playing yet on the first hole than on the ninth.[14] Many individuals seem prepared to take a famous quip by Arnold Palmer at face value: "I have a tip that can take five strokes off anyone's golf game. It's called an eraser."[15]

The following discussion begins with an overview of cheating techniques. It then explores such behavior in two contexts that are particularly problematic: doping in professional sports and misconduct in college sports. These are situations in which the pressures to cheat are particularly intense and the societal consequences particularly significant. The high visibility of college and professional athletics and the cult of sports celebrities make their cheating scandals especially salient and culturally corrosive. Prominent athletes are role models for the nation, and society has a stake in reinforcing their honesty, integrity, and sportsmanship.[16]

Although the discussion that follows talks about athletics in general, that should not obscure the differences among sports. Each has its own culture and implicit moral norms, just as each sports team develops its own ethical subculture.[17] Still, as the breadth of examples cited below indicate, cheating is a problem that is widely shared. Its prevalence among the most prominent athletes should be a matter of broad public concern.

## Techniques of Cheating

One of the oldest techniques of cheating involves rigging matches and betting on the outcomes. The frequency of the problem in international soccer received renewed attention in 2014, when the sport's governing body sent new guidelines to its members titled "Specific Recommendations to Combat Match

Manipulations."[18] The increasing commercialization of college sports has generated about $100 billion annually in gambling revenues, and with it problems of corruption.[19] According to one overview, "Fixing a college game is like shooting fish in a barrel. You can pretty much fix any college game you want to. And it wouldn't take a lot of money to do it."[20] *Cheating the Spread* describes a common system. The spread is a gambling handicap favoring the underdog team. The bet is on how many points a favorite will win by. An athlete on a team that is favored to win can intentionally miss a layup or free throw to shave points off the score so as not to beat the spread. His team can still win the game while corrupt gamblers can win their bets on the opposing team. This kind of lead-footed play is difficult to prove. It often takes catching a player on electronic surveillance.[21] Given the difficulties of detecting such cheating, the result is what one expert calls "a perfect storm for criminal conspiracy . . . [Y]ou've got young athletes with uncertain futures and financial hardships who feel they're not going to be hurting anybody if they shave a few points."[22]

Cheating with equipment is another common technique. According to some commentators, cheating is baseball's oldest profession.[23] Batters have used corked bats, and pitchers have put graphite, baby oil, pine tar, or Vaseline on baseballs.[24] When accused of using a foreign substance on the ball, Don Sutton responded, "Not true at all. Vaseline is manufactured right here in the United States."[25] Gaylord Perry was notorious for throwing illegal spitballs to achieve the wins that gained his membership in the Hall of Fame.[26] In racing, jockeys have resorted to buzzers that give horses an electric shock to increase their speed.[27] Tennis players have used rackets of illegal string tension, and golfers have used clubs of illegal weight or size. In football, Hall of Fame player Jerry Rice admitted to having "stickum" on his hands throughout his career to make the ball easier to catch, a practice he characterized as "a little illegal."[28]

In 2015, the National Football League charged that footballs supplied by the New England Patriots in their lopsided victory over the Indianapolis Colts were underinflated, making them easier to throw and catch.[29] A subsequent investigation found that it was "more probable than not" that quarterback Tom Brady was aware that the balls were doctored, and suspended him for four games.[30] That penalty was first overturned and then reinstated on appeal to the courts.[31] However, the Patriots did not appeal a fine of $1 million and denial of two draft choices, a sanction described by the Chair of the Santa Clara Institute of Sports Law and Ethics as "on the low side of meaningful," but more than "a slap on the wrist."[32] And, he noted, the reputational consequences were perhaps more significant. " 'Cheater' is an indelible adjective."[33] Yet it is by no means clear how much Brady's or his team's reputation actually suffered. In commenting on the scandal, four-time Superbowl champion Joe Montana acknowledged that if he'd known that deflating was effective, he might have tried it. He also noted that his own teammates "until they got caught" used to spray silicone on their shirts to make it harder for an offensive linesman to hold them. If Brady was guilty, "so what. Just pay up and move on. It's no big deal."[34] After all, Montana added, "If you ain't cheating, you ain't trying."[35]

Cheating through violation of eligibility and recruiting guidelines is also common. It begins early, in youth sports, and it is adults as much as children who are to blame. A textbook case was the 2015 scandal involving the Jackie Robinson West Little League team, which lost its World Series title because it included players who did not live or attend school in the team's district.[36] Violations of age restrictions occur with depressing regularity, but significant sanctions do not. An exception was the father of a winning pitcher for the Little League World Series. His celebrity won him an indictment for fraud after he for entered his 14-year-old son in a competition restricted to 9- to 12-year-olds.[37] The boy, Danny Almonte, pitched a perfect game, and received considerable public adulation until officials learned that his father had falsified his Dominican Republic birth certificate.[38]

Equally common are illegal recruitment bribes and related misconduct. Amateur Athletic Union basketball coaches have funneled illicit payments from colleges to influence athletes' decisions of which school to attend.[39] College coaches have provided meals, transportation, lodging, clothes, and even tuition in violation of NCAA rules. They have also gambled on tournaments and used ineligible players.[40] Although non-compliance with these rules strikes many perpetrators as trivial, it fosters corrosive attitudes. Each violation makes the next one easier to rationalize, and honest athletes bear the cost.

Some cheating involves intentional assaults, which also start early. Organizers of a California Pop Warner football team of 10- and 11-year-olds allegedly gave cash rewards for particularly violent hits.[41] High school football coaches have explicitly or implicitly echoed the view that if players "ain't cheating, they ain't trying."[42] An Emory ethics professor told a reporter that the Atlanta Falcons should "go for [the] ankle" of an opponent who had recently recovered from breaking that ankle, and 45 percent of newspaper readers agreed.[43] The New Orleans Saints rewarded such attitudes; the team had a bounty system in which defensive players received slush fund payments for deliberately injuring opponents.[44] In hockey, some players are expected to act as "enforcers" by injuring opponents, and are allowed to continue playing despite serious assaults.[45] Violence is so common that it has inspired a widely repeated quip: fans come to see fights and are disappointed when hockey breaks out. In 2014, soccer player Luis Suarez received a four-month suspension for biting a World Cup opponent; it was his third offense.[46] Perhaps the most celebrated incident of violence involved the ex-husband and bodyguard of figure skater Tonya Harding. They hired a hit man to break the leg of her main competitor. Harding pled guilty to conspiring to hinder prosecution of the attacker and was sentenced to 500 hours of community service and a $160,000 fine. After conducting its own investigation, the US Figure Skating Association concluded that Harding knew of the planned attack before it occurred. As a consequence, it stripped her of her championship title and banned her for life from participating in USFSA-run events.[47]

Another form of cheating involves misleading an umpire. In soccer, some players engage in diving or "flopping" to the ground, sometimes pretending to be injured, to make it seem as if their opponents have committed a foul.[48] Yale Law School professor Stephen Carter describes similar deception by a football player who failed to catch a pass.

> [The player] hit the ground, rolled over, and then jumped up, celebrating as though he had caught the pass after all. The referee was standing in a position that did not give him a good view of what had happened, was fooled by the player's pretense, and so moved the ball down the field. The player rushed back to the huddle so that his team could run another play before the officials had a chance to review the tape.[49]

What was most dispiriting about the incident was the broadcaster's only comment: "What a heads-up play!" The implication, argues Carter, is "Wow, what a great liar this kid is! Well done!"[50] "That in a nutshell," Carter concludes, "is America's integrity dilemma: we are all full of fine talk about how desperately our society needs it, but when push comes to shove, we would just as soon be on the winning side."[51]

Some cheating occurs at the highest levels, by those who should be setting an example of fairness and impartiality. In one celebrated case, a high school principal changed the math grade of a football player to prevent him from failing and becoming ineligible to participate in state playoffs.[52] New England Patriots coach Bill Belichick was fined $500,000 for improperly videotaping opposing coaches' signals from their own sidelines.[53] The Olympics have been tainted by scandals surrounding illegal payments to influence committee members' choice of a site and judges' evaluations of performances.[54] Even candidates to be judges have cheated on qualifying exams.[55] Government officials have also been implicated, as subsequent discussion of doping scandals indicates. So too, at least 14 current and former top-ranking employees of the International Federation of Association Football (FIFA), along with sports-marketers, have been indicted for racketeering, wire fraud, and money laundering that spanned over a decade. Officials accepted bribes to decide who would hold and televise games, and who would run the organization overseeing soccer worldwide.[56] Some FIFA leaders arranged to pay themselves more than $80 million.[57] The charges earned well-deserved parodies of the "World Cup of Corruption."[58]

In an incident that speaks volumes about the problematic attitudes in professional sports, cheating by soccer goal keeper Briana Scurry gave the U.S. women's team a five-to-four victory over China in the 1999 World Cup championship. Scurry illegally blocked a penalty kick by moving a few steps to secure a better angle. Although that rule violation went undetected by referees, Scurry acknowledged the misconduct to reporters with the observation, "Everybody does it. It's only cheating if you get caught."[59] As Michael Josephson, head of the Josephson Institute of Ethics, noted, "the fact that she made the statement is more troubling than her conduct."[60] And the fact that the secretary general of U.S. soccer had "no comment on this whatsoever" is more troubling still.[61]

Of course, not all forms of cheating are equally problematic. Feigning an injury stands on different moral footing from deliberately causing one. Some cheating, such as Perry's spitballs, seems to have been widely known and tolerated by fans. And off-the-field cheating that involves violations of technical eligibility rules may not threaten the competition to the same extent as on-the-field cheating that is widely observed. But all of these violations undermine the integrity of sports. And as Chapter 1 noted, even minor forms of cheating often pave the way for more serious misconduct. If, as is often claimed, athletics are a training ground for life, they should reinforce values that reflect our best selves and serve societal interests.

## Doping

The most pervasive cheating in professional athletics involves doping, the use of performance-enhancing drugs. The term comes from dop, a stimulant drink common in South Africa.[62] Given the prominence of the war against doping in recent decades, one might assume that there is a clear definition of what doping is. There is not.[63] The World Anti-Doping Agency (WADA) avoids definitional difficulties by stating simply that "Doping is defined as the occurrence of one or more of the antidoping rule violations set out in the . . . [World Anti-Doping] Code."[64] Although there is clear consensus that substances such as amphetamine, anabolic steroids, growth hormones, and erythropoietin (EPO) constitute doping, there is no corresponding agreement concerning other substances and practices.[65]

### The Ban against Doping

The ban against doping rests on three primary rationales. The first is that it is harmful to athletes' health. Steroids in high doses pose risks of liver damage, hypertension, and arteriosclerosis. Human growth hormone increases the risk of cancer, cardiac and thyroid problems, and impairment of reproductive health.[66] The second rationale for prohibition is that if doping were legal, athletes who were concerned about their health would nonetheless feel pressure to take injurious substances in order to remain competitive. The third justification is that professional and college athletes are role models for younger athletes who may lack the capacity to make informed judgments about long-term health risks. Accordingly, sports ethicists argue that rational and unbiased athletes would prefer a ban; otherwise, any individual's advantage from performing-enhancing drugs would be nullified when others followed suit, and the harms ultimately would be felt by all.[67]

Yet not all prohibited drugs constitute a significant danger to health: ephedrine is a case in point. And other practices that are harmful to health, such as painkilling injections, are allowed.[68] To be added to the list of prohibited substances, a substance must meet two of the following three criteria;

1. It must be performance-enhancing.
2. It must be harmful to health.
3. It must run counter to the spirit of sport.[69]

The spirit of sport is characterized by a broad range of values: ethics, fair play, and honesty; health; excellence in performance; character and education; fun and joy; teamwork; dedication and commitment; respect for rules and laws; respect for self and other participants; courage; and community and solidarity.[70] Such an inclusive list does little to justify the lines that have been drawn regarding certain drugs and practices.

## Historical Background

Doping has an extended history. Greek athletes, Roman gladiators, medieval knights, and eighteenth-century Amsterdam canal swimmers experimented with various methods, including strychnine, cocaine, ether, and alcohol.[71] Pud Galvin, one of nineteenth-century America's most renowned pitchers, drank monkey testosterone before a key victory, and earned an endorsement for the method in the *Washington Post*.[72] In the Olympics, Thomas Hicks, a British runner, won the 1904 marathon with the aid of a life-threatening dose of strychnine.[73] Four years later, an Italian runner, also under the influence of strychnine, collapsed before the finish line. In the 1920s, a Tour de France competitor complained openly to the press that the increasing difficulty of the course had caused cyclists to "run on dynamite."[74] The International Association of Athletics Federation banned stimulants in 1928, but the prohibitions were meaningless in the absence of testing.[75] In the 1950s and 1960s, the East German government's provision of powerful steroids to thousands of athletes drew attention to the problem. That doping had created an Olympic powerhouse with horrific side effects, including heart and liver damage, and birth defects among children of German athletes.[76]

However, what put the issue on the agenda of professional associations was the death of Danish cyclist Knud Jensen during the 1960 Olympic Games. Although some facts surrounding his death are disputed, it was commonly attributed to the use of amphetamines. Two of his teammates also collapsed.[77] When controls came into force in 1965, over a third of cyclists tested positive.[78] The death of English cyclist Tom Simpson, in front of whirring cameras in the 1967 Tour de France, drew support for tighter prohibitions. An Olympic gold medalist testified in congressional hearings that "by 1968, athletes in every event were using anabolic steroids and stimulants."[79] In response, the International Olympic Committee introduced systematic doping tests in 1968. Because the tests were directed at familiar substances, athletes had incentives to use new and potentially more dangerous ones.[80] Shortly after the enforcement structure came into effect, Olympic shot-putter Jim Doehring told the *Los Angeles Times* that "everyone's using something and I'm not excluding myself from that."[81] In the late 1980s, fourteen Dutch and four Belgian riders, all young and apparently healthy, died suddenly. At least some deaths were attributed to EPO. It increases the production of oxygen-carrying red blood cells, but also increases the risk of lethal blood clots.[82] According to one cyclist, "if a rider who couldn't tell his arse from his elbow went to the right physician with the wrong morals and paid what it took, then he could in principle buy his way to victory."[83]

In the United States, doping remained widespread. In 1989 congressional testimony, one expert testified that when the U.S. Olympic Committee announced drug tests in a variety of sports in 1984 and 1985, it found that 50 percent of the athletes tested positive for steroid use. Officials were informed that "if we could not select an athlete taking steroids, we simply wouldn't have a team."[84] Such evidence caused the National Collegiate Athletic Association (NCAA) to begin random testing for performance-enhancing substances and recreational drugs in the mid-1980s.[85] However, abuses remained common at both the professional and collegiate level. A decade later, estimates of the frequency of doping were as high as 30 percent.[86] In many sports, athletes were living in a "culture of tolerance."[87]

## Current Challenges

That culture began to change as officials improved testing regimes and cracked down on violators. Still, few sports have been untainted by scandal. In 2014, the world's top-ranked badminton player failed a drug test, and in 2016, Maria Sharapova, the world's highest-paid female athlete, acknowledged taking a banned substance.[88] Deaths and breakdowns on the track prompted Congress to consider, although not pass, the Horseracing Integrity and Safety Act, which would have given the U.S. Anti-Doping Agency jurisdiction over horseracing.[89]

The sports in which doping has received the greatest prominence are track and field, cycling, and baseball. The most celebrated case in track and field involved Marion Jones, winner of five medals at the 2000 Olympic games. In 2007, Jones was sentenced to six months in prison for lying to a grand jury about her use of performance-enhancing drugs, and was stripped of her medals.[90] "It's the destruction of a heroine of the day," said Dick Pound, the chair of the World Anti-Doping Agency.[91] Jones had appeared on the cover of *Vogue, Time,* and *Newsweek,* and it was in part her celebrity status that caused the trial judge to impose the maximum penalty. As he noted, "athletes in society . . . serve as role models to children around the world. When there is a widespread level of cheating, it sends all the wrong messages."[92]

Jones was not an isolated case. In 2017, a confidential report by the United States Anti-Doping Agency revealed widespread abuses in Nike's Oregon Project, an effort to enhance performance by American distance runners.[93] According to the Agency investigators, a lead coach for the Project teamed up with an endocrinologist to give athletes illegal drug infusions and to lie to them about the legality of the procedure. The report faulted the "win-at-all-costs culture that exists across all levels of sport."[94]

As to cycling, a 2013 *Washington Post* article ran under the title "Is Lance Armstrong the World's Biggest Liar?"[95] What prompted the question was not only Armstrong's confession to Oprah Winfrey that he had consistently lied about his use of performing-enhancing drugs, but also his gall in previously filing a successful libel suit against London's *Sunday Times* for its claims about his possible drug abuse. Prior to his confession, Armstrong was legendary for battling testicular cancer at the age of 25 and winning seven straight Tour de France titles. What is most dispiriting about the scandal is Armstrong's subsequent acknowledgment that "if you take me back to 1995 when doping was completely pervasive, I would probably do it again."[96] And no wonder. Despite being stripped of his titles, Armstrong's net worth has been estimated at $100 million.[97]

For many cyclists, the financial incentives to cheat have been compounded by peer pressure. In his autobiographical account *Rough Ride,* British athlete Paul Krimmage recounts the role that money, fear of humiliation, and expectations of teammates played in his decision to dope. Most of all, he wanted to be "one of the boys," and in that culture, it meant doing whatever it took to get a performance edge.[98]

There is, however, some indication that the situation has changed substantially since Krimmage and Armstrong began their doping regimen. As the independent commission appointed to investigate Armstrong's conduct noted, it had not heard from anyone

> credible in the sport who would give cycling a clean bill of health in the context of doping today. However, the general view was that doping is either less prevalent today or that the nature of doping practices has changed such that the performance gains are smaller. There was a general feeling that this has created an environment where riders can now at least be competitive when riding clean.[99]

A similar point could be made about Major League Baseball. Like cycling, the sport has a sorry history of ignoring the problem. Major League officials and team managers long engaged in what Chapter 1 described as "willful ignorance" or "motivated blindness"[100] Enhanced performance drew crowds, and no one wanted to know that doping was responsible. Not until 2004 did the league institute random drug testing; it was one of the last major professional associations to do so.[101] Before the testing regime, estimates of the pervasiveness of performance-enhancing drugs ranged from 40 to 80 percent.[102] Players felt pressure not only to enhance their own records, but also, as one pitcher put it, to not "let [their] team down."[103] As a consequence, many of contemporary baseball's iconic figures have been implicated in doping, including Roger Clemens, Jose Canseco, Mark McGuire, and Barry Bonds.[104] These revelations became fodder for comedians, as when Chris Rock announced at the Academy Awards, "We've given out ten awards so far and not one of the winners has tested positive for steroids."[105] In 2005, Canseco's blockbuster, *Juiced,* described widespread drug use. And in 2007, *Game of Shadows,* a bestselling expose by two investigative journalists, chronicled the rise and fall of the Bay Area Laboratory Cooperative (BALCO), a San Francisco nutrition supplement and drug supplier. Its involvement in doping implicated 27 prominent athletes, including Barry Bonds.[106] Bonds was convicted of obstruction of justice for giving an incomplete answer to a question in a grand jury proceeding. Although the decision was reversed on appeal, his home run record remains under a cloud.[107] As one commentator described the celebration of Bonds's achievement, "it's like a man robbing a bank and then having a giant party to watch him count the money."[108]

No reliable recent estimates of the extent of the problem are available. According to a prominent 2003 study conducted by former senator George Mitchell, anonymous tests found that 5 to 7 percent of Major League players were using anabolic steroids.[109] The total number of athletes engaging in doping was undoubtedly higher because the tests were incapable of detecting human growth hormone. The problem persists because tests are inadequate and the incentives to evade them are substantial. A major loophole is the therapeutic use exemption (TUE), which allows an athlete with a legitimate medical condition to use a banned substance under medical supervision.[110] As experts note, if the priority is to combat doping and level the playing field for competitors, then individuals seeking such exemptions should be sidelined until their conditions no longer require banned substances.[111]

Instead, under the current regime,

> if athletes have expert advice and if their use of doping is carefully organized and timed, the risk of being caught is slight. For an initiative whose aim is to promote equal competitive conditions for all, it clearly presents a problem that those who can afford to work with the best doping doctors run less of a risk of testing positive than competitors with more modest means trying to find their own way to climb the last few rungs of the ladder.[112]

Another sports columnist similarly notes that in football, "There are ways to beat the tests. Players are sophisticated enough to find them. They will always find them when their career, not to mention millions of dollars, are on the line. It's easy for NFL owners to say they are against performance-enhancing drugs. It's a lot harder to believe them. Bigger and faster bodies make for more brutal collisions. In football, brutality is a big seller."[113]

Yet most surveyed athletes have negative attitudes toward performance-enhancing drugs and support mandatory testing.[114] In two studies of elite athletes, "not a single one, whether they had doped or not, believed that the anti-doping campaign should or could be abandoned . . . . "[115] A common observation was that "[c]ompetition has to be on an equal footing."[116] As one athlete put it, testing is "a necessary evil. I will do anything to make sport clean. And if that means I have to pee in a cup 20 times a year, then that's a small price to pay."[117]

Officials need to capitalize on that support and to strengthen penalties and enforcement structures. The World Anti-Doping Agency has been notoriously ineffective in responding to allegations of cheating, as a recent widespread scandal involving Russian athletes made clear.[118] A 2016 independent investigation implicated Russia's Ministry of Sport and Federal Security Service in operating an extensive doping program.[119] In response, the International Olympic Committee (IOC) required the country's athletes to demonstrate that they had not been doping before the 2016 Games.[120] That process excluded over a hundred athletes from competition.[121] It also drew attention to the need to strengthen enforcement, and the IOC has responded by creating a new drug-testing authority to operate under WADA and handle doping control at the games.[122] That is clearly a step in the right direction, but whether it will go far enough will depend on the authority's resources, technical capabilities, and enforcement powers.

## Strategies for Professional Athletics

Addressing the full variety of cheating techniques in professional athletics will require an equally varied set of strategies. The most obvious and probably most effective response is to substantially strengthen penalties and enforcement structures. As one researcher concludes, "baseball detects and punishes only the most stupid and obvious perpetrators," and penalties are often lax.[123] The same is true in other sports. The four-month suspension for a repeated soccer offender such as Luis Suarez sent the wrong message.[124] Pitcher and manager George Bamberger captured the prevailing ethos among many players:

> We are paid to win games. There are rules, and there are consequences if you break them. If you're a pro, then you don't decide whether to cheat based on if it's "right or wrong." You base it on whether or not you can get away with it, and what the penalty might be.[125]

NFL player Jeremy Shockley similarly observed that "I feel like I've been coached that way my whole life—to play dirty and to play mean."[126]

If that is the mindset, then penalties need to be more substantial. The current practice of suspending cheaters for a specified period is inadequate if they can reap the advantages at contract renewal time. When baseball player Melky Cabrera tested positive for performance-enhancing drugs, he was suspended for 50 games. Then, two months later, he was rewarded with a two-year $16 million contract, by far the best of his career. Other guilty athletes have re-signed with the same teams and received raises.[127] That incentive system needs to be reversed.

More attention also needs to focus on suppliers, not simply athletes. For example, one commentator has proposed that new, potentially performance-enhancing medicines should only be released once the producer had provided an effective testing method. Athletes could be required to have their doctor registered and certified by the national anti-doping agency, and penalties could include fines and removal from the medical register.[128]

Reputational sanctions also need to be greater. One reason cheating remains common is that fans are complicit. As David and Daniel Luban argue, "far from becoming incensed by cheating in baseball, fans tolerate it and—truth be told—fans enjoy it."[129] They attribute this enjoyment to our nation's

> love-hate relationship with formal rules and authority. At one level, Americans understand the importance of laws and extol the rule of law. At another level, we hate red tape and despise robotic rule-following. It's a cultural contradiction engraved in our national psyche. We know

> that we need speed limits and state troopers, but we speed all the time and we don't like troopers who ticket us. A moment's reflection on that flash of sullen anger everyone feels when they get pulled over for speeding explains a lot about why baseball fans boo the umpires . . . . We tolerate rule breaking as long as it's equal opportunity and doesn't violate some deeper principle, and we admire the audacity of players who care more about the game than the rule book . . . If players never cheated, it would show that baseball doesn't deserve passion; in a curious way, cheating shows respect for the game.[130]

In recognition of that ambivalence, Luban and Luban argue for a distinction between "good cheating and bad cheating." Bad cheating is the kind that undermines fundamental fairness and "threatens to make baseball a worse game."[131]

But drawing that line is a tricky business, and one difficult to explain to an eight-year-old, who needs to internalize respect for rules. We can, to be sure, recognize better and worse forms of cheating. It is worse to drill the batter than cork the bat, and better to feign injury than to cause it. But our culture in general and sports in particular would be fairer if we declined to recognize a category of "good cheating" and if fans were less tolerant of those who engage in it.

We also need to combat the mindset, expressed by Olympic chief Jacques Rogge, that "Hoping for a drug-free Olympic Games is naive; cheating is embedded in human nature."[132] It may well be that some individuals will always try to game the system, but it does not follow that we should let them get away with it. We need to remember that professional athletes are role models for the nation, and even actions that are not harmful to them or don't seem to undermine "fundamental fairness" set the wrong example for others.

In a celebrated Nike ad, Charles Barkley claimed that he should not be considered a role model simply because he could put a basketball through a hoop.[133] Parents and teachers, he pointed out, were better suited for that role. But the reason he was in the commercial in the first instance was precisely because he served as an example, like it or not. And that role carries corresponding ethical responsibilities that society has an interest in enforcing.

## College Athletics

In 1928, after a long career as a college coach and administrator, R.H. Jordan wrote:

> If one wishes to know the soundness or weakness of a school, he or she should examine the athletic program . . . If there is dishonesty,

> selfishness, hypocrisy, the story will be told in athletics. If there is truth, honor, courage, self-control, these will be manifested in the games.[134]

By that standard, too many institutions fall short.

Cheating in college sports persists along three dimensions. First, coaches and administrators have cheated in ways large and small. As noted earlier, they have provided meals, transportation, lodging, clothes, and tuition in violation of NCAA rules; they have also gambled on tournaments, and used ineligible players.[135] At some schools, boosters, with the knowledge of the athletics department, have paid players under the table, in amounts sometimes totaling $10,000 annually.[136] Schools have also compensated athletes for jobs they never performed.[137] Second, athletes have cheated in courses to maintain their eligibility to play. And third, institutions have cheated athletes out of a genuine academic experience in order to ensure their eligibility and undivided attention to competition.

In chronicling a scandal at the University of North Carolina (UNC), Jay Smith and Mary Willingham concluded that too many athletes are "handed a cheap knockoff of the academic experience their typical nonathlete classmates can reliably expect to receive."[138] What makes the situation worse is that

> the athletes thus defrauded come disproportionately from socioeconomically disadvantaged positions, and they are also disproportionately African American . . . . By systematically neglecting the true educational needs of some of their most academically challenged students, precisely so as to facilitate their own pursuit of profits and wins, universities carry out the greatest of all scandals in big-time college sports.[139]

Richard Southall, director of the College Sport Research Institute at the University of South Carolina agrees. "We pretend that it's feasible to recruit high school graduates with minimal academic qualifications, give them a full-time job as a football or basketball player at a Division 1 NCAA school, and somehow have them get up to college-level reading and writing skills at the same time they're enrolled in college-level classes . . . . [W]e're all kidding ourselves."[140]

UNC is a sobering case history. Its estimated national revenues from athletics have totaled over 16 billion annually. To sustain that enterprise, athletic and academic officials worked together for over two decades "to relieve hundreds of athletes of the burden of having to follow an authentic and educationally sound curriculum."[141] African and Afro-American studies courses, particularly those offered in the summer or as independent studies, provided high enough grades to offset the often dismally poor GPA earned in required courses. Students in African and Afro-American courses averaged a solid 3.0 although their average in other classes was 1.89.[142] There was apparently no expectation that people would do the reading in these athlete-friendly courses. According to one professor, "about 60 percent of the class clearly had no idea what was going on."[143] Eventually, at least for a certain subset of their courses, the department chair "simply eliminated the expectation that [students would] be present for anything at all."[144] All told, between 1990 and 2011, the department offered more than 200 lecture classes that never met.[145] In courses that did meet, a 10- or 20-page paper earned three credits and a good grade, and was often recycled from earlier semesters or cobbled together by tutors.[146] It was unclear whether anyone actually read the papers.[147] One academic counselor frequently served as a ghostwriter for football players; she would have them talk about what they wanted to write while she did the actual composing.[148] An internal investigation also revealed some 560 grade changes that were suspected to be unauthorized.[149]

UNC was not alone.[150] At Auburn, the chair of the sociology department supervised 250 students in independent studies projects. Football players averaged a 3.3 grade in his classes, compared with 2.1 in other courses.[151] At Syracuse, an academic counselor and receptionist wrote a paper for a Brazilian basketball player whose eligibility was at stake.[152] At the University of Washington, a Swahili instructor faxed examinations to coaches and received faxed answers in return.[153] At the University of Tennessee, a professor who headed the university's tutoring program blew the whistle on cheating and paid the price in hate mail and threats of physical violence by disgruntled fans.[154] At the University of Minnesota, a former office manager for the Academic Counseling Unit in athletics confessed to having written papers for at least 19 basketball players over a period of five years; the team's coach warned her that "the papers can't be too good."[155] A tutor who insisted on remedial tutoring for a star basketball player and refused to write his papers was not renewed; an investigation revealed that athletic department personnel were "actively plotting to subvert academic standards."[156]

At the University of Michigan, a psychology professor offered at least 250 independent study courses for athletes over a three-year period in addition to his regular teaching load. They were widely viewed as a "safety net" for academically challenged students.[157] When questioned, a university dean claimed that "this is the kind of faculty experience we aspire to provide for all of our students."[158] The *Ann Arbor News* found that two football players were able to add one of these independent study courses with only four weeks to go in a 14-week semester. This was seen as unproblematic because there was not much catching up to do.[159] Students reported spending 15 to 25 minutes a week in the professor's office, although a three-credit-hour course is supposed to require an average of six hours of work outside the classroom in addition to three hours in class each week.[160] One hockey player disclosed that his three independent study courses were conducted primarily through email. A football player similarly acknowledged that his professor was not really "work oriented, he's not just bringing you in to write papers and all that stuff."[161]

In schools' most profitable sports of basketball and football, many athletes "come from challenging school and home environments [that do] . . . not always prepare them well for college."[162] Some are reading only at the elementary school level.[163] These athletes are under enormous pressure to do whatever it takes to maintain their academic eligibility to compete. As one UNC basketball player put it, "I'm my family's lottery ticket . . . I have to succeed."[164] Counselors have often steered these athletes toward an undemanding curriculum that leaves them in essentially the same "academically undernourished state in which they had arrived on campus."[165] Faculty who need a stipend for teaching in the summer have incentives to create athlete-friendly courses to boost enrollment. One UNC professor, after promising a course with no tests, got 30 athletes to enroll in his Naval Weapons class.[166] Some research suggests that athletes in football and basketball grow "increasingly cynical about and uninterested in academics" the more time they spend on campus.[167] What these players are told, "in so many subtle and not-so-subtle ways, is that they should regard their academic experiences either as a necessary evil or as a fringe benefit to enjoy only as time allows."[168]

The solutions are obvious. If schools admit athletes with deficient academic skills, then adequate programs of remedial education should be available.[169] Other proposals include extending scholarships to cover five years, shortening athletic schedules, avoiding games during exam periods, and placing academic counseling and tutoring programs under independent leadership outside departments of athletics.[170] Stiffer sanctions are also necessary. The NCAA's response to egregious violations by North Carolina's football program was only a postseason ban for one year, reductions of 15 scholarships, and three years of probation.[171]

## Missed Opportunities

Participation in sports has an ethical dimension. It can reinforce values such as fairness, responsibility, and honesty, as well as personal characteristics such as teamwork, loyalty, self-sacrifice, discipline, and perseverance.[172] Yet this potential too often goes at least partly unrealized. According to some research, the longer persons are in organized sports, the more morally callused they become, and the less respect they show for opponents, officials, coaches, and teammates.[173] Other evidence similarly suggests that athletic participation is often accompanied by less mature moral reasoning, which reflects the self-interested nature of the activity.[174] Vince Lombardi's celebrated claim that "winning isn't everything, it's the only thing" has a corrosive effect on ethical values. Peanuts' Charlie Brown added his own dispiriting gloss. When told that "Winning isn't everything," he responded, "That's true, but losing isn't anything."[175]

Society can ill afford that message. As Stephen Carter puts it, "what turns competitiveness into sportsmanship is a respect for one's opponent and one's teammates, and the rules by which the game is played. Sportsmanship implies a desire to win but a willingness to lose, to accept defeat is also a part of the game."[176]

Elite athletes are role models for the nation, and both they and their coaches should encourage all that is best in athletic endeavors.[177] The younger the athlete, the more influence the coach has over attitudes affecting cheating, and an emphasis on mastery rather than winning can have positive impact.[178] Too many youth sports programs lack that focus.[179] Coaches and parents should direct participants' attention towards self-improvement, effort, and the intrinsic quality of the experience.[180]

Organizations such as the Positive Coaching Alliance, which is designed to give youth and high school athletes a "character building" experience, are part of the solution.[181] Fans and parents can also play a more positive role, and avoid the tacit tolerance of cheating that remains common. Sportsmanship should involve more than platitudes dutifully recited on ceremonial occasions. It should be an integral aspect of the athletic culture.

Two celebrated events in collegiate football bring that point home. In 1940, Cornell University played Dartmouth for the top ranking in the nation. Dartmouth led 3-0 with a minute to go in the game. Cornell was stopped short on the fourth down, which should have ended the game. But confused officials ruled that Cornell could run another play. Cornell scored on the fifth down and won the game. The following Monday, a newsreel showed the mistake. However, officials of the Eastern Intercollegiate Athletic Association interpreted the rules to prevent a change in score. Cornell's athletics director and head football coach Carl Snavely forfeited the victory and sent a telegram to Dartmouth extending congratulations. Fifty years later, a similar mistake occurred in the Big Eight game between Colorado and Missouri. Colorado scored on a fifth down to win the game and go on to share the national championship. Bill McCartney, Colorado's coach, and leader of the Promise Keepers, a religious organization, refused to forfeit the victory and claimed, "Only the Lord can judge me. I'm confident HE will find that we did the right thing."[182]

That game was a missed opportunity. It is not only the Lord that does the judging. When values play out on a public stage, athletic leaders should embody what is best in sports. They need every opportunity to reinforce ideals to which all competitors should aspire.

# 3

# Cheating in Organizations

The cost of cheating in organizations is staggering. The typical organization loses an estimated 5 percent of its revenues each year to fraud, amounting to a global total of some $3.7 trillion annually.[1] When employees cheat on safety-related matters, the price may be paid in human lives, as recent scandals involving car manufacturers attest.

Cheating in organizations occurs with depressing regularity. Studies cited in Chapter 1 find that between one-third and one-half of employees observe unethical conduct on the job.[2] When Americans contemplate the losses resulting from workplace cheating, they tend to blame rogue individuals and rogue institutions: "bad apples" and "bad barrels."[3] By contrast, when experts describe the same behaviors, they tend to emphasize the normality of deception in everyday life.[4] Some of the country's leading corporations have the sorriest records. During one recent four-year period, the world's top 16 financial services institutions (including Bank of America and JPMorgan Chase) paid $300 billion in penalties, fines, settlements, and legal costs resulting from fraud, money laundering, rate rigging, and related activities.[5] Many individuals involved in that misconduct were otherwise upstanding members of their communities. As one researcher notes, "[a]lmost all the studies have agreed on one point: White-collar offenders are psychologically normal."[6] And they almost always fail to see themselves as corrupt.[7] The individuals victimizing others are often victims themselves as well—victims of their own self-deception.[8]

Part of the reason is that individuals are less likely to view a decision to cheat as involving ethical issues when it arises in workplaces rather than in other contexts.[9] As one manager put it in Robert Jackall's famous case study on organizational misconduct, "What's right in the corporation is not what is right in a man's home or his church."[10] When employees cheat their organization, for example by taking company property, they frequently reason that the "company can easily afford it," or "they'll never miss it."[11] In a study of pilfering at an electronic factory, four-fifths of those surveyed believed that their peers did not feel guilty about their conduct.[12] As one worker explained, "It's a corporation . . . It's not like taking from one person . . . . [P]eople justify it [on grounds] that the corporation wouldn't be hurt by it . . . they just jack the price up and screw the customer. They're not losing anything . . . . [Pilfering] gives them a nice big tax write off." Another similarly noted, "A company won't miss it like a person would. This don't make it right but it justifies it in their mind."[13]

Cheating in organizations comes in three forms. One involves misconduct that benefits the employee at the expense of the organization. Cheating an employer out of funds, property, or productive work time are common examples. A second form of misconduct occurs by leaders at the expense of workers. Cheating employees out of overtime or benefits are textbook cases. A third form of cheating serves the organization at the expense of third parties, and often occurs at the request or with the tacit support of its managers. In effect, too little organizational loyalty can shortchange the entity; too much can shortchange the public.[14] Although these different types of cheating have somewhat different dynamics, they are all driven by self-interest and facilitated by organizational culture.

## Forms of Cheating

In *From Hire to Liar: The Role of Deception in the Workplace,* David Shulman describes a wide variety of cheating for which organizations pay the price. Workers in his study, like those in other research, spent hours talking on the phone to friends, doing personal errands, and "cyberloafing"—surfing the Internet, shopping online, social networking, and playing video games.[15] Online slacking has become increasingly common. Studies of United States workers have found that between 64 and 90 percent acknowledge using the Internet for recreational purposes during work hours, and that organizations lose a staggering amount of productive time as a consequence.[16] In one typical case, an employee set up his computer so he could play games but switch the screen to a financial spreadsheet with a single click if someone walked by.[17]

Another way to cheat organizations involves resume fraud. Studies find that between 40 and 53 percent of resumes include false claims, most often involving educational credentials, work experience, and prior salaries.[18]

Other workers shortchange organizations in less conventional ways. One individual in Shulman's study worked for the state during the summer clearing a river of debris. When he and his colleagues failed to find enough debris, they arranged with the fire department to bring them wood that they could hose down and pretend to have found in the river. Their supervisors were aware of the deception. But in their view, "wood was being found, jobs were being saved, and that's all that mattered."[19] In another case, a software consultant summarized common attitudes with uncommon candor: "My real goal at work is to do as little work as possible while getting paid as much as possible. That's it, and I don't feel bad about it at all." If questioned about his delays in completing a task, he simply explained that "I ran into a problem," and his colleagues were too busy with their own work to notice that he was not busy with his.[20]

Other forms of cheating occur at much higher and costlier levels. On Wall Street, some traders have engaged in what they call "pump and dump." They encourage clients to bid up the stock price of a company above its market value. They then sell their own stock, held illegally under assumed names by fellow conspirators, before the price tumbles. Investors can lose hundreds of millions of dollars.[21] In *Moral Mazes,* sociologist Robert Jackall recounts the unhappy history of an accountant who stumbled on pension fund fraud orchestrated by the CEO. When the accountant reported it, a vice president told him "to forget the whole thing. Everyone does it. That's just part of the game in business today."[22] William Aramony, the CEO of United Way, evidently held the same view. His personal use of organizational funds resulted in convictions for fraud, conspiracy, and money laundering. He diverted money donated for charitable causes to fund a European vacation and pay an $80,000 salary for his girlfriend's "hour or so" of work.[23] In the aftermath of the scandal, donations dropped by over 15 percent in some United Way chapters.[24]

In other cases, managers cheat their own employees. A national survey of some 4,000 low-wage workers found that more than two-thirds experienced at least one pay-related legal violation in the previous week, totaling about 15 percent of earnings. Three-quarters were not paid the required overtime rate, and another quarter were paid less than the applicable minimum wage. Of those who complained, over 40 percent experienced illegal retaliation.[25] Notorious examples of such conduct involve Walmart, which once paid over $640 million to settle 63 class action suits charging various forms of wage theft.[26] Organizations owned by Donald Trump have a similarly sorry record of stiffing low-level workers and making litigation too expensive for them to recoup their losses.[27] A classic example was a suit for lost wages by a dishwasher against Trump's Mar-a-Lago Club resort in Palm Beach. The company ultimately settled the claim for $7,500, an amount that hardly justified the employee's legal costs.[28] In another celebrated example involving a Trump organization, the company dragged out a case for 16 years before settling claims that it cheated 200 undocumented Polish workers out of wages and medical and pension benefits.[29] Undocumented immigrants are particularly vulnerable to such exploitation because they fear that complaints will expose them to risks of deportation.[30]

A third form of cheating benefits the organization as well as the employee, at least in the short term. In *Liar's Poker,* Michael Lewis describes a mutual reward system at Salomon Brothers. While in training to become a Wall Street trader, Lewis learned that clients were "exploitable," and that their vulnerability could pave the way for organizational profits and personal bonuses. The firm conveyed its priorities through "Hoot and Holler," a public address system that announced successes by traders and salespersons. When one of the firm's traders manipulated Lewis to sell a bundle of poorly performing Salomon-owned AT&T bonds to an unsuspecting German banker, the sale was announced in glowing terms on Hoot and Holler. Lewis then realized that he had "inadvertently swindled a customer and that this was considered a noteworthy achievement by the firm."[31] When Lewis complained to the trader who had misled him, the trader responded, "Look, who do you work for, this guy or Salomon Brothers?"[32]

In other cases of organizational misconduct, the participants do not receive direct financial benefits; rather, their reward comes in status, job security, and relationships with peers and supervisors. As Columbia Law professor John Coffee has long noted, corporate misconduct is often attributable to the pressure placed on mid-level employees who know that they can be readily replaced if they fail to cut corners.[33] An increasing number of in-house lawyers and other professionals have faced criminal prosecutions because, as a Securities and Exchange Commission official put it, they "twisted themselves into pretzels to accommodate the wishes of company management."[34] One WorldCom accountant reported making improper accounting adjustments requested by her superiors because she was her family's primary breadwinner, and she doubted her ability to find another job with an equivalent salary in the same city.[35] So too, a marketing official at JP Heinz explained deceptive bookkeeping as a response to profit goals that were impossible to meet: "everybody knew that if you missed the targets enough, you were out on your ear."[36] In commenting on automotive employees' willingness to fake airbrake tests, one observer noted the risks of termination and pointed out that "Your conscience doesn't pay your salary."[37]

So, too, Wells Fargo placed bank employees under what investigators titled "excruciatingly high pressure" to open new accounts; the result was that over 5,300 employees lost their jobs for misconduct associated with creating unauthorized accounts.[38] To make their quotas, bankers preyed on the most vulnerable customers: immigrants, elderly individuals with memory issues, and college students opening their first account. One ex-employee analogized the practice to "lions hunting zebras. [Bankers] would look for the weakest, the ones that would put up the least resistance."[39] Undocumented immigrants were particularly inviting targets because they would be unlikely to complain to authorities.[40] Supervisors had their own incentives to look the other way and ignore complaints.[41] A *New York Times* account ran under the title, "Pervasive Sham Deals at Wells Fargo, and No One Noticed?"[42] The response seemed to be along the lines famously coined by novelist Upton Sinclair: "It is difficult to get a man to understand something [is unethical] when his salary depends upon his not understanding it."[43]

Sometimes instructions to cheat are explicit.[44] An employee told one subordinate in Shulman's study to "just fake the signature," then paused and added "unless you're uncomfortable with that." The employee interpreted her as saying "just do it—what's the big deal? Don't bug me about it or you'll regret it."[45] Walmart managers reported instructions to engage in illegal practices such as shaving time off employees' payroll records. As one explained, "I screwed plenty of people in my career there. Honestly you have to. Its either you do it or there's the door. They told us in meetings, 'I can go hire anyone off the street and pay them fifty thousand dollars to run a store.' "[46]

In other instances, the message is more indirect. As Chapter 1 indicated, euphemisms often help make cheating more palatable. One employee recalled, "The boss will usually say something like 'Come on, you can find a way to do this, can't you?' And you know he wants it done."[47] Under these circumstances, employees learn that to be valued, they need to be "reasonable," "flexible," or "creative."[48] Such euphemisms encourage the kind of "ethical fading" described in Chapter 1. At General Motors, employees were told not to use terms such as "defect," "safety," or "problem" in writing reports, which prevented open discussion of ignition switch failures.[49] At Volkswagen, falsified emissions test results were partly attributable to managers who reportedly said something like "Please think again on that, and if you don't find a solution, we may need to find another engineer."[50] When litigation was immiment, in-house lawyers advised employees that emission-related data should be kept "only if necessary," which led to illegal destruction of thousands of documents.[51]

## The Organizational Conditions of Cheating

All of the forces that drive cheating discussed in Chapter 1 also operate in organizations. Individuals are influenced by the costs and rewards of misconduct, the social consensus concerning the behaviors at issue, and the proximity and magnitude of their consequences.[52] People are also subject to the cognitive limitations and biases that foster ethical disengagement.[53] In addition, however, they respond to an organization's culture, climate, dynamics, leadership, and structure.

### Workplace Culture, Climate, and Financial Pressures

An organization's ethical culture involves its formal and informal systems of behavioral control. Also important is its ethical climate, which involves perceived values, moral meanings given to policies and practices, and shared beliefs that certain forms of ethical reasoning and conduct are expected.[54] So for example, a climate may be predominantly principled (driven by laws, rules, and procedures), egoistic (driven by self-interest), or benevolent (driven by concern for employees, customers, and the public).[55] Cultures and climates are closely related because governance systems give rise to perceptions about values. And for obvious reasons, cheating is more common in egoistic climates.[56]

Organizational cultures are affected by larger institutional and national environments. Cheating is most likely when individuals find that legitimate means of achieving goals are blocked, and illegitimate means carry relatively low risks of sanctions.[57] Leniency in oversight makes cheating more economically profitable, and political and financial constraints often work against effective governance.[58] For multinational corporations, operating in a corrupt foreign environment increases tendencies to engage in corrupt practices themselves.[59] Complexity, vagueness, or perceived unfairness in regulations also compromises compliance.[60] Executives of a large drugstore chain rationalized submission of false Medicare prescription claims on the grounds that their legitimate requests for reimbursement had been denied. In their view, cheating was simply a way to "expedite the money the state owed to us."[61] Enron's leaders similarly blamed an inappropriate regulatory structure for their difficult circumstances and reasoned that cheating was a justifiable response. According to one senior executive, "if they're going to put in place such a stupid system, it makes sense to try to game it."[62]

Competitive pressures and market forces play an equally important role.[63] Managers from Fortune 500 companies have reported that the most important cause of unethical practices in their corporations is the pressure applied by superiors to show profits and reduce costs.[64] And those superiors feel themselves under similar pressure. The recent spate of scandals involving falsified test data by car manufacturers has been attributed partly to fierce competition coupled with stringent new regulations.[65] So, too, Enron's fraudulent accounting and finance practices were in part driven by Wall Street's unrealistic growth expectations. Managers feared that they would fail to hit the market's earnings targets and that this failure would undermine investor confidence. The result would be to erode the price of the stock, on which some of the firm's key financial transactions depended.[66] Outside firms that served Enron were under their own competitive pressures to acquiesce in its misleading accounting techniques. As one top Merrill Lynch executive put it, "Enron is a top client to Merrill Lynch. Enron views the ability to participate in transactions like this as a way to differentiate ML from the pack and add significant value."[67] Arthur Andersen accountants similarly worried about losing consulting business if they raised too many audit issues.[68] Outside lawyers were also silenced by the realization that legal work went to those who were, in the words of Enron employees, "flexible," rather than "difficult."[69]

When circumstances become particularly bleak, individuals may be driven to what white-collar crime experts term "desperation dealing."[70] A congressional committee investigating the savings and loan implosions during the 1980s concluded:

> Normally honest bankers (including thrift insiders) . . . resorted to fraud or unsafe practices in efforts to save a battered institution. In those cases an incentive existed to turn an unhealthy financial institution around by . . . making even more speculative investments, hoping to "make it big."[71]

Desperate circumstances led to desperate measures, many of them fraudulent. That created a climate of opportunity for other cheaters who were motivated more by greed than by concern for the institutions. These offenders concluded that, as the Commissioner of the California Department of Savings and Loans put it, "[t]he best way to rob a bank is to own one," and cheated Americans out of billions of dollars in life savings.[72] So, too, contemporary Silicon Valley entrepreneurs face substantial temptations to inflate sales and earnings and suppress countervailing information in order to justify high stock prices in public offerings. As one entrepreneur put it, after working for years to get a start-up ready for the offering, "the temptation to hide any last-minute adverse surprises is overwhelming."[73] In many cases of corporate misconduct, deviant norms become part of workplace cultures and convince otherwise ethical individuals to engage in illegal activities.[74] To a CEO in one of these cultures, "morals go out the window when the pressure is on."[75]

Organizations construct their cultures and climates in multiple ways: the content and enforcement of their ethical standards, their criteria for promotion and compensation, and their treatment of employees and stakeholders. Unrealistic performance goals undermine employee ethics.[76] Participants in an MCI accounting scandal cooked the books in part because their superiors established unreachable targets for collection of past bills.[77] Leslie Fay accountants falsified their ledgers in response to excessive profit expectations.[78] Wells Fargo employees opened sham accounts that customers did not authorize or want in order to meet unrealistic quotas. Those who failed to meet their targets risked termination, mandatory unpaid overtime, or other forms of retaliation.[79] Skewed reward structures also encourage unethical behavior.[80] Enron's hypercompetitive, profits-at-any-cost culture and reward structure had a predictably corrosive impact. Under the company's "rank and yank" evaluation system, employees who rated the lowest in financial performance were terminated, demoted, or passed over for promotion.[81]

How organizations respond to employees' moral concerns also affects cheating behavior. Shooting the messenger was the standard response to unwelcome ethical tidings in companies such as Enron, and ultimately, it was not just the messenger who paid the price.[82] Nor is Enron an isolated case. A former Arthur Andersen partner who brought up the subject of internal ethics in accounting practices recalled being "looked at as if [she] had teleported in from another world."[83] At Wells Fargo, one former employee recalled that "everybody knew there was fraud going on and the people trying to flag it were the ones who got in trouble."[84] Lawyers' fraudulent billing practices described in Chapter 1 persist not only because firms impose sweatshop hourly quotas, but also because "nobody wants to kill a rain maker."[85]

Employees' perceptions of organizational justice similarly influences their tendencies to cheat.[86] The most common rationalization that workers offer for stealing company property is unfair treatment by the employer.[87] Surveys of a wide variety of contexts including factory work, nursing, and fast-food restaurants find that employees cheat more when they can reframe their actions as a legitimate response to organizational injustice.[88] Wage cuts that employees feel are unfair also encourage theft.[89] Even when inequitable treatment is not directed at them personally, individuals often seek to "balance the ledger" and "even the score."[90] People reason in terms of retributive justice and view their own misconduct as a justifiable response to organizational norms. Surveyed cyberloafers are quite explicit about their retaliation. As one put it, "My boss is not the appreciative kind; I take what I can and whenever I can. Surfing the net is my way of hitting back." Another similarly reasoned that "It is OK to surf the net for non-work reasons because my boss is biased and does not treat us well."[91] Conversely, employees feel indebted to organizations that are fair, and are less likely to cheat in ways that serve their own interests at the expense of their employers.[92] Perceptions of fairness also increase individuals' willingness to report misconduct.[93]

Group loyalty is another powerful driver of ethical behavior. Individuals who identify strongly with their organization may be willing to cut corners on its behalf.[94] People who feel well treated by their employer often feel pressure to reciprocate even at the expense of their own ethical principles.[95] Perceptions of peer behavior also exert a strong influence on ethical choice. They establish a standard for appropriate workplace conduct, and can socialize otherwise moral individuals into immoral activities.[96] Having a close psychological connection to others makes their unethical actions seem less problematic.[97]

The concerns of fellow group members are often more salient than those of distant or abstract victims.[98] Compensation structures that reward team performance can thus compound peer pressure to cheat, as was true at Volkswagen during the emission test scandal.[99] People are more likely to rationalize cheating behavior when the benefits are shared with others.[100] And although Volkswagen's violation of safety standards increased the public's risks of lung disease, those responsible would never confront individuals who paid the price.[101] So too, in many financial scandals, fraudulent practices that make firms appear stronger lull executives into feeling that their actions are not actually harmful. "There's no uncomfortable dissonance."[102] There are no visible victims; "all the shareholders, they love you."[103]

Individuals also feel uncomfortable raising ethical issues that make others feel uncomfortable. As Jackall reports in *Moral Mazes*, employees generally want to be viewed as "our kind of guy" and "someone who can be trusted."[104] When individuals acquiesce in wrongdoing in response to peer pressure, they often attempt to reduce the cognitive dissonance between their behaviors and values by readjusting their values and internalizing group norms. They then socialize others to conform to prevailing standards, which helps perpetuate a culture of misconduct.[105]

The importance of collective approval, well-documented by behavioral psychologists, was also well-captured by essayist C.S. Lewis in "The Inner Ring."[106] He describes how our need to belong to a favored circle eclipses moral commitments:

> Just at the moment when you are most anxious not to appear crude, or naif, or a prig—the hint will come. It will be the hint of something which is not quite in accordance with the rules of fair play: something which the public, the ignorant, romantic public would never understand . . . but something, says your new friend, which "we"—and at the word "we" you try not to blush for mere pleasure—"we always do." And you will be drawn in, if you are drawn in, not by desire for gain or ease, but simply because at that moment you cannot bear to be thrust back again into the cold outer world . . . . And then, if you are drawn in, next week it will be something a little further from the rules, and next year something further still . . . . It may end in a crash, a scandal, and penal servitude; it may end in millions [and] a peerage . . . . But you will be a scoundrel.[107]

As Lewis suggests, incremental acts of misconduct can help to institutionalize and normalize cheating.[108] Individuals feel pressure to engage in slightly deviant acts, and then, to relieve the cognitive dissonance between their behaviors and their values, they engage in rationalizations. Those rationalizations, in turn, license more substantial wrongdoing, and people end up embroiled in cheating behaviors that they would have initially rejected outright.[109] In some instances, group dynamics can create a "social cocoon," a subculture where deviant norms take hold.[110]

## Ethical Leadership

Leaders have a powerful influence on organizational culture by modeling ethical behavior, setting appropriate standards, and holding employees responsible.[111] Studies find that the most important determinant of workplace climate is the day-to-day behavior of its leaders.[112] The presence of moral role models at all levels of the organizational hierarchy tends to reduce immoral conduct, including cheating.[113] Employees who see leaders willing to follow through on formal ethics policies are also more likely to report misconduct.[114] In describing ethical leaders, individuals emphasize a willingness to communicate clear ethical boundaries and to look beyond the "bottom line."[115] Such leadership has been particularly critical in environments where cheating has been tolerated. Top management in one corporation saw a strong stance against bribery as crucial in an industry in which "graft, payoffs, trips to Bermuda . . . and less obvious deal sweeteners are a way of life." Leaders' own policies and practices helped others internalize "personal codes of honor; they speak privately of the importance of not being known as men or women 'who can be had.' "[116]

By contrast, leaders who pay only lip service to ethics and ignore, condone, or reward cheating have the opposite effect.[117] Enron's "tone at the top" was "profits at all costs."[118] Ethics rules were treated as niceties made to be stretched and circumvented when necessary. Those who advanced were those able to "stay focused" on financial objectives "unburdened by moral anxiety."[119] That untroubled state could often be reached only by willful ignorance, a deliberate avoidance of compromising information.[120] One automobile executive similarly explained that in his industry, "The rules are meant to be broken. If you aren't willing to test the limits of what's acceptable . . . you'll never make it to the next level of performance."[121] An oil company leader echoed that view: "If you're too afraid of stepping over the foul line, you'll never figure out how close to it you can get."[122] So, too, Salomon Brothers CEO John Gutfreund was notorious for overlooking misconduct by those who delivered short-term profits, and getting rid of those who fell short.[123] Although he sometimes "talked about values, . . . his conduct often sent a contrary message."[124] The hypocrisy of some leaders' moral posturing was apparent in the shamelessly candid response by Goldman Sachs to a fraud suit. Shareholders alleged that the firm had misrepresented the nature of a deal by failing to live up to its frequent public statements about the importance of integrity to the firm. In seeking to have the suit dismissed, Goldman Sachs lawyers argued that "misstatements alleged in the complaint—e.g. regarding the firms' 'integrity' and 'honesty' —are nothing more than classic 'puffery.' "[125]

Other examples of failed leadership involve individuals who trivialize misconduct or short-circuit ethical discussion. Wells Fargo CEO John Stumpf seemed blindsided by customers' fury over paying for unwanted accounts because in his view, the amount of money they lost wasn't significant and the fraud wasn't "orchestrated."[126] According to the bank's internal investigation, the perception was that Stumpf was not "someone who wanted to hear bad news." Nor did he want to reduce or eliminate unrealistic sales quotas, for fear that employees would be "under motivated."[127] When presented with evidence of misconduct, Stump and other senior leaders, were "disinclined . . . to see the problem as systemic. It was common to blame employees who violated Wells Fargo's rules without analyzing what caused or motivated them to do so. Effect was confused with cause."[128] So, too, at a corruption trial that convicted one Volkswagen executive, the CEO referred to the widespread use of company funds on prostitutes as mere "irregularities."[129] Another company that invested significant resources in an ostensibly "world class" ethical compliance program had leaders who failed to take it seriously. As one disillusioned senior manager noted, at monthly two-hour meetings with the chief operating officer "we spend 5 minutes on compliance and 115 minutes on profitability. So, you tell me—what matters here?"[130]

## Diffusion and Displacement of Responsibility

A related problem involves diffusion and displacement of responsibility. Either responsibility is so widely shared that no one feels accountable, or individuals shift their obligations to others in the organization. In one study of white-collar offenders, "virtually every one [interviewed] . . . pointed out, even complained that it was not he who was the true villain—it was always someone else."[131] A highly publicized example ended with proceedings by the Securities and Exchange Commission (SEC) against the CEO, top officers, and general counsel of Salomon Brothers.[132] The case arose from the firm's failure to discipline and disclose securities law violations by one of its top traders, Paul Mozer. To settle the case, the firm ended up paying almost $300 million in fines, which at the time was the second-largest penalty ever imposed on a financial institution. During a brief suspension, Salomon lost major clients and over $4 billion in trades, and its stock price and market share subsequently plummeted. According to the CEO who came on after the SEC charges, the events constituted a "billion-dollar error of judgment."[133] How that error occurred provides an illuminating case history of diffusion of responsibility and failed leadership.

The culture at Salomon was highly competitive. Mozer was a thirty-four-year-old trader whose aggressive style fit right in. He was very rich, but from his perspective, not rich enough. To increase his earnings, he exceeded Treasury limits on bids for government securities by placing a false bid in someone else's name. When the matter came to light, his supervisor, Vice President John Meriwether, discussed the matter with General Counsel Donald Feurstein, President Thomas

Strauss, and CEO John Gutfreund. Without further investigation of some other red flags, the group accepted Mozer's characterization of the bid as an isolated incident. However, Feurstein believed that the conduct was probably criminal, and the group agreed it should be reported to the New York Federal Reserve Bank.[134] A subsequent SEC report described the decision-making as follows:

> [E]ach of the four executives who attended meetings . . . placed the responsibility for investigating Mozer's conduct and placing limits on his activities on someone else. Meriwether stated that he believed that once he had taken the matter of Mozer's conduct to Strauss and Strauss had brought Feuerstein and Gutfruend into the process, he had no further responsibility to take action with respect to the false bid unless instructed to do so by one of those individuals. Meriwether stated that he also believed that, though he had the authority to recommend that action be taken to discipline Mozer or limit his activities, he had no authority to take such action unilaterally. Strauss stated that he believed that Meriwether, who was Mozer's direct supervisor, and Feuerstein, who was responsible for the legal and compliance activities of the firm, would take whatever steps were necessary or required as a result of Mozer's disclosure. Feuerstein stated that he believed that, once a report to the government was made, the government would instruct Salomon about how to investigate the matter. Gutfreund stated that he believed that the other executives would take whatever steps were necessary to properly handle the matter. According to the executives, there was no discussion among them about any action that would be taken to investigate Mozer's conduct or to place limitations on his activities.[135]

The result was that Meriwether admonished Mozer and told him that the firm would report his conduct to the government. However, the firm failed to do so. Some speculated that Gutfreund was concerned that public disclosure might trigger fines, lawsuits, and adverse publicity, which would jeopardize his already precarious leadership position.[136] According to one insider, Gutfreund "went to sleep hoping it would just go away."[137] It did not. Mozer submitted further illegal bids that finally triggered an internal investigation. But it took three months for the company to notify the SEC and to issue a press release acknowledging the misconduct. That release did not disclose management's prior awareness of the incident.

No one lived happily ever after. Gutfreund, Strauss, and Meriwether resigned and settled securities charges by accepting fines and suspensions. Mozer was fired and pled guilty to lying to the Federal Reserve Bank. He served four months in prison and was banned from the securities industry for life. The case illustrates the form of bureaucracy that Hannah Arendt described as the most dangerous of all: "rule by Nobody."[138]

Salomon was not an isolated example. Displacement of responsibility often leads to the moral disengagement described in Chapter 1.[139] And it has been partly responsible for ethics scandals plaguing the automobile industry. In a case involving a fraudulent brake report at BF Goodrich, test laboratory employees who prepared its false exhibits explained that "we're just drawing some curves and what happens to them after they leave here, well, we're not responsible."[140] So too, an expert's report on the 2015 faulty ignition switch scandal at General Motors described

> a troubling disavowal of responsibility made possible by a proliferation of committees. It is an example of what witnesses called the "GM salute," a crossing of arms and pointing outward towards others, indicating that the responsibility belongs to someone else. Here, because a committee was "responsible," no single person bore responsibility or was individually accountable.[141]

There was also evidence of a "GM nod," in which employees agreed to a course of action but failed to follow through. One example involved a junior attorney who asked whether there should be a recall. According to an expert's report on the scandal, the lawyer "was told that the issue had already been raised with engineering, that the engineers were working on it, and that they had not come up with a solution. This lawyer got the 'vibe' that the lawyers had 'done everything we can do.' "[142]

A fragmentation of information as well as responsibility can also help obscure the full ethical dimensions of an issue. GM and other car manufacturers have been notorious for creating "information silos" that mask patterns of defects that should raise alarms.[143] The result, as General Motors CEO Mary Barra summed it up, was that in her company, "Nobody took responsibility" for the ignition switch problem.[144] The cost for the corporation was over a billion dollars in legal liability.[145]

## Whistle-Blowing

Silence is the default option in most organizations because of the risk employees associate with whistle-blowing.[146] Organizations generally don't want their dirty linen washed in public, and even internal whistle-blowing can make others feel uncomfortable.[147] The message they send is "get with the program or find another company."[148] The problem was well illustrated in a celebrated case involving Walmart executives who bribed Mexican officials to get permits for new stores. There, a culture of silence led to suppression of a whistle-blower's report and prevented the company's leaders from hearing of the corruption.[149] Wells Fargo's indifference and retaliation against those who complained about sham accounts had similar effects.[150]

Enron's response to whistle-blower Sherron Watkins was another textbook case of what not to do. After meeting privately with Watkins, CEO Ken Lay directed the company's outside law firm Vinson & Elkins to investigate her charges, but not to explore the accounting issues that were at the core of her concerns. The law firm did not object to these restrictions on its inquiry. Nor did it support her call for a probe by independent lawyers and accountants. Instead, the firm found no need for further investigation, although it did acknowledge "bad cosmetics," and the risk of adverse publicity and litigation.[151]

Punitive responses to such reports effectively deter other individuals from speaking out.[152] Studies of whistle-blowing find that those who seek to expose ethical violations routinely encounter harassment, ostracism, and retaliation; some become permanent pariahs in their fields.[153] Although retaliation is greatest for those who report to external agencies or the media, it can also be substantial for those who use internal channels.[154] Sadly, retaliation is most likely for disclosures of misconduct that is pervasive and severe, and all too often, these reports go largely unheeded or produce no lasting change.[155] Fear of reprisals, along with lack of confidence that reports would be productive, are the major reasons that employees give for not airing ethical concerns.[156] Many doubt that anonymous or confidential disclosures will remain so, or that paper protections against job retaliation will prove effective.[157] As one employee summed it up, "Nobody likes a whistle-blower. I thought it would end my career."[158]

## Remedial Strategies

### Culture and Climate

Organizations that seek to reduce cheating need to focus first on ethical culture, the interplay between the formal rules, policies, and reward structures and the informal norms and expectations that influence members' behavior. Equally important is ethical climate—the perceptions that members have about the moral content of practices and procedures. Because informal social controls are more effective in deterring unethical behavior than formal compliance structures, organizations need to assess their climates and cultures, and to ensure that informal norms match formal commitments.[159] Fostering ethical infrastructures requires integrating ethical concerns into all activities, particularly performance evaluation and reward systems. Organizations that place overwhelming influence on bottom-line concerns encourage employees to do the same and to "put their moral values on hold."[160]

Among the most effective strategies for promoting ethical culture are ethical leadership, fair treatment of employees, and open discussion of ethics.[161] As noted earlier, leaders are crucial both as moral role models and moral managers. They can set a personal example, establish appropriate policies, design effective reward structures, and hold others accountable for ethical performance.[162] Followers who perceive leaders as honest, trustworthy, fair, and caring are more likely to respond in kind.[163] It is not just the tone at the top that is important. Supervisors at all organizational levels need to convey high expectations for ethical behavior and zero tolerance for cheating.[164] Those who do so should be identified, rewarded, and reinforced.[165]

Understanding cultural norms is essential to ensuring organizational justice. As previous discussion made clear, employees' ethical conduct, job performance, and loyalty to the organization partly depend on its perceived fairness.[166] Employees care about both procedural and distributive justice. Their perceptions depend on whether reward structures seem equitable, whether performance standards seem reasonable and impartially applied, and whether workers are respected and valued in decision-making processes.[167] Because individuals often retaliate in response to unfairness, leaders need to monitor perceptions of organizational justice. And they should reward managers who treat subordinates with dignity and interpersonal sensitivity.[168] Unpalatable decisions are less likely to provoke retaliatory responses if employees feel that their concerns have been heard and that they have been treated with respect. As Winston Churchill famously explained the surprisingly genteel tone in his declaration of war against Japan, "If you have to kill a man, it costs you nothing to be polite."[169]

Organizations also need to know how employees respond to surveillance. In some contexts, an absence of oversight signals trust and fosters exemplary behavior; in other circumstances, it is an invitation to misconduct.[170] As Chapter 1 noted, instituting a weak but intrusive compliance system is particularly likely to be counterproductive. Such monitoring can trigger resentment, erode moral motivations, and encourage employees to view their behavior in expedient rather than ethical terms; their focus becomes not what is right but what is the likelihood that they will get caught and what will it cost them if they do.[171] So, for example, employees often perceive organizational surveillance of their Internet usage as an indication that their employer doesn't trust them or respect their privacy.[172]

Other strategies carrying fewer risks include ethical climate surveys, hotlines, and ethics officers or ombudspersons. Organizations should ask employees whether their workplace has a culture of integrity and whether they can raise concerns without fear of retaliation.[173] By preserving confidentiality, such interventions can encourage reporting by individuals wary of retribution.[174] Taken together, these initiatives can help to identify patterns of misconduct and possible "ethical sinkholes."[175]

Under the Obama administration, troubled organizations increasingly had what experts label a "culture moment."[176] Part of the reason was that government regulators were pushing them to do so. According to one banking CEO, "culture is the new rabbit Washington is chasing."[177] If that is the right metaphor, there is reason behind the chase. Decades of research underscore the importance of workplace culture in driving ethical behavior. It is long past time for organizations and their regulators to get with the program. If Trump's administration reverses course and mirrors his own disregard for business ethics and regulatory oversight, the public will pay the price.[178]

## Ethical Leadership

As noted earlier, one consistent finding of research on organizational culture is the significance of leaders' own ethical commitments. That commitment is critical in several respects. First, leaders set a moral tone and a moral example by their own behavior.[179] Employees take cues about appropriate conduct from those in supervisory positions.[180] Whether workers believe that leaders care about principles as much as profits significantly affects the frequency of ethical conduct.[181] Employees who see superiors follow through on formal ethics policies are more likely to report misconduct.[182] Leaders also play a crucial role in establishing appropriate reward and monitoring structures and in responding to cheating incidents. Oversight of those with oversight responsibility is particularly critical. Gatekeepers need to be held accountable.[183]

Lawyers have a special role to play as the "guardian of . . . corporate integrity" and the "conscience of the corporation."[184] Sometimes this requires reminding employees that, as Nike's general counsel put it, "making money is only good if you keep the money;" pursuing profits through cheating is not a sustainable business model.[185] To bring that point home to his staff, a lawyer who served as chief compliance officer of York Capital Management hedge fund had golf shirts made to order. On one side they read: "Your Capital Management Compliance Department." The other side read: "We Take the Fun Out of Funds."[186]

Wells Fargo offers a case history in what not to do. For over a decade, despite evidence of widespread fraud, the only individuals fired were low-level employees.[187] Carrie Tolstedt, the vice president in charge of the retail branches where misconduct occurred, was never penalized. Indeed, in justifying her high compensation, the bank's proxy statements cited her high "cross selling ratios," which had been possible only through sham accounts.[188] At her retirement, she walked away with over $124 million in stock and options, and Wells Fargo CEO John

Stumpf praised her as a "standard-bearer of our culture, a champion for our customers, and a role model for responsible, principled, and inclusive leadership."[189] Had she been fired instead, she could have been forced to give back at least $45 million.[190] Although Stumpf was ultimately asked to resign, he too left with a whopping financial reward, estimated at over $130 million; when combined with earlier stock payments, he gained close to $250 million.[191] When asked by members of the Senate Banking Committee about why he had not returned any of his compensation package, he claimed that the decision was not up to him but was a matter for the bank's board of directors. Committee members reminded him that he was the board's chair.[192] Only after strong public outcry and plummeting stock prices did the board demand a forfeiture of $135 from Stumpf and $19 million from Tolstedt, which still left them with a tidy reward for their moral myopia.[193]

It should not take such external pressure for internal leaders to respond decisively to evidence of systemic misconduct. Major scandals should become moments for organizations to forge a new ethical identity. These are occasions for asking "what do we want to be," and for giving reputational concerns a higher priority.[194] To make that happen, leaders must encourage candid dialogue on ethical issues. Having someone to consult "outside their immediate circle . . . can foster more effective leadership."[195] Every individual's moral compass needs to be checked against external reference points, and leaders are no exception. Recognizing ways in which they might be wrong is crucial in determining what is likely to be right.

Consistency between words and actions is particularly important in conveying a moral message.[196] Day-to-day decisions that mesh poorly with professed values send a powerful signal. No corporate code or mission statement can counter the impact of seeing leaders stifle dissent, implement corrosive reward structures, or pursue their own self-interest at the organization's expense. Hypocrisy may be the tribute that vice pays to virtue, but it is a singularly unsuccessful leadership strategy.

## Ethics Codes

Over 90 percent of large American companies have ethics codes, and they are common in other organizations as well.[197] These formal rules can be useful in clarifying what constitutes unethical behavior, but research has been mixed about how much they influence workplace conduct.[198] As Chapter 1 noted, their effectiveness depends on whether they are seen as more than window dressing.[199] To that end, they need to be enforced through disciplinary sanctions, and reinforced by informal norms and reward structures. An article on Enron put the takeaway in its title: "Culture Matters More than Codes."[200] In one study, leading researchers Linda Treviño and Gary Weaver found that none of the middle managers surveyed were aware of their company's code, even though all of them had signed it as a condition of employment.[201]

Accordingly, asking employees to attest that they have read and complied with formal rules may be helpful in contexts where cheating has been a problem.[202] Shell requires its managers to certify that "neither the company nor its authorized representatives has been party to the offering, paying, or receiving of bribes." If such assurances are not possible, managers must discuss the reasons and submit follow-up reports.[203] Involving employees in drafting and revising ethics codes can also create greater buy-in as well as raise awareness.[204]

## Ethics Training

Ethics should be included in training and orientation programs that address workplace dilemmas as well as the structural pressures, cognitive limitations, self-interest, and self-deception that compromise decision-making.[205] Educating individuals on the biases that impede honest evaluation of their actions can help mitigate the effect of these biases.[206] Having people engage in structured moral conversation and rehearse ways of coping with concrete challenges can strengthen moral resolve and prepare them for encountering temptations in practice.[207] So, too, inviting employees to think about a prospective action from the perspective of stakeholders and the public can reinforce ethical values.[208] Open discussion of cheating can raise moral awareness, expose self-serving rationalizations, and highlight its human as well as legal, reputational, and economic costs.[209] Publicizing the losses attributable to misconduct, and making victims identifiable can be particularly effective.[210]

That was the case for Noreen Harrington, a Goldman Sachs employee who blew the whistle in a mutual fund trading scandal. The illegal practices at issue involved buying and selling funds after the market closed and exploiting time zone differences affecting the prices of international funds. Initially, she accepted it as simply part of a "nameless faceless business." Her view changed when her sister asked her for advice on her 401(k) account: "then I saw the faces of everyone whose only asset was a 401(k). At that point, I felt the need to try and make the regulators look into these abuses."[211] By incorporating such case studies in their training programs, organizations can bring home the human consequences of cheating. For similar reasons, some companies have found it useful to bring in ex-offenders, who can describe the paths that led to their convictions.[212]

Equally important is evaluation of such educational initiatives. We know that corporations spend millions of dollars annually on these training programs. What we don't know is how well they work in deterring or remedying unethical conduct, and which approaches are most effective.[213] Clearly some programs have fallen short. When the federal government instituted ethics briefing in the 1990s, one senior official at the Office of Government Ethics described a common format:

> The trainer walks into the classroom and in effect says to the class, "Look, *you* don't want to be here and *I* don't want to be here. So let's get this over with. Here's what you need to know: last year you could skate *this* close to the law, but now you can only skate *that* close. Any questions? Good."[214]

Although we might hope that such examples are now rare, we have no reliable way of knowing. To the extent that evaluation occurs, it generally involves asking participants to rate their satisfaction with the educational experience.[215] It would be far more useful to know whether they do anything differently as a result. Had Wells Fargo undertaken that inquiry, it would have learned that its ethics training was falling short. The problem was not that employees were unaware that their conduct was fraudulent, but rather that they believed their paychecks depended on it.[216] As long as the bank's corrosive reward structure remained in place, educational initiatives were unlikely to be adequate.

## Whistle-Blower Protections

An effective response to organizational cheating also requires more safe spaces for moral disagreement and more protection for whistle-blowers. As noted earlier, the problem in too many organizations is "not only does no one want to listen but no one wants to talk about not listening."[217] It is, of course, true that some dissenters are unbalanced or vindictive employees who air self-serving grievances. Bur even those whose motives are tainted may have valid concerns. Whatever the costs of coping with unjustified internal dissent, the price of suppression is likely to be greater.

Support from leaders, supervisors, and peers is all crucial in encouraging reports of misconduct. As the subtitle of one article on whistle-blowing noted: "It takes a village."[218] Best practices include: establishing and publicizing multiple channels for complaints, including confidential hotlines; assigning responsibility for prompt investigation and follow-up; ensuring a thorough review process that addresses not only individual wrongdoing but also underlying causes; and providing appropriate discipline for misconduct and protection from retaliation.[219] Some experts recommend reinforcing employees' responsibility to report abuses by sanctioning non-compliance, rewarding whistle-blowing, and treating reprisals as a prima facie firing offense.[220]

Expanded legal safeguards for whistle-blowing are equally important. The current patchwork of federal and state law leaves far too many private-sector workers unprotected from retaliation.[221] We need to strengthen legal prohibitions against reprisals, and expand resources for governmental agencies that enforce them. Investigations of retaliation have long been hampered by excessive caseloads and lack of basic training and support structures.[222] In addition to legal protections, whistle-blowers need greater public support. More resources should be available to organizations that provide publicity, advice, and legal assistance.

## Sanctions

Stiffer penalties for both individuals and organizations involved in cheating are also necessary. Traditionally, organizations have often been reluctant to identify high-level offenders, and white-collar criminals have received much more lenient sentences than street criminals.[223] However, that has begun to change, and the lack of individual prosecutions in the aftermath of the 2008–2009 financial crisis brought calls for greater accountability.[224] Occupy Wall Street demonstrators carried signs in the financial district with slogans such as "Go Directly to Jail," and "Hungry? Eat a Banker."[225]

Although recent research on the severity of sanctions paints a mixed picture, some studies still reveal disturbing disparities between street criminals and white-collar offenders.[226] One comparison of federal sentences found that the mean fraud penalty was 23 months, compared with 70 months for drug trafficking, and 83 months for robbery.[227] Defendants convicted of auto theft were four times more likely to receive a prison sentence than embezzlers, and their sentences were longer.[228] Another study of defendants convicted of grand theft found that white-collar offenders (those who cheated Medicaid) were less than half as likely to be incarcerated as blue-collar offenders. Yet the median financial losses from the Medicaid offenses were more than 10 times the median losses from the blue-collar crimes.[229]

One reason for the disparities in sentences involves the disparities in resources available to offenders. Those accused of organizational crimes can often afford expert legal assistance, because either they have adequate personal resources or their employers are required to indemnify their legal costs. So, for example, large mortgage companies advanced almost $50 million dollars over a three-year period to defend executives accused of various offenses.[230] The legal talent available to white-collar defendants often enables them to negotiate favorable pleas, or to mount massive letter-writing campaigns arguing for leniency in sentences.[231]

These efforts are frequently successful. All too often, judges have empathized or identified with offenders whose backgrounds and status are similar to their own and who seem to have been punished enough by the humiliation of prosecution.[232] In one example so egregious that it was reversed on appeal, a federal trial judge sentenced a former chief executive who had been found guilty of conspiracy, fraud, and money laundering to just seven days in prison. The court justified its 99 percent departure from sentencing guidelines on the grounds of the defendant's family and community involvement as well as his business expertise.[233] Another case of leniency involved a clerk who looted a municipal retirement fund; she was placed in a probation program that permitted expungement of her criminal record once she paid restitution.[234] A third example concerned a financial services advisor who gambled away the $700,000 he stole from a state health program; he was sentenced to one to two years in alternative housing and five years of probation.[235]

Yet many of the common assumptions underlying leniency toward such cheaters are unfounded. Contrary to conventional wisdom, white-collar criminals are not less likely to be repeat offenders than street criminals.[236] So, too, the widespread view that reputational sanctions are punishment enough for financial crimes is inconsistent with the limited data available. For example, a *Forbes* survey found that Americans are usually "forgiving and often forgetting about white-collar convictions."[237] Research by the Securities and Exchange Commission similarly showed that most rogue brokers had little difficulty securing jobs in the financial sector after their convictions.[238]

That is not to suggest that white-collar offenders should be treated as permanent pariahs. But it is to suggest that too many cheaters see too little to lose from cheating. If fines are levied only on organizations, shareholders pay the price, and those responsible for misconduct often escape without serious penalties. Given the difficulties of proof, and the lack of resources and heavy caseloads of many enforcement officials, serious sanctions are necessary in the relatively few cases that end in conviction. More high-visibility criminal prosecutions are necessary, such as the one involving the Volkswagen emissions scandal. Not only did the company end up paying more than $22 billion in fines and legal settlements, but six executives also faced criminal charges.[239] So, too, in the financial sector, as Senator Elizabeth Warren noted in the aftermath of the Wells Fargo scandal, "the only way that Wall Street will change is if executives face jail time when they preside over massive frauds."[240] They should also be subject to more stringent clawback requirements that force them to return compensation that is the fruit of fraud or excessive risks.[241] A majority of Americans seem to agree; they believe that white-collar criminals are not punished appropriately.[242]

Two-thirds of the public also think that the enforcement resources available to address white-collar crime should be at least as great as those available for street crime.[243] Although systematic data comparing expenditures are not available, it is clear that agencies charged with addressing organizational cheating are grossly understaffed.[244] In many contexts, resources have not kept pace with the growth in regulatory responsibilities. To take just one example, the number of oversight staff at the SEC per trillion dollars in investment advisor assets has dropped by half over the last decade.[245] As SEC Chair Mary Jo White summed it up in 2016 congressional testimony, "The need for significant additional resources . . . cannot be overstated."[246]

For similar reasons, we need greater shaming of guilty organizations through not only criminal penalties but also through civil liability, reputational sanctions, and consumer boycotts.[247] The recent scandals involving the automotive industry are a reminder of the human costs that occur when the public fails to punish habitual offenders and modest legal fines are seen as just another cost of doing business. The Wells Fargo debacle is a similar wake-up call. "I think we have gone too far" in terms of regulation, Wells Fargo CEO John Stumpf told an interviewer in 2013. That was the same year that the bank's sham accounts hit their peaks, and he was named Banker of the Year by a major trade publication.[248] If anything, the moral of this story is that regulation has not gone nearly far enough to change the culture of Wall Street.

## Research and Reassessment

Empirical evidence on the effectiveness of ethical initiatives has been limited, partly due to the difficulties of convincing organizations to allow data collection.[249] We lack systematic research on whistle-blowing, training, and other responses to cheating.[250] Persuading more organizations to share information and benchmark performance would be beneficial for all concerned.

Not only should we be collecting more data, we should also be questioning how best to present them. In particular, we need to challenge prevailing definitions of organizational success. All too often, researchers lionize corporations based solely on their short-term bottom-line performance.[251] Two widely acclaimed books are cases in point. Jim Collins's *Good to Great* analyzed what has enabled "good" organizations to become "great" performers over a sustained period. "Great," as Collins's research team defined it, involved exceptional stock returns independent of industry performance for 15 years. Although the team considered including measures such as "social impact" and "employee welfare," they settled on a definition of success that reflected only financial measures.[252] Among their "great" companies was Philip Morris, which had the "longest record of exceptional performance" of any of the businesses profiled.[253] Researchers did make an oblique acknowledgment that not everyone would define "greatness" to include maximizing sales of deadly carcinogens by suppressing information about their addictive qualities. However, they concluded that it is not the "content of a company's values that correlate with performance but the strength of conviction with which it holds those values."[254]

Similarly, *Lasting Leadership* profiled 25 executives whom a panel of experts considered the most influential business leaders of the past quarter-century. The criteria for selection focused on the ability to create new business ideas or opportunities and cause dramatic political, social, or industry changes. Like *Good to Great,* the index to *Lasting Leadership* provides no listings under ethics, corporate social responsibility, or related topics. Although a few individuals are singled out for leadership with a moral dimension, the vast majority are not.[255] Several have personal histories or business records that are anything but distinguished in ethical terms. For example, the account of Sam Walton's transformation of Walmart omits discussion of the company's labor and financial cheating scandals.[256]

We urgently need more balanced definitions of success, which include ethical commitments as well as financial profitability. Researchers and thought leaders have unique opportunities and corresponding obligations to underscore the importance of moral values in assessing organizational performance. Those who establish cultural standards cannot afford to treat issues of ethical responsibility as someone else's responsibility.

# 4

# Cheating on Taxes

"Tax day," quipped comedian Jimmy Kimmel, "is the day that ordinary Americans send their money to Washington, D.C., and wealthy Americans send their money to the Cayman Islands." Many Americans believe that he is right, and perceptions of the unfairness of the tax system fuel widespread cheating. The Internal Revenue Service (IRS) estimates the annual tax gap—the difference between the tax collected and the tax owed—at around $450 billion, or 16.9 percent, and other estimates are higher.[1] The federal gap has tripled over the last two decades and continues to grow.[2] Moreover the IRS figure excludes revenue from illegal activities and from evasion of state income taxes, so the actual gap is far wider.[3] California alone estimates that it experiences annual losses of $10 billion.[4]

The discussion that follows reviews the frequency of cheating on taxes, the dynamics that perpetuate it, and the strategies to combat it. Cheating here refers to evasion, which involves the willful attempt to misrepresent income or mislead authorities. That is different from tax avoidance, the exploitation of legal loopholes.[5] Avoidance suggests the need to close the loopholes; cheating raises more serious ethical concerns. Not all of the tax gap is, of course, attributable to cheating. Part of the shortfall reflects honest errors or unconscious tendencies to resolve doubts in a self-interested direction.[6] But for many Americans, tax evasion is a way of life, and society as a whole bears the cost. Although cheaters often view their conduct as a victimless crime, the harms are in fact substantial. The victims are intended beneficiaries of public funds and honest taxpayers who must make up for the lost revenue. When evasion is widespread, public confidence in the system is eroded, potential tax evaders are emboldened, and the rule of law is compromised.[7]

## The Nature and Frequency of Cheating

As long as there have been taxes, there has also been tax evasion and efforts to control it. In ancient Rome, cheaters could be put to death.[8] In 1916, three years after America's enactment of the income tax, a syndicated series ran in newspapers across the country under the title "The United States Income Tax Steal!." The series chronicled fraud and evasion by many of the nation's most prominent citizens and corporations.[9] Fast forward a century, and the same is still true. Ed McCaffrey, head of the University of Southern California's Tax Institute, put it bluntly: "The rich are getting away with more and more things."[10]

Occasionally they get caught. Dennis Kozlowski, former head of Tyco International, was charged with failing to pay $1 million in sales taxes on artwork, and former tennis star Boris Becker was forced to pay a fine of nearly $3 million to avoid jail time for extensive tax evasion. One Los Angeles couple wrote off pool service, cable television, and yard maintenance as part of home office expenses. The husband, a would-be screenwriter, deducted their vacation trips, including movies, concerts, and plays, as business expenses, on the theory that they would provide inspiration for a Broadway musical comedy that he never wrote.[11] A New York strip club attempted to avoid paying over $3 million in state taxes by claiming that its dancers were not providing entertainment but "rather a nontaxable service similar to . . . personal services provided by a sex therapist."[12]

Donald Trump has been one of the nation's most prominent offenders. A *USA Today* investigation revealed that Trump and his companies had been involved in over one hundred lawsuits and legal disputes concerning taxes during the decade before his election as president.[13] New York state alone has had to file over three dozen cases to collect overdue taxes.[14] Some of his most blatant cheating has involved property value disputes involving golf courses. For example, in a financial disclosure form prepared for his presidential campaign, Trump valued a Westchester golf club at over $50 million, while at that same time arguing in a tax assessment dispute that it was worth only $1.4 million.[15]

Cheaters often receive assistance from lawyers or preparers who take a "don't ask, don't tell" approach to their clients' dishonesty, or who sometimes actively facilitate it.[16] One Panama law firm that specialized in secretive shell companies and offshore tax shelters helped some 14,000 clients in 100 countries before a leak of 11 million documents revealed the abuses.[17]

The Internet has democratized offshore tax evasion. Americans can open a bank account, establish a personal holding company, or create a trust in some distant location with the click of a few keys. In the words of one Internet promoter, "your assets will be safe from the Tax Authorities in your local country."[18] A *Wall Street Journal* analysis of IRS records indicated that some ten billion American dollars had found a home away from home in hidden Swiss bank accounts. This criminal conduct was facilitated by asset management firms, insurance companies, and investment advisory groups.[19] A former Deputy IRS Commissioner has also estimated that as many as two million Americans have moved assets offshore to places such as the Cayman Islands in order to escape taxes.[20]

The 2016 presidential campaign put issues of tax evasion and avoidance front and center. Presidential candidate Donald Trump refused to release his returns, and a few pages obtained by the *New York Times* suggested that the reason may have been that he had avoided paying personal taxes for over a decade through a strategy of dubious legality.[21] What distinguished Trump's behavior from that of other politicians involved in tax scandals was his aggressively unapologetic stance. When asked about his strategy to escape any tax liability, Trump responded that of course he had taken advantage of that option, that Clinton's donors had as well, and that it suggested that he was "smart."[22] Forty-five percent of surveyed Americans agreed, although 61 percent also thought it was "unpatriotic."[23] The tax filings for Donald Trump's Foundation revealed more clearly illegal activities, including transferring assets to a "disqualified person," such as Trump himself, a member of his family, or one of his businesses.[24] For example, the Foundation served as a slush fund to settle legal disputes by making charitable contributions in lieu of paying fines.[25] It also made illegal political contributions to an organization supporting Florida's attorney general while she was investigating Trump University, and it purchased lavishly priced items (including oversized portraits of Trump), which were given to Trump as gifts.[26]

Another celebrated tax scandal involved Zoe Baird, the first woman to be nominated as U.S. attorney general. Baird, a wealthy corporate lawyer, had knowingly hired illegal immigrants to perform childcare and domestic work. Baird and her husband, a Yale law professor, paid no Social Security and Medicare taxes for the workers. Given that the Justice Department prosecutes violators of tax and immigration laws, one would think that the Clinton administration would have been concerned about appointing a violator of those laws to head the Department. But after learning about the nonpayment, President Clinton forwarded Baird's nomination to the Senate. According to Press Secretary Dee Dee Myers, the matter was "fully disclosed. [The President] considered it and did not think it was a problem."[27] Orrin Hatch, the top-ranking Republican on the Senate Judiciary Committee, agreed. In his view, "It's no big deal. No one is above the law, but people make honest mistakes and that should not deprive her from serving her country."[28] Joseph Biden, the Democrat heading the Judiciary Committee, saw the matter differently. He told Baird, "There are tens of thousands, millions of Americans out there who have trouble taking care of their children . . . with one fiftieth [of] the income that you and your husband have, and they do not violate the laws."[29] With public opinion running strongly against the nomination, Baird asked that her candidacy be withdrawn. She faded from view, but the incident set off a string of confessions by other candidates, belated payments to the IRS, and withdrawn nominations.

Although it is scandals involving the wealthy that gain public attention, they are by no means the only Americans who cheat on their taxes. Hotel magnate

Leona Helmsley is credited with claiming that "Only the little people pay taxes."[30] But many of these "little people" do not. They cheat in ways large and small. They inflate their itemized deductions for everything from medical bills to charitable contributions. They manufacture deductions to cover expenses never incurred. They understate their income and do not declare cash revenue. They deduct their personal living costs as business expenses.[31] One IRS-sponsored study concluded that 42 percent of all returns had some understatement of taxable income.[32] Surveys that ask taxpayers about past tax compliance similarly suggest that cheating is common. In one study of middle- and upper-income taxpayers, 57 percent acknowledged overstating deductions or understating income.[33] In another survey of taxpayers at all income levels, 38 percent reported definitely or probably leaving income off their return, and another 8 percent reported definitely or probably overdeducting. Many of these individuals asserted that they had paid what they legally owed, perhaps by compensating for deductions that they did not take because they did not keep receipts.[34] Other research finds more modest but still substantial rates of non-compliance. In a Harris poll conducted for the IRS, 22 percent of taxpayers reported either overstating deductions or understating income on their tax returns in the last five years.[35]

The majority of tax evasion involves underreporting taxable income.[36] Underreporting consists of "understated income, improper deductions, overstated expenses and erroneously claimed credits."[37] This underreporting accounts for 83.5 percent of tax evasion, whereas simple non-filing and underpayment accounts for the rest.[38] Most of understated income comes from business activity, not wages or investments.[39] The compliance rate for wages, which are subject to withholding and third-party reporting to the IRS, is 99 percent.[40] By contrast, business taxpayers are more likely to cheat on their taxes because of the difficulty of audit.[41] These taxpayers may be individuals who are self-employed or are members of a partnership, but the category also includes corporate entities more generally.[42] Although other taxpayers' income is typically reported to the IRS via third parties, most of business taxpayers' income is not.[43] As law professor Daniel S. Goldberg describes it, "[t]ax cheating by business taxpayers comes in all sorts of sizes and varieties. Income items are omitted, personal expenses are claimed as tax deductions, capital expenditures are deducted."[44] Estimates suggest that more than half of partnerships, closely held corporations, and self-employed individuals cheat.[45] Overall, the compliance rate for business income is 44 percent. Within this group, the lowest rate, 20 percent, is for informal suppliers, such as moonlighting professionals, childcare workers, and other independent contractors.[46] The self-employment tax is also underreported, with a compliance rate estimated at 48 percent.[47] The reporting rate for tip income is slightly higher, at 60 percent.[48] Detecting such evasion is difficult because it mainly involves understatements of cash.[49]

## Causes of Cheating

Decisions to cheat are influenced by taxpayers' honesty, risk assessment, and opportunities and potential rewards for evasion.[50] In explaining non-compliance with tax laws, experts suggest two main models: the deterrence model and the norms model.[51] The deterrence framework builds on classic economic theory; people pay their taxes in order to avoid legal sanctions, and they do so only when the expected cost of sanctions exceeds their tax obligations.[52] The cost of sanctions includes both financial penalties and nonmonetary consequences, such as the unpleasantness, invasion of privacy, and expenditure of time connected with an audit.[53] In this view, individuals are rational economic actors who only cheat when it is worth it, given the penalty they expect to receive, adjusted by the likelihood that they will be caught and punished.[54] From a deterrence standpoint, it is economically rational for Americans to cheat. Only between 1 and 2 percent of returns are audited, and the percentage is even lower for individuals who have primarily wage income and take standard deductions.[55] As one commentator notes, detection "requires an IRS audit of the payer, [and] a curious and energetic agent . . . [T]he IRS must poke and prod, look and question. The limited IRS budget in the face of an overwhelming number of tax returns makes the verification process spotty and haphazard."[56] The problem is compounded by cutbacks in enforcement budgets and resources at times when the complexity and number of returns have been increasing.[57]

Under these circumstances, expected fines would have to be quite high to deter cheating.[58] They are not. A case in point involves an opera singer who claimed $126,000 for unauthorized business expenses and $90,000 in other deductions that were disallowed. She filed returns one to five years late, ignored appointments with tax examiners, and failed to show up at a tax court hearing. Her fine was only $15,000.[59] The leniency of penalties often drives behavior even by professionals who should have some responsibility to promote compliance. So, for example, a senior partner at a prominent accounting firm advised the firm not to register a tax shelter with the IRS as required by law. As he explained to colleagues, "the rewards of successful marketing of the product . . . far exceed the financial exposure to penalties that may arise."[60] Not only did he fail to see cheating as an ethical issue, he seemed oblivious to the potential sanctions that he faced for participation in fraud: loss of his CPA license.[61]

Moreover, taxpayers can avoid a penalty for inaccuracy if their position has substantial authority, which, for practical purposes, means a two in five likelihood of success if the matter proceeded to litigation.[62] Considering the low risk of detection, even when maximum penalties are imposed, an expected fine is only 3.5 percent of the expected liability.[63] The temptation to fudge is further fueled by media accounts such as "2015 Is the Best Year Yet to Cheat on Your

Taxes," with examples of successful deductions ranging from pet food to breast enlargements.[64] Under the current system, Americans concerned only with economic costs and benefits have every reason to cheat on their taxes.[65]

By contrast, the norms model assumes that Americans comply with their tax obligations because they want to adhere to specific social or personal standards of conduct. Many taxpayers have commitments to values such as reciprocity, fairness, and respect for the rule of law, which prompt them to pay what they owe.[66] Research finds that taxpayers tend to internalize the norms of a group with which they strongly identify.[67] Accordingly, some proponents of the norms view worry that dramatically increasing fines for non-compliance could be counterproductive by signaling to taxpayers that cheating is widespread and requires greater deterrence.[68]

Neither the norms model nor the economic model fully explain tax behavior. Some people may cheat on their taxes because they find the tax system unfair. According to researchers Joel Slemrod and Jon Bakija, "complying with our labyrinthine tax regulations is frustrating, costly, and intrusive."[69] The complexity of the United States tax code means that Americans, in total, spend a huge amount of time and money on their tax affairs: 3 billion hours a year, and $12 billion in tax preparation services and software.[70] The average American spends 27 to 30 hours.[71] And no wonder, given the arcane and convoluted instructions in much of the tax code. T.R. Reid recent's indictment of the American tax system offers abundant examples. His favorite reads: "Go to Part Iv of Schedule I to figure line 52 if the estate or trust has qualified dividends or has a gain on lines 18a and 19 of column 2 of Schedule D (Form 1041)(as refigured for the AMT, if necessary)."[72] The instruction book for low-income taxpayers seeking to claim the earned income tax credit is 59 pages long.[73]

Moreover, at the end of the process, many individuals are unsure whether they have complied. Even experts are confused by many tax questions. In one survey, 46 tax professionals attempted to calculate a sample tax liability.[74] Each one found a different level of liability, from $34,420 to $68,192, when the actual liability was $35,643.[75] Some evidence suggests that complexity not only increases frustration, it encourages the belief that others are taking advantage of complexity to avoid paying their fair share.[76] Such perceptions may also discourage compliance.[77] Research summarized in chapters 1 and 3 made clear that a sense of unfairness often prompts retaliatory cheating. And as noted below, the American tax system strikes many individuals as inequitable. That perception builds on celebrated examples. The amount that President Clinton owed in taxes was less than that of a working woman whose income was one-twentieth of his. [78] Billionaire Warren Buffet famously pointed out that he was paying a lower rate than his secretary, because capital gains are taxed at a lower rate than other earnings.[79]

A wide variety of research on procedural justice finds that willingness to comply with laws depends on perceptions of their fairness. These perceptions affect attitudes and behaviors independent of the objective outcomes of encounters with the laws.[80] A sense of fairness is crucial in maintaining the legitimacy of the tax system. When people think that the system is unjust, they may

> spend less time reporting carefully and may be motivated to produce what they perceive to be a fair outcome even when this does not conform to the law . . . . [By contrast,] people may be motivated to work hard to report accurately and pay what they owe by their sense that the laws and their application are fair in terms of the distribution of tax payments, the way taxes are spent, the process of reporting and paying, and the way they are treated by the IRS."[81]

If, as is often the case, people hear only from individuals who have had an adverse experience with the IRS, it can fuel their sense of injustice. The minority of taxpayers "who think the IRS treated them unfairly may vent their anger by talking in more detail and to more people than taxpayers who evaluate the IRS's performance more favorably."[82]

In short, cheating is partly but not solely a function of the expected risks and benefits of non-compliance. People are also less likely to view tax evasion as morally wrong if:

- they believe that their friends and neighbors are engaged in such evasion;[83]
- they believe that the IRS expects to be cheated;[84]
- they believe that the tax revenues are being used unwisely;[85]
- they believe that the tax system is unfair.[86]

Public opinion research finds that large percentages of Americans share such beliefs. To be sure, the vast majority of Americans condemn cheating on taxes. A 2014 CNN poll found that 90 percent considered it morally wrong.[87] An earlier PEW poll similarly reported that 79 percent of taxpayers believed that failing to report all income was morally wrong; only 14 percent thought it was not a moral issue; and just 5 percent considered it morally acceptable.[88] However, when another poll asked if "you think any of your friends or neighbors cheat on their taxes," 38 percent said yes, 35 percent said no, and 28 percent weren't sure.[89] So too, when asked, "do you think most people cheat on their taxes, some people cheat on their taxes, or only a few people cheat on their taxes," 21 percent said "most," 46 percent said "some," and 29 percent said "only a few." When asked how much people cheat, 40 percent said "a lot," 52 percent said "a little," and the rest said they "don't know."[90]

Most Americans also think that tax burdens are too high and that the tax system is somewhat or quite unfair.[91] When a Pew survey asked Americans "which of the following bothers you most about taxes," 11 percent said the amount, 28 percent said the complexity, and 57 percent said "the feeling that some wealthy people get away not paying their fair share."[92] When a Gallup poll asked whether upper-income people were paying a fair share of their taxes, only 26 percent thought that they were; 61 percent thought they were paying too little.[93] Similarly, 66 percent thought that corporations were paying too little; only 21 percent thought they were paying their fair share. And in an ABC/*Washington Post* poll, 68 percent agreed that the tax system favored the wealthy.[94] In evaluating the enforcement process, 51 percent of Americans would prefer a root canal at the dentist to being audited by the IRS. Only 34 percent would prefer an audit.[95] Only 49 percent of Americans had a favorable opinion of the IRS; over a third (38 percent) had an unfavorable opinion.[96]

The influence of these perceptions comes through in David Callahan's *The Cheating Culture.* One would-be artist, who made most of her income in cash through private teaching and tutoring, reported submitting a "work of fiction" to the IRS. She couldn't afford to continue her career in the arts if she paid what she owed in taxes. As she explained,

> I don't think it's the "right" thing to do, but personally I don't really care. I know that one wrong doesn't right another wrong, but until I see any sign of a real move to . . . the closing of loopholes for the rich, or increased benefits for those making their living in the arts, I don't feel particularly inclined to be honest. When I read about the IRS going after those in lower-income brackets, it makes my blood boil.[97]

A student who put himself through school by driving a cab similarly acknowledged that "I hardly reported any of my income. I was barely making enough money as it was and there was no way I was going to hand it over to a government that doles out tax breaks to the rich and leaves students like me to starve."[98] Another man who claimed false charitable deductions confessed, "I rationalize it by saying that wealthy people and big businesses have much larger loopholes that they're taking advantage of, so that [my offense] is very low down on the scale of crimes. The only guilty feeling I have is the fear of getting caught."[99]

## Strategies

Strategies to address tax evasion fall into three main categories. One, drawing on the deterrence model noted earlier, is to increase penalties and audit rates.

A second approach builds on the norms approach and aims at creating more positive attitudes toward compliance. A third strategy involves more fundamental changes in the tax structure.

The first approach would seek to enhance deterrence by dramatically heightening penalties and risk of audit. As noted earlier, under the current system, sanctions are often limited to back taxes or modest fines, and the likelihood that they will be imposed is remote.[100] Experimental evidence indicates that greater efforts to detect and to penalize tax evaders will increase compliance if individuals perceive the enforcement changes to be significant.[101] In a controlled field study in Minnesota, taxpayers who received a letter indicating that their returns would be closely examined significantly increased their reported income.[102] Another study estimated that doubling the funding for audits would increase taxes by as much as 60 times the cost of the additional oversight.[103] According to Reid's recent review, the IRS spends only 35 cents for every hundred dollars it brings in.[104] To reduce political opposition to increased oversight, the government could reimburse at least some of the expenses of audit for taxpayers who are found to have paid substantially all of the taxes they owe.[105] A related option would be for the IRS to check most or all returns and require taxpayers to provide some justification for key items. In the Netherlands, the tax authority subjects every personal income return to at least a cursory audit.[106]

Yet as noted earlier, some commentators worry that an increase in auditing and penalties might prove counterproductive if the only way to gain political support for the reform is to publicize the magnitude of evasion.[107] They argue that the government would be better off trying to reinforce norms of compliance by publicizing the fact that most Americans are honest on their tax returns.[108] A compromise position is both to publicize taxpayer honesty and to argue for enhanced enforcement on the grounds that it would increase the fairness and cost effectiveness of the process. In any case, however the audit and penalty issues are resolved, it seems clear that more enforcement directed at preparers involved in their clients' evasion could help detect and discourage such misconduct.[109]

Another deterrence-oriented strategy is to reduce the wiggle room that enables evasion. Currently, sanctions for underreporting income do not apply if the taxpayer's position is supported by "substantial authority," which requires only that the position have about a 40 percent likelihood of being correct.[110] University of Virginia law professor Michael Doran has proposed imposing an inaccuracy penalty on any understatement of taxes attributable to a position that the taxpayer does not reasonably and in good faith believe to be correct.[111] Faced with uncertainty, taxpayers could resolve the issue in their favor as long as they believed in reasonable good faith that their position was likely to prevail and they described the uncertainty on their return.[112] Return preparers and tax advisors could be held to corresponding standards.[113]

To encourage third parties to report relevant information, the government could strengthen whistle-blower programs at both the federal and state levels.[114] One possibility would be to create a private right of action that would give whistle-blowers a share in any recovery.[115] Such approaches have been highly successful in other contexts. For example, the federal False Claims Act enables individuals who report fraud against the government to receive 15 to 25 percent of any recovery resulting from the information. Since amendments strengthening the act were adopted in 1986, the Department of Justice has recovered over $33 billion dollars in such whistle-blower cases.[116]

A related approach is to change the way that penalties are assessed. As Columbia Law School law professor Alex Raskolnikov points out, existing sanctions "fail to take into account variations in the probability of detection."[117] Cheating on taxes takes many forms, each of which has a different likelihood of detection, yet fines are constant across all types of evasion. The result is inadequate deterrence for some violations.[118] One reform strategy would be to change penalty or audit rates to match expected levels of detection.

But, as many experts argue, "policymakers would be mistaken to attempt tax penalty reform by adopting the implications of the simple deterrence model."[119] That model cannot account for current compliance rates, given that expected fines are so much lower than liabilities. As earlier discussion noted, other considerations such as reciprocity and respect for law are motivating taxpayers. Moreover, deterrence strategies do not always produce the desired results. Bank Leumi, for instance, "hit the accelerator even harder" when regulators cracked down on international banks for helping Americans establish tax shelters.[120] Rather than viewing increased enforcement as a sign it should cease its illegal behavior, Bank Leumi "urged bankers 'to suggest to [prospective clients] that they transfer their accounts' " from the punished banks to Leumi.[121]

Drawing on the norms model, these experts advocate more rewards and reinforcement for compliance. Promoting "pleasant, efficient contacts with the tax collection agency" is one strategy.[122] Other methods include reinforcing taxpayers' sense of their responsibilities as citizens.[123] Enhancing trust in the justice system and legislative process could also increase tax compliance.[124] To that end, outreach efforts should remind people of how they benefit from tax revenues. Such benefits, law professor Joshua Rosenberg notes,

> tend not to be anywhere near our consciousness at the time we pay attention to tax. . . . When we drive on the freeway, rarely do we think "here are my tax dollars at work." On April 15, we are not usually focused on the fact that without taxes, we would have no ability to enact or enforce product and food safety requirements; and when we sit down to eat,

> few of us think "I am so glad I paid tax, because some of the money went to make sure that the food we are about to eat is not dangerous.[125]

By contrast, in Japan, on National Firefighters Day, children get to sit in firetrucks and their parents see thank you signs reminding them that "your taxpayments suppliled our equipment."[126] The American government needs to do a better job of underscoring benefits of tax revenues. Experience with a pilot program in Minnesota suggests that just sending taxpayers a letter describing the educational, healthcare, and other services supported by state income tax dollars is not enough.[127] A much more systematic and sustained effort is necessary.

One concrete example of a norms-oriented strategy is to shame tax evaders. Researchers Ricardo Perez-Truglia and Ugo Troiana suggested this approach in a widely circulated *New York Times* op-ed. [128] India and the United Kingdom employ this strategy, as do some states in this country that publish lists of tax evaders online. To test the power of shaming, Perez-Truglia and Troiana sent letters to tax delinquents. The authors "divided recipients into two groups. In the first, only the recipient was chosen to get information about an online list of tax delinquents. In the second, the recipient and other people from the same community were given that information."[129] The second group knew that their continued non-compliance would be apparent to friends and family. This potential exposure made the second group of taxpayers 20 percent more likely than the first group to repay their tax debts. Repayment was particularly likely when these debts were relatively small and easy to repay. These results led the authors to conclude that "shaming policies are an effective tool and should be part of the effort to make citizens pay their fair share."[130]

Columbia professor Alex Raskolnikov advocates a combination of deterrence and norm-based enforcement.[131] He argues that the government should "abandon its current one-size-fits-all strategy and begin to target enforcement based on particular taxpayer motivations."[132] Under his proposed framework, taxpayers would choose between a deterrence-based and a norms-based oversight system. The deterrence system would mirror the current, fine-based regime, but with higher penalties.[133] The norms-based system would enable taxpayers to retain lower fines in exchange for certain concessions if a dispute arises. Raskolnikov suggests, for example, that a taxpayer who elected the norms-based regime would concede that "the government's position will be presumed correct unless proven otherwise by clear and convincing evidence."[134] Because taxpayers motivated by norms rather than deterrence aren't inclined to cheat in the first place, they presumably would not object to concessions that enhanced the government's advantage in a dispute.[135]

Reformers have also drawn lessons from social psychology to suggest ways of strengthening compliance norms. Stanford professors Joseph Bankman and

Clifford Nass, and University of Michigan economist Joel Slemrod, argue that the IRS should "redesign the tax forms and on-line filing process to elicit more truthful responses from taxpayers."[136] In effect, their proposal is to deter cheating by raising the psychological cost of lying.[137] "This can be done," they argue, "simply by asking more direct questions, thereby forcing taxpayers who wish to evade to do so through explicit, clearly false statements, as opposed to giving deceptive answers to more general questions."[138] The revised questions should be detailed and specific, so that taxpayers cannot lie without paying a significant cognitive cost.[139] As the authors note, "the more explicit a lie the taxpayer is required to tell to avoid taxes, the harder it is to rationalize away."[140] At the same time, making taxpayers swear under penalty of perjury that they are telling the truth before they fill out the form primes taxpayers to focus on their obligations, making it more uncomfortable for them to lie.[141] As Chapter 1 noted, fewer individuals cheat when they must sign a statement affirming their honesty at the top of a form.[142] Because research also indicates that appeals not to be a cheater can somewhat reduce cheating, the IRS could experiment with including such language on the tax return.[143] Whatever approach the IRS takes, Bankman, Nass, and Slemrod suggest that it institute a "regular system of pilot programs to test different question designs and evaluate their impact on taxpayer behavior."[144]

A third group of strategies involve more fundamental reforms. One is radical simplification, designed to make the system easier and fairer.[145] The government could, for example, eliminate most or all itemized deductions, credits, and exclusions, and lower the marginal tax rates. Or it could substantially increase the standard deduction, which would reduce the number of itemizers.[146] In arguing for eliminating itemized deductions and exemptions, Reid points out that they disproportionately benefit higher-income individuals. For example, only about 20 percent of homeowners take the deduction for mortgage interest, and about three-quarters of all those deductions go to taxpayers making more than $100,000.[147] And other well-off countries that do not allow such deductions have home ownership rates comparable to the United States.[148] Similarly, most other other countries have curtailed or eliminated deductions for charitable contributions and have not experienced a significant drop in such gifts.[149] Some reformers also advocate treating all income the same whether from wages or capital gains, and expanding the scope of withholding to include all income, including dividends, interest, and capital gains.[150]

Although simplification would reduce taxpayers' frustration with the tax code, it is by no means clear how much it would reduce evasion. Taxpayers who underreport income for income tax purposes also underreport sales for sales tax purposes, even though the sales tax is quite simple.[151] However, if one of the strategies to achieve simplification is to expand withholding, that would reduce opportunities to cheat. Some countries, including Japan and Great Britain, have a system of "precision withholding" under which the amount the government withholds is, for most taxpayers, the amount due.[152] Japanese taxpayers get an accounting of what officials believe is due, and if it looks correct, as is true in 80 percent of cases, the amount is automatically credited or debited. [153] In the United States, even without simplifications and expanded withholding, the IRS has enough information to complete tax forms accurately for between 30 to 40 percent of taxpayes.[154] If the agency had the staff and authority to complete those forms, opportunities for cheating would diminish.

Other reformers believe, as did then Senator Bill Bradley, that "you can't just tinker. Your goal has to be to fix the whole damn thing."[155] The most radical approaches seek to do what former House Ways and Means Committee chair Bill Archer advocated: "tear the income-tax system out by its roots. We have to remove the Internal Revenue Service from the lives of Americans totally."[156] Consumption taxes are the most commonly suggested alternative, either in the form of a "flat tax" or a national sales tax. A flat tax, as Slemrod and Bakija describe it, has three main characteristics:

> First, the tax base would include wages, salaries, and pension benefits, but all other kinds of income . . . would be completely excluded from taxation at the personal level. Second, all taxable income above an exempt level, based on family size, would be subject to a single, "flat" rate of tax. Finally, tax returns would allow no itemized deductions or other special preferences of any kind . . . . Proponents emphasize that, as a result of this clean tax base, the flat-tax return for individuals could fit on a postcard![157]

Advocates of a flat tax see benefits both from a deterrence and a norms perspective. In proponents' view, the flat tax would save taxpayers hundreds of billions in direct and indirect compliance costs. If the cost of filing goes down, more taxpayers will allegedly choose not to evade. As taxes are seen as easier and fairer, compliance rates will rise. However, as Slemrod and Bakja also note, the "the degree to which [the flat tax] would accomplish these goals is subject to much debate among economists."[158] Most tax experts reject this approach on the ground that it would shrink revenue and exacerbate inequality. A flat tax is regressive and seems less equitable than a "personal income tax with rates that rise with income."[159]

An alternative that somewhat responds to this concern is a national sales tax, sometimes referred to as a value added tax (VAT). It would operate much like traditional state sales taxes, and would either supplement or replace the income tax. Most other rich democratic countries rely more heavily on consumption taxes than does the United States, partly because they evoke less resistance and evasion; they are paid in small increments, so the taxpayer doesn't see their total annual amount.[160] Although such taxes are regressive, that effect could be partially offset by exempting or reducing rates on subsistence items and using revenues to provide credits for low-income taxpayers or to subsidize programs that reduce inequality.[161] In *The Death of the Income Tax,* Daniel Goldberg advocates an electronic version of this approach. It would include a progressive tax on wages, and a consumption tax that would incorporate lower rates on staples than on luxury items.[162] Such an automated system would make cheating far less possible.

The political challenges to achieving such reforms in the current political climate are daunting. Donald Trump campaigned on tax reform, but the plans he proposed both before and after the election focused on cuts for corporations and wealthy Americans that are widely unpopular even among his own supporters.[163] Only 18 percent of Trump voters and 13 percent of the general public favor cuts for the rich, and only 39 percent of Trump voters and 22 percent of the general public favor decreases in corporate taxes.[164] Sixty-one percent of Americans say upper-income individuals pay too little in taxes, a percentage that has remained fairly constant for the last quarter century.[165] Moreover, the bare-bones plan that Trump announced months after his election included what the *New York Times* described as a "huge loophole" for "people with creative accountants."[166] It would allow individuals to establish a limited liability company or "pass through entity" as their employer. That would allow them to receive income as business earnings rather than wages and be taxed at a lower corporate rate.[167] Many experts believe that such an option would increase popular perceptions that the system is unfair and encourage further gaming of its requirements.[168]

How the Trump proposals will fare remains unclear. What is clear is the electorate's desire for substantial modification of the current tax structure. In both Pew and NPR/Kaiser Family Foundation surveys, over half of Americans agreed that "there is so much wrong with the federal tax system that Congress should completely change it."[169] When asked by an ABC/*Washington Post* poll about the importance of tax reform, 56 percent thought it was a high priority and 31 percent placed it as among the nation's highest priorities.[170]

The stakes in this reform effort are substantial. Former Supreme Court Justice Oliver Wendell Holmes Jr. noted that "taxes are what we pay for civilized society."[171] We need to do a better job in ensuring that the burden is spread fairly, that cheaters do not prosper, and that the culture reinforces compliance.

# 5

# Cheating in Academia and Plagiarism in Professional Settings

Academic cheating has an extended history. For fourteen hundred years, China was governed largely by bureaucrats selected by highly competitive civil service exams.[1] Proctoring was rigorous and penalties for cheating were severe, including execution. Yet cheating was pervasive. Candidates bribed officials, hired substitutes to take the test, and purchased model essays. Notes were put inside loaves of bread and copied on underwear in invisible ink.[2]

Plagiarism also has deep historical roots. The term as we now understand it appeared in first-century Rome. The poet Martial accused another poet of claiming verses that Martial had written.[3] Other early plagiarism complaints involved Shakespeare, who borrowed lines verbatim, along with plot details, from other authors.[4]

In the United States, academic dishonesty prompted occasional expressions of concern in the nineteenth and early twentieth centuries. An 1869 cheating scandal involving half the student body at Yale attracted considerable, but apparently ineffectual, attention. In 1931, Yale's dean declared cheating to be so pervasive as to demand "instant and sweeping measures of reform."[5] Around the same time, sociologist Robert Angell's influential profile of American universities observed that "many young men and women who are scrupulously honorable in other relationships of life seem to have little hesitancy in submitting themes and theses which they have not written, in bringing prepared 'cribs' to examinations, and in conveying information to one another during the course of an examination." Angell attributed the problem to the failure of undergraduates to "appreciate the value . . . of serious . . . intellectual effort and achievement."[6] Similar failures were apparent among their professors. Scandals involving faculty misconduct during the 1960s and 1970s led to ethics codes, rules for human subjects research, and research integrity programs and offices.[7]

The contemporary era brought renewed focus on academic integrity as pressures and opportunities for cheating escalated. Increased competition for financial aid and for admission to colleges and graduate programs also increased temptations for cheating. Techniques grew more inventive. Cheat sheets have been discovered in bags of potato chips and rolls of toilet paper; information has been concealed on labels of bottled water.[8] After passage of the No Child Left Behind Act, which imposed sanctions for low public school test scores, increasing numbers of teachers and administrators became implicated in cheating.[9] Misconduct involved everything from prepping students to changing their answers and altering poorly performing students' identification numbers so that their scores would be excluded.[10] Eleven Atlanta educators were even found guilty of racketeering for their roles in systemic cheating.[11]

Many scandals have involved high-achievers who had options other than cheating. In 2012, Harvard investigated 125 students for engaging in unauthorized collaboration on a take-home final.[12] That same year, at New York's Stuyvesant High School, one of the country's most prestigious public schools, 70 students were implicated in a pattern of cheating on state exams.[13] At another prestigious Long Island high school, 20 students faced charges involving hiring students to take the SAT and ACT for them.[14]

The Internet has provided additional resources for academic misconduct. Instructional videos and websites on how to cheat have gone viral.[15] Several software companies specialize in devices for high-tech cheating, such as tiny concealable earpieces and Bluetooth pens that connect with electronic devices.[16] Online material can easily be cut and pasted into student essays. Completed papers, even customized graduate theses, are readily available for purchase.[17] Students who "couldn't write a convincing grocery list" have gained assistance on everything from lab reports to college admission essays; even papers on academic dishonesty are for sale.[18] One employee of a cheating site spent a year completing all of a student's homework and take-home exams, and did "everything short of laying out his [client's] jammies before bed."[19] Ironically enough, even sites that facilitate plagiarism provide customized papers that are themselves plagiarized.[20] Dan Ariely and Aline Gruneisen, two Duke researchers who purchased essays on academic dishonesty, discovered that half of those they received were pilfered. They were also of a quality "that would best be described as gibberish."[21] The essays' authors appeared to have a "tenuous grasp of the English language." When the researchers requested refunds, the sellers insisted that they "had not plagiarized anything." As Ariely reported, one company even threatened litigation and claimed that it would get in touch with the dean's office at Duke to "alert him to the fact that I had submitted work that was not mine."[22]

Cheating in academia should be a matter of serious concern. Integrity is a cornerstone of educational institutions and the fairness of their evaluation processes. Today's students are tomorrow's leaders.[23] The years they spend in school are a critical period in ethical development, and those who cheat are developing patterns that persist in adult life.[24] Scholars are role models for students, and plagiarism by either group compromises fundamental values of honesty and integrity.

## The Frequency of Cheating

Estimates of the frequency of academic dishonesty vary widely. As few as 1 percent and as many as 95 percent of students report behaviors such as using others' words and ideas without attribution, collaborating on independently assigned work, and copying from other students during examinations.[25] The lower rates are usually associated with serious forms of cheating such as hiring an examination proxy or writing an assignment for another student. One compilation of surveys found that the average rate of reported cheating was 70 percent.[26] Among high school students, a large national study found that 80 percent acknowledged some form of cheating.[27] In a survey of college alumni, who arguably had less of a vested interest in concealing their misconduct than undergraduates, 82 percent reported having engaged in some form of cheating during their college years.[28] Among graduate students, between 39 and 46 percent report having cheated. Figures are higher for business students (56 percent) than for law students (30 percent).[29]

Relatively little research measures actual cheating as opposed to self-reports, and its results vary. One study found that 61 percent of students in its sample engaged in plagiarism.[30] Another study of resume fraud found that 41 percent included information that was contradicted by official records.[31]

Whether cheating is becoming more common is difficult to assess. Conventional wisdom is that the problem is increasing. In a national survey of a thousand chief academic officers, more than two-thirds believed that cheating had escalated recently, although fewer than a quarter thought that it was on the rise on their own campuses.[32] Over 90 percent of faculty believe that cheating is a problem at their university.[33] However, the best available evidence does not find clear increases when controlling for different methodologies. There has been a significant drop in students acknowledging serious cheating since 2002, although that decline may in part reflect a change in research methodology and a reduction in response rates. Surveys are now administered online, and not all students believe that their responses will remain confidential. As a result, leading scholars such as Donald McCabe, Kenneth Butterfield, and Linda Treviño note that chronic cheaters may be reluctant to participate in studies or to be honest about their misconduct.[34] Other evidence suggests that students also underestimate what constitutes cheating. Rates of reported misconduct increase when definitions are given.[35]

Individuals who begin cheating early in life are more likely to cheat later, and most individuals start early.[36] In a large national survey by the Josephson Institute of Ethics, about half of high school students reported that they had cheated on an exam in the past year, a third reported copying an Internet document for a classroom assignment, and three-quarters reported copying a homework assignment. [37] Other large scale research finds that four-fifths of public school students reported plagiarism or exam misconduct.[38] When students were asked whether they were satisfied with their ethics and character, 92 percent said yes, even though 64 percent acknowledged cheating on a test at school, and 82 percent had copied homework from someone.[39] Half of the students didn't think that cheating was wrong.[40] In an interview with CBS News, one student put common attitudes with uncommon candor: "It probably sounds twisted, but I would say that in this day and age, cheating is almost not wrong."[41]

Cross-cultural research finds that cheating in academia varies widely. One study of undergraduate economics and business students found that rates ranged from around 5 percent in Nordic countries to 88 percent in Eastern European countries. The United States was in the middle, at 39 percent.[42] Other research finds a greater frequency of reported cheating on exams among students in the United States (21 percent) than in Finland (14 percent), but lower than in China (83 percent), Russia (70 percent), and Portugal (62 percent).[43] In a survey of students in introductory accounting classes, 62 percent of the U.S. students reported having cheated, compared with 72 percent of the Japanese, 71 percent of the Chinese, 57 percent of the Australian, and 51 percent of the Irish students.[44] In some instances, parental pressure compounds the problem. In a widely publicized recent incident, photographers captured parents in Bihar, India, scaling the wall of a multistory school building in order to hand cheat sheets through a classroom window to their children taking an exam inside.[45] That scene elevated family values to new heights.

## Who Cheats and Why

The three main drivers of academic misconduct are individual characteristics, organizational factors, and social context. Although a common tendency is to attribute cheating to fundamental character flaws, research shows no consistent causal relationship between moral development and student cheating.[46] As Chapter 1 noted, although individuals clearly differ in their responses to temptation, contextual pressures have a substantial effect independent of any generalized predisposition.[47] In 1928, Hugh Hartshorn and Mark May published classic studies, subsequently replicated with some reinterpretation. They found that students who were honest in one context were not necessarily so in others. It was not possible to accurately predict cheaters in French from cheaters in math; even the slightest change in situational factors dramatically altered tendencies toward deceit.[48]

Nor are demographic characteristics predictive of cheating. Academic misconduct bears no relation to race, ethnicity, or political ideology.[49] Studies on gender and cheating have mixed findings.[50] A meta-analysis of surveys found that men report more favorable attitudes toward cheating and more cheating behavior.[51] However, some recent data suggest that women may have caught up, perhaps because they are increasingly likely to major in areas such as engineering and business that used to be more male dominated and that have relatively high rates of cheating. Within similar majors, gender differences in cheating are typically very small.[52]

However, certain other individual characteristics do correlate with higher rates of cheating. Academic misconduct is most common among the lowest and highest-achieving students, measured by grades and test scores.[53] Students cheat both to survive and to thrive.[54] Students with significant extracurricular activities, particularly athletics and fraternity or sorority involvement, also have higher levels of cheating. One reason is that these students have less time to devote to coursework, and have correspondingly greater temptations to cut corners. Another reason is that they also have greater assistance in cheating. Some fraternities and sororities keep copies of prior exams and papers that can be plagiarized.[55] And as Chapter 2 noted, some schools have been complicit in enabling academically unprepared athletes to maintain their required grade point average. Motivation also matters in predicting misconduct. Students who perceive grades or jobs as the ultimate goal of education are more likely to cheat than those who value learning or personal development.[56] Unsurprisingly, students with high motivation to achieve extrinsic rewards but low motivation to work hard have higher rates of cheating.[57]

Social context plays an even greater role. Perceptions of peer attitudes and behavior are among the strongest predictors of cheating.[58] Seeing others cheat and go unpunished is strongly correlated with academic dishonesty.[59] Many students take the view that "It's cheat or be cheated: Because everyone is doing it, you don't want to be the only one not doing well."[60] Where cheating is widely accepted, it can also be a bonding ritual among friends. Alejandro Zambra's short story about cheating in a Chilean high school captures that dynamic. As the narrator puts it, "Thanks to our cheating, we were able to let go of some of our individualism and become a community. It's sad to put it like that, but copying gave us solidarity."[61]

The perceived quality and fairness of instructors is also important.[62] If the teacher seems "indifferent or permissive, the subject matter seems unimportant or uninteresting, or tests seem unfair or confusing, students feel more justified in cheating."[63] One Duke student rationalized copying a classmate's work because she found the assignment "mindless." She understood how to do what was asked; she "just didn't have time."[64] Course work that appears overly difficult or burdensome encourages students to cut corners.[65] So does the pressure to maintain or keep scholarships.[66] Parental pressure to obtain high grades plays a similar role.[67] These factors give rise to students' "neutralizing" attitudes, the tendency described in Chapter 1 for individuals to neutralize the wrongfulness of conduct by blaming external conditions.[68]

The frequency and severity of punishment also influences misconduct. Students are more likely to cheat when they perceive little risk of being caught and/or receiving severe sanctions.[69] Part of the reason that cheating is so pervasive is that the likelihood of detection is so minimal. The highest reported rate of apprehension is 3 percent.[70] Predictably, students are also influenced by social conditions that facilitate cheating, such as close seating during exams or ready access to online materials.[71] Conditions that actively discourage dishonesty, such as honor codes, also matter. Schools with these codes generally have lower levels of cheating. However, honor codes "must be more than mere window dressing;" they must be "well implemented and strongly embedded in the student culture."[72] Effective codes work in two ways. They increase students' perceptions of the risk involved in cheating, and remind them of its moral dimensions at a relevant moment.[73]

## Responses to Student Cheating

Any adequate response to academic misconduct requires a comprehensive set of strategies to build a culture of integrity and an environment conducive to learning.[74] Because one strong predictor of cheating is prior cheating, interventions need to begin early. For young children, general discussion of honesty can be helpful in preventing misconduct.[75] Schools should partner with parents in emphasizing the value of learning and integrity, minimizing pressure to succeed at all costs, promoting time management skills, and disciplining children who engage in cheating.[76]

At the high school and college level, institutions need systems to detect and deter cheating, to provide clear, consistent, and fair application of sanctions, and to ensure strong support from faculty and administrators.[77] Honor codes can be a partial means to those ends, although in their strictest forms, they may not be the optimal choice. The most rigorous code systems include:

- Unproctored exams,
- A pledge to abide by standards of academic integrity;
- Mandatory student reporting of infractions of the code;
- A judicial process involving students in addressing violations.[78]

Such systems have not been wholly successful because they have never quite managed to persuade students that it is "honorable to inform on their fellow students who have committed infractions."[79] Students are reluctant to report because they fear making an enemy, they don't want to snitch on friends, or they believe that there are extenuating circumstances.[80] One study of college students found that three-quarters had witnessed cheating during an examination. More than half ignored it. Fewer than 1 percent reported the incident to the instructor. When asked why not, the most common response was that they didn't want to get involved; individuals thought "it's the [cheater's] problem not mine."[81] In other research, common explanations included:

- "I think there's a lot that goes overlooked here, that people just pass off as 'Oh well, I was just helping him on his paper,' . . . rather than actually cheating;"[82]
- "There is an "unspoken code . . . that you don't rat other people out . . . . I think you want to be liked."[83]
- "I guess it's just a hierarchy . . . of values in the sense that my loyalty would outweigh my sense of fair play . . . . "[84]

Given the low likelihood of student reporting, many institutions have adopted less stringent systems, with codes that include an honor pledge and student-run honor councils, but not unproctored exams or the obligation to report.[85] Donald McCabe, a leading expert on academic misconduct, supports such modified approaches, and with reason. As he notes, a reporting requirement that most students disregard may just give them a rationale "to ignore other aspects of the policy or to be cynical about the academic integrity culture."[86]

Convincing faculty to report misconduct poses related challenges. Many professors are uninformed of procedures regarding cheating or unwilling to follow them.[87] In one faculty survey, 60 percent had witnessed cheating, but only a fifth of those had complied with requirements that called for an initial meeting with the student and department chair. Typical reasons included:

- "I wasn't 100% sure the student was cheating;"
- "It wouldn't help;"
- "It was a large class and I couldn't deal with the magnitude of the problem;"
- "It was the first time the student cheated."[88]

In other surveys, about 40 percent of faculty acknowledged having ignored suspected cheating.[89] When asked how they would react if they "were convinced . . . that a student had cheated on a test or assignment in [their] course," only 19 percent would report the incident to the appropriate authority. Most would fail the student on the test or assignment, or require the student to redo it.[90] Yet if faculty don't report suspected dishonesty to a centralized office, they reduce the possibility of sanctions stringent enough to deter misconduct, and the opportunity to track repeat offenders. Inadequate responses not only "embolden students who are willing to cheat," they also create a dilemma for other students "who worry about competitive disadvantage."[91]

Part of the problem is that procedures for reporting dishonesty are unduly burdensome. "Make it easier for faculty to report cheating," one professor advised. "The way it is now it is like the faculty member is on trial."[92] Others agreed that there were "too many hoops to jump through," and that "there is no reward for taking the time, effort and energy."[93] Some faculty members even deny that dealing with issues of student integrity is part of their role. According to one professor, students who cheat are "cheating themselves, wasting their money etc. If they are concerned with their bottom line grade rather than actually learning something, then they have missed the whole point of college and I feel sorry for them, but it is not my job to change their value orientation in that regard."[94] Yet such responses ignore the faculty's opportunity to foster students' moral development and their obligation to ensure fairness for those who play by the rules. If students do not learn how to cope with achievement pressures without cheating, their patterns of dishonesty may persist into adult life, at a cost not only to them but also to society as a whole.[95]

Faculty have a corresponding responsibility to create a classroom environment that encourages learning as well as integrity, because, as noted earlier, the two are related.[96] Assignments should be interesting and challenging, and designed to foster mastery of the subject rather than rote memorization. Professors should solicit student feedback, and intervene with poor performers by directing them to appropriate support services.[97] Expectations of honesty can be made explicit in class discussion and written materials on the syllabus.[98] Most students think that an emphasis on ethics and fairness would be effective in reducing cheating, and more research is needed to test that assumption.[99]

Administrations also must do their part to support a culture of integrity and an effective learning environment. At a minimum, that requires self-assessment. Traditionally, few institutions have sought to measure the extent of academic dishonesty; one now-dated survey found that only 15 percent did so, and systematic research is unavailable about current efforts.[100] That needs to change, and accrediting bodies should demand information about academic integrity as part of the review process.[101] Even without such pressure, colleges and universities should take a hard look at how well they are responding to dishonesty and what they could do better. They also should ensure that academic integrity is included in important school communications, such as the institution's mission statement, website, admissions materials, orientation programs, and presidential addresses.[102] Administrations also should do more to assist faculty in creating effective learning environments, and to help at-risk students become effective learners. Skills programs in writing, time management, and research can address the performance problems that encourage cheating.

So, too, administrators need better communications concerning the procedures for detecting and reporting dishonesty and the importance of using them.[103] Following a recent year in which 84 Stanford students violated the honor code, the provost sent a letter to faculty noting that "with the ease of technology and widespread sharing that is now part of a collaborative culture, students need to recognize and be reminded that it is dishonest to appropriate the work of others."[104] Reporting policies need to be user-friendly, and sanctions need to be significant.

All too often, first violations are treated leniently; students escape with a written reprimand and probation.[105] Some administrators take the view that "we've all been there."[106] In the Stuyvesant cheating scandal, students received relatively brief suspensions that could be expunged from their records and not reported on college applications.[107] Research suggests that such leniency is often a mistake.[108] It is important to combat what psychologist Dan Ariely describes as the "what the hell effect." As he notes,

> Once you commit your first act of dishonesty, you are more likely to commit others. One experiment found a sharp point of transition where people suddenly graduated from engaging in a little bit of cheating to cheating at every opportunity they had. Once people begin to think of themselves as cheaters, they become more likely to engage in cheating.[109]

Administrations should also take responsibility for creating conditions that discourage cheating. Proctoring during exams has been shown to decrease cheating directly, by means of a physical presence, and indirectly, by conveying the expectation that integrity is highly valued.[110] Leaving empty seats between students, and preventing access to backpacks and electronic devices is also prudent.[111] Ready access to web-based plagiarism detection services should also be available to all faculty. But institutions should not be lulled into thinking that such services are a solution to the problem; at best, they can simply identify its symptoms. One study found that just telling students that plagiarism software would be used to check their work did little to affect their attitudes toward such dishonesty.[112] Much more needs to be done, including all of the strategies noted earlier, to reinforce cultures of integrity on American campuses.

In addition, administrations should do more to support national initiatives. The Center for Academic Integrity, founded in 1992, has played a key role by sponsoring research, disseminating best practices, and providing a support network. But it is small and underfunded, and needs more members from among the 90 percent of U.S. colleges that have yet to join. There are also several dozen higher education associations that could focus more attention on academic integrity. Jump-starting these initiatives is no easy task. Unless and until a scandal surfaces, most administrations face little pressure to address cheating. Yet to let such dishonesty become part of the fabric of education disserves our nation and its future leaders.

## Research Misconduct

Less is known about the frequency of misconduct among scholars than among students. Almost no systematic empirical surveys are available, and academic institutions generally treat reports of faculty cheating as confidential.[113] In one of the rare efforts to assess such misconduct, a Stanford University researcher pooled data from 18 sources and found that almost 2 percent of scientists admitted to fabricating or falsifying their work or manipulating data. Fourteen percent said that they had seen misconduct among peers.[114]

In a recent example of such cheating, *Science* retracted a widely reported article based on evidence that one of the coauthors had cooked data and lied about funding. The article, which purported to show that gay canvassers could change voters' minds about gay marriage, drew on a purported survey that the identified polling company had never conducted.[115]

Most experts believe that such blatant fraud is infrequent but that the bending of norms is common.[116] In some instances, the cheating is simply a matter of "convenience," to avoid "extra work" or unhelpful results.[117] Resume fraud is common; one review of medical fellowship applications found that 29 to 35 percent of candidates had lied about their research, scholarly presentations, and articles.[118] The federal government's Office of Research Integrity reports that the number of institutions responding to allegations of research misconduct has grown steadily since the early 1990s and is expected to continue to do so.[119] On average, retraction of a scientific paper occurs daily because of misconduct.[120] Industry sponsorship compounds the temptations to skew results. One meta-analysis found that researchers with such sponsorship were over three times as likely to reach conclusions favorable to industry as those without such financial support.[121] Some articles published by prominent academics have even been drafted by industry consultants.[122]

These examples point up the need for more stringent disclosure policies and effective enforcement structures. Harvard University, in the wake of concerns over conflicts of interest at the medical school, developed stricter rules for all its faculty, which could serve as models for other institutions. Among other things, the revised rules require public disclosure of all relevant financial interests. Increasing numbers of academic journals have required similar disclosures, and other publications should follow suit.[123]

## Plagiarism

Plagiarism is a form of academic misconduct that has become increasingly problematic, although as federal judge Richard Posner notes, it is "not clear whether this is because it is more common, because its boundaries are more contested, or because it is easier to commit and detect through digitization."[124] According to dictionary definitions, plagiarism is the wrongful appropriation of the ideas or the expression of the ideas of another without attribution.[125] If the material is copyrighted, and the copying exceeds fair use, the conduct might also constitute illegal infringement, a problem discussed at greater length in Chapter 6.

Difficulties arise for several reasons. First, disputes center on whether copying or failure to attribute must be intentional to constitute misconduct. Some ethical codes prohibit only knowing plagiarism, others prohibit unintentional copying as well, and many are ambiguous.[126] Conventions also vary concerning attribution.[127] In many European countries, scholars frequently publish material written by their assistants, and that practice is not viewed as wrongful. In the United States, it is generally considered plagiarism for faculty to appropriate the work of their students, unless they are paid research assistants. However, such conduct occurs with depressing frequency in everything from published articles to grant proposals and patent applications.[128]

Conventions concerning ghostwriting are also problematic. Books nominally written by celebrities or politicians are often the work of someone else. Contracts with ghostwriters frequently forbid disclosure of their role, as was the case with Hillary Clinton's *It Takes a Village*.[129] Even medical professors have escaped sanctions for letting their names be used on articles ghostwritten by drug companies.[130] Authors often justify the practice on the ground that ghostwriters have consented to the appropriation. But consent is not the touchstone of harm for plagiarism. A student who buys a term paper and submits it as his own has the consent of the author. The real question is whether readers are misled. In the case of celebrity publications, the audience expects authors to have help.[131] In the case of scholarly publications, the audience expects authors to do their own work and to acknowledge any assistance.

How explicit that acknowledgment should be raises further questions. A common but contested practice is for faculty to appropriate work by paid research assistants without any attribution other than a single footnote expressing gratitude for their aid.[132] If that appropriation is substantial, it meets the Modern Language Association's definition of plagiarism. That definition encompasses giving "the impression that you have written or thought something that you have in fact borrowed from someone else."[133] Applying this standard, law professor Lisa Lerman concludes that a "professor who uses a substantial chunk of writing by a research assistant is engaged in plagiarism. He is implicitly stating 'I wrote this' when he did not."[134] Yet under other professional association guidelines, the issue is less clear. The Association of American Law Schools' standard states:

> When another's scholarship is used—whether that of another professor or that of a student—it should be fairly summarized and candidly acknowledged. Significant contributions require acknowledgment in every context in which in which ideas are exchanged. Publication permits at least three ways of doing this; shared authorship, attribution by footnote or endnote, and discussion of another's contribution within the main text. Which of these will suffice to acknowledge scholarly contributions by others will, of course, depend on the extent of the contribution.[135]

That leaves ambiguous whether the common convention is sufficient. Is it enough for an author to acknowledge a research assistant's contribution without explaining how extensive that contribution was? Some argue that the employment relationship makes the practice acceptable. In their view, just as judges don't credit law clerks, and law firm partners don't credit associates, academics shouldn't be required to do more than identify students who have assisted a work. But it would be good to have greater clarity about best practices, and the point at which extensive student contributions should be disclosed or recognized through coauthorship.

Some fuzziness also surrounds the practice of citing primary sources that authors have not found or read themselves but instead have copied from secondary sources that they do not identify. The practice is widespread for several reasons: it is rarely possible to detect, it keeps footnotes to a manageable length, it usefully identifies the origin of material, and it embellishes the author's academic reputation. As Posner notes, "most scholars in a culture that prizes originality give as little credit to their predecessor as they can decently get away with."[136] But the practice is problematic, because it appropriates another's work without attribution and falsely implies that the author did the hard work of finding the original sources.[137]

Another difficulty involves sanctions. Responses to plagiarism vary considerably within and across scholarly communities.[138] Particular controversy involves the appropriate remedies for sloppy scholarship. That issue has arisen with even some of the nation's most prominent scholars. Two examples involve Harvard Law School professors. Lawrence Tribe acknowledged plagiarism when the *Weekly Standard* found that he had copied one passage verbatim and over 20 passages almost verbatim without attribution to the work of a University of Virginia law professor.[139] Tribe blamed the oversight on his "well meaning effort to write a book accessible to a lay audience through the omission of any footnotes or endnotes."[140] A university investigation concluded that this conduct constituted "a significant lapse in proper academic practice," but that the plagiarism was unintentional. Harvard expressed its "conclusions and concerns" to Tribe and declared the matter closed.[141] Law professor Charles Ogletree copied six full paragraphs nearly verbatim from a Yale Law School professor. Ogletree claimed that he had not read the passage from the Yale author; a pair of research assistants reportedly had inserted it into the manuscript and had accidently dropped the quotation marks and cite.[142] No sanctions for the conduct were ever disclosed.[143]

Another celebrated example of sloppy scholarship involved Doris Kearns Goodwin. This Pulitzer Prize–winning historian was accused of plagiarizing large amounts of material—passages on 91 pages—for her book *The Fitzgeralds and the Kennedys*.[144] Goodwin claimed that her copying was inadvertent; she had forgotten having written out in longhand verbatim passages from those works. Yet when outed, she failed to acknowledge the extent of her copying or her payment of an undisclosed amount of money to the original author, presumably in settling claims of copyright infringement. Even so, many prominent historians rallied to her defense after she hired a leading political consultant to manage the spin. Their position was hard to reconcile with the admonition by the American Historical Association that "the plagiarist's standard defense—that he or she was misled by hastily taken and imperfect notes—is plausible only in the context of a wider tolerance of shoddy work."[145]

Many other leading figures have been guilty of plagiarism and have emerged largely unscathed. While annotating the papers of Martin Luther King Jr., researchers discovered pervasive copying without attribution that went undetected during his life.[146] Alex Haley settled with an author from whom he pilfered passages for *Roots*.[147] Julius Kirshner, a University of Chicago historian, published under his own name a book review written by his graduate student; the sanction was simply a ban on teaching other graduate students for five years. Kirshner responded to the censure by saying "I feel exonerated. There was no finding of academic fraud. I'm still teaching here."[148] Popular historian Stephen

Ambrose was similarly unapologetic for copying large swaths of materials from other authors, some of it verbatim. Although he agreed to correct his books, he told the *New York Times* that "I tell stories. I don't discuss my documents. I discuss the story . . . . I am not writing a Ph.D. dissertation."[149] Although he wished he had "put the quotation marks in," he defended his approach. "If I am writing up a passage and it is a story I want to tell and this story fits and a part of it is from other people's writing, I just type it up that way and put it in a footnote."[150] He also noted on his website that the copied words that investigative reporters had discovered in his works amounted to only "10 pages of some 15,000 pages in print."[151]

Several incidents of plagiarism by nominees for governmental positions surfaced early in the Trump administration.[152] One involved Monica Crowley, who had been selected for a high-profile post on President Trump's National Security Council. She withdrew after disclosures that she had plagiarized key passages of her widely circulated book and her doctoral dissertation. Her explanation that she had decided to "pursue other opportunities" did not mention plagiarism; her publisher, Harper Collins, announced that the book would be released again after proper corrections.[153] Betsy DeVos, Trump's nominee to head the Department of Education, submitted a 62-page written answer to questions that Senator Patty Murray had not had time to ask during the confirmation hearings. Many of DeVos's answers copied text verbatim from federal statutes, Education Department materials, and other sources without attribution. Ironically enough, Murray's questions also included language that, as her staff noted, "did not include proper citation to their original source."[154] Of course, staff are working under considerable pressure under tight time constraints in preparing these materials. But that is the excuse that students and scholars often use in rationalizing their plagiarism. Someone seeking to head the Department of Education has a responsibility to set the right example of academic integrity. Her failure to do so, and the relatively little concern it engendered, are themselves cause for concern.[155]

Equally problematic is the lack of public attention concerning plagairism by Trump's nominee for the Supreme Court, Neil Gorsuch. Before his confirmation vote, Politico and *Buzzfeed* identified multiple plagiarized sections of Gorsuch's 2006 book and his 2000 article on assisted suicide.[156] Several sections of the book lifted language almost verbatim from someone else's law review article without crediting its author, and instead citing the sources that she relied on. In a number of other instances in the book and the 2000 article, Gorsuch borrowed from other scholarly publications without attribution.[157] Although the White House responded that "highly regarded academic experts" had refuted the "false attack" on Gorsuch's integrity, other independent experts viewed Gorsuch's conduct as plagiarism.[158] The most charitable description was "sloppy," scarcely the standard appropriate for a Supreme Court Justice. [159]

Even more disturbing than these cases are the large number of incidents that go unreported or unpunished because the victim fears retaliation or the institution fears adverse publicity and the risk of litigation.[160] These concerns are not unfounded. In one celebrated example, a scientist fired for plagiarism sued the University of Dayton on 13 counts, alleging everything from libel and slander to civil conspiracy and intentional infliction of emotional distress. The university prevailed, but its costs totaled close to $200,000.[161] The result is that many colleges operate with an academic version of "don't ask, don't tell."[162] Peter Charles Hoffer, the author of a book on academic fraud, views the problem as "like cockroaches. For every one you see on the kitchen floor, there are a hundred behind the stove."[163] A rare effort by the *Chronicle of Higher Education* to look behind the stove exposed countless examples of unsanctioned pilfering. In one instance, it took three public charges of plagiarism, and misconduct in 23 of 26 articles, before a literature professor was finally fired.[164] In another case, a University of Oklahoma regents professor had a quarter-century record of repeated academic offenses. When confronted by the *Chronicle*, he responded, "You've probably heard the old adage 'publish or perish' . . . I'm not saying the ends justify the means, but maybe it's a shortcut, using someone else's words."[165] The *Chronicle* reporter pointed out that he was no longer under such pressure and asked why, at the age of 60, he had stolen the introduction to an essay. His response was "Maybe it sounded good."[166]

Other frequent excuses for plagiarism are equally unconvincing. One professor who lifted a third of a graduate student's article claimed that such "cutting and pasting" was a common practice and a way to "conserve energy."[167] Many faculty blame sloppy research assistants or pressures stemming from too many writing commitments.[168] Some scholars simply deny the charges without any plausible reason. A University of Missouri dean whose commencement address appropriated language from a speech by Princeton professor Cornel West claimed never to have seen West's speech. When confronted with the two identical texts, he acknowledged that his ideas were not "original" and that the replication of West's prose was "unfortunate" and "a shocker."[169]

Identifying the problem is, however, far easier than formulating solutions. Part of the reason plagiarism persists is that many academics are reluctant to throw the first stone. Few feel entirely blameless, for reasons that David Plotz describes:

> I frequently imitate the style of writers I admire. I surely have recycled snappy phrases I've read. I can't tell you what they are, but I bet they're out there. I have a fear—which I suspect is shared by most writers—that somewhere, in something I wrote, I may have even stolen a sentence. I don't remember doing it. I would never do it intentionally. But

> could I swear that it never happened? No. This is—to steal a phrase—our "anxiety of influence.[170]

As I can personally confirm, even writing on the subject of plagiarism is an invitation to paranoia.

Moreover, psychological research suggests that some plagiarism is unconscious. "Cryptomnesia" describes a condition in which individuals erroneously believe that they have produced a new idea when they have instead retrieved an old one from memory.[171] Particularly when authors attempt to improve on another's ideas or prose, they may come to think that the material originated with them.[172] Given the blurred boundaries of plagiarism, and the risk that many scholars may have inadvertently crossed them, some degree of underenforcement may make sense.

Yet even so, there is considerable room for improvement in the way that academic institutions handle plagiarism. Most obviously, they can take charges more seriously, and deny tenure or terminate employment of those found guilty of serious or repeated violations. Lesser, but still substantial, sanctions should be available for even inadvertent plagairism. Given the difficulties of proving intentional misconduct, it should not be necessary to demonstrate willfulness. Deliberate indifference to norms of attribution should carry serious consequences. Scholars whose work is stolen are harmed just as much by sloppy scholarship as by deliberate theft.

Journals, presses, and professional organizations also should take appropriate action when they discover plagiarism. Responses include notifying an author's home institution, issuing a corrected version, barring future submissions from the author, withdrawing a book from the market, and removing an article from electronic databases.[173] Professional associations should publicize offenders' misconduct and deny them memberships. Outreach to the media could enhance the deterrent effect of sanctions.

Plagiarism, notes Posner, "has sometimes a comical air, as when the University of Oregon plagiarized the section of Stanford's teaching assistant handbook dealing with—plagiarism. Both Jonathan Swift and Laurence Sterne denounced plagiarism in words plagiarized from earlier writers."[174] A more recent ironic example is a theology professor who stole material for a book on ethics.[175] Yet the consequences of plagiarism are generally anything but humorous, both for individuals whose stock in trade is stolen, and for the academic profession generally, whose public credibility depends on a reputation for integrity. Society as a whole also suffers if plagiarism becomes widespread and diminishes incentives for original work. The author of a World War II book, from which popular historian Stephen Ambrose appropriated material, gave voice to the injury: "I agonized over every word in my book . . . . [Ambrose] just typed in the words, changing a pronoun or a comma here and there. What took me 20 years took him 15 minutes. If that."[176]

Such incidents will continue if the culture fails to take them more seriously. Ambrose remained a bestselling author, whose legacy was barely tarnished by the controversy surrounding plagiarism. Other famous offenders such as Doris Kearns Goodwin have continued to thrive. When Melania Trump's 2016 campaign convention speech plagiarized part of Michelle Obama's 2008 convention speech, there was little lasting damage, even though she was reportedly familiar with the origin of the quoted passages.[177] Yet Donald Trump got humorous mileage out of the incident at a charitable fundraiser by using it as an example of media bias. "You want the proof?," he asked. "Michelle Obama gives a speech. And everyone loves it, it's fantastic. They think she's absolutely great. My wife, Melania, gives the exact same speech and people get on her case . . . . And it wasn't her fault."[178] Ironically enough, as Rachel Maddow noted, Trump stole the joke from a political cartoon.[179] Just as the American public quickly forgave Melania, it also forgave Vice President Joseph Biden for a celebrated incident of appropriating passages from a British politician's speech.[180]

Yet these incidents are symptomatic of a deeper problem: a culture that attaches too little importance to integrity. Plagiarism and academic cheating undermine core values and deserve more serious responses.

# 6

# Copyright Infringement

Although copyright infringement is not always framed as cheating, it fits the dictionary definition. Those who illegally download music and videos cheat copyright owners out of legitimate profits. This form of piracy is nothing new. In the early recording industry, illegal copying was a widespread problem.[1] What is, however, new is the democratization of dishonesty. The emergence of tapes, CDs, and the Internet made it possible for ordinary Americans to copy and distribute music in violation of copyright laws. Moreover, the same technological advances that made piracy easier also made it easier to detect. Through the growth of peer-to-peer file sharing, enforcement has become at least technically possible for copyright holders. Internet Service Providers have retained Internet protocol addresses and log databases that make previously undetectable "sharing" both "visible and traceable."[2]

The result has been a conflict between legal and social norms. Copyright law provides severe penalties, including fines of up to $150,000 for each infringing act. But the average American engages in multiple activities that qualify as infringement.[3] Part of the problem is lack of knowledge of what exactly constitutes a legal violation. A national sample of Americans answered an average of only 4 out of 10 basic intellectual property questions correctly, a proportion just slightly better than chance.[4]

A more serious problem, however, is that on some issues, such as peer-to-peer file-sharing, the public simply doesn't care what the law is. Most people think that current statutory protections are too broad.[5] Almost two-thirds of Americans believe that providing proper attribution to creators should enable the free copying of their intellectual property works; knowledge of what the law is does not affect their opinions of what the law should be.[6] In *Digital Life*'s survey of some 2,600 Americans, "while 78 percent of respondents said stealing a DVD from a store was a serious offense, only 40 percent viewed downloading a movie the same way."[7] Many Americans believe that "ripping off the music industry is just part of the culture."[8]

## The Frequency of Infringement

The amount of such copyright infringement is staggering. Tru Optik, a media analytics firm, estimates that only 6 percent of nearly 10 billion movies, television shows, and other files downloaded in the second quarter of 2014 were legal.[9] One study by the American Assembly at Columbia University found that 70 percent of young adults between 18 and 29 had illegally copied or downloaded music or videos, and almost 30 percent got most of their collections that way.[10] In a survey of younger children, those between the ages of 8 and 18, 88 percent understood that peer-to-peer music downloading is illegal but 56 percent admitted engaging in it.[11] The hit HBO show, *Game of Thrones*, "is sometimes downloaded illegally more times each week than it is watched on cable television."[12] The show broke television piracy records when it was downloaded 3.2 million times in the 24-hour period after it hit piracy sites.[13] Some 2.7 billion file-sharing Web searches occur annually.[14] A 2013 survey from NetNames found that in one month, 432 million Internet users worldwide sought copyright-infringing content online. "It just shows how embedded this particular activity has become in people's lives," said NetNames director of piracy analysis David Price.[15]

The impact on profits has been dramatic. Music industry revenues have declined from nearly $20 billion to $7 billion a year.[16] As to film and television piracy,

> Security Firm Irdeto says that it detected almost three times as many instances of pirated content (14 billion) in 2012 as it did in 2009 (5.4 billion). This despite the "content cops" that networks and others are employing, whose sole job is to detect, contest, and eliminate as many unauthorized content links as possible. Their task is a bit like trying to shore up a leaky hull. You're never going to plug up every leak; the goal is just to stay afloat.[17]

The U.S. government estimates the cost of piracy to total much as $250 billion per year.[18]

## The Causes of Infringement

As these figures suggest, consumers care less about legality than about cost, quality, and convenience.[19] People resist seeing their conduct as theft, which they view as involving scarce, tangible objects capable of physical possession; intellectual property, they believe, is none of the above.[20] One social computing researcher at Microsoft found that young Internet users became angry when peers used their works without permission, but saw no problem in lifting images from shows or movies for use in their own work. As his survey suggested, "the farther removed you feel from the source, the more likely you are to disregard the copyright and the intellectual property."[21] In a Pew poll, 78 percent of Internet file sharers didn't think that they were stealing.[22] In a *New York Times*/CBS poll, 29 percent of Americans under 30 believed that file-sharing is always acceptable and 64 percent believed that it is at least sometimes acceptable.[23]

Although many individuals say they care about whether artists receive a fair share of revenues, they manage to resist seeing a connection with their own theft.[24] Infringers rationalize their conduct on the ground that "artists aren't making the money, just the CD makers."[25] Other excuses are that "the record companies don't need my fifteen dollars as much as I do," or that "I know the artists need to get paid, but the record companies are so rich."[26] One of the busiest threads on the piracy site Oink asked "Why do you pirate music?" Thousands of answers came in, many expressing contempt for the major labels, others reflecting "good old fashioned greed."[27]

## Responses to Infringement

### Deterrence

In dealing with the widespread gap between legal and social norms, society has four basic options: deterrence, adaptation, persuasion, and surrender. The recording and movie industry's initial response to widespread infringement was deterrence. It sought broader protection and sued more individuals for violations. American copyright law became more stringent from the 1970s onward; it imposed stiffer penalties for infringement and provided longer copyright terms. The assumption appeared to be that more copyright was better copyright, and that stricter rules were necessary to protect the creative industry. The Copyright Term Extension Act of 1998 added an extra 20 years onto all copyrights. Critics dubbed it the Mickey Mouse Protection Act, because it extended copyrights for the earliest Mickey Mouse cartoons that were created in 1928.[28] The industry also lobbied unsuccessfully for legislation such as the Stop Online Piracy Act (SOPA), which would have given rights holders the ability to proceed against allegedly infringing sites without any judicial oversight.[29]

Armed with greater legal protection, the industry went after thousands of small violators in an attempt to make examples of them. One Boston University student was ordered to pay $675,000 for illegally downloading and sharing 30 songs (that's $22,500 a song).[30] In another case, the industry sued a middle-aged, terminally ill Mexican immigrant on welfare who could not speak English, for the alleged file-sharing activities of his son. The copyright holders demanded that he divert funds from his welfare checks to finance a settlement.[31] Founders and operators of file-sharing sites were also targeted. The founder of NinjaVideo, a site for illegally streaming and downloading television shows and movies, was sentenced to 16 months in prison for criminal copyright infringement. "I know it's naive," the founder said, "but I never imagined it going criminal . . . . Even if it is wrong."[32] In the most celebrated suit, 13 record labels sought $75 trillion dollars in damages against the file-sharing network Limewire. They calculated damages by counting every time someone downloaded or uploaded a file from the site. In effect, the judge concluded, the labels wanted "more money than the entire recording industry has made since Edison's invention of the phonograph in 1877."[33] Many saw the claim as a "perfect symbol of [the recording industry's] boundless avarice."[34]

The strategy was not effective. As Stanford Law School professor Mark Lemley noted, "the content industry sued tens of thousands of file sharers, and may well have deterred those it sued, but there were tens of millions of people sharing files . . . It sued and shut down dozens of software providers, but there were always more who stepped in to take their place."[35] One researcher calculated that, even at the peak of industry suits, file-sharers were about "as likely to be sued as to be struck by lightning."[36] The result, as another commentator put it, was that "Stopping online piracy is like playing the world's largest game of Whack-A-Mole. Hit one, countless others appear. Quickly."[37]

The reason, psychologist Tom Tyler suggests, is that the severity and certainty of punishments have a "clear but minor influence on law-related behavior."[38] People comply with laws primarily based on their perceived morality and legitimacy. Compliance depends on whether individuals think that the law is right and fairly administered.[39] In the context of copyright, "people need to believe that the rules . . . serve reasonable social purposes and are not simply efforts to create profits for special interest groups, such as large corporations."[40] When most individuals lack such a belief, increased enforcement has little effect, as is clear from America's experience with alcohol under Prohibition.[41]

## Adaptation

In the face of massive resistance, the industry has tried strategies of adaptation, which involve indirect ways to combat piracy or mitigate its consequences. One approach has been to enlist universities in discouraging infringement. Because campus networks often have been overburdened with students using them for file-sharing, administrators have been willing to threaten file-sharers with loss of network privileges and other academic sanctions. The Higher Education Opportunity Act of 2008 requires universities to warn students of sanctions for copyright infringement and to develop plans to "effectively combat the unauthorized distribution of copyrighted material . . . ."[42] "To the extent practicable," campuses also must provide alternatives to illegal downloading or peer-to-peer sharing of copyrighted material.[43] Some universities have temporarily disconnected Internet access to known infringers. For example, when Rightscorp notified Columbia University that a junior had illegally downloaded Taylor Swift songs through the campus Wi-Fi network, administrators terminated the student's access.[44]

The industry has also enlisted some American Internet service providers to send warning notices to file-sharers on their networks. But providers have refused to implement a three-strikes plan to cut off customers who are repeat offenders, and the warnings are widely viewed as ineffective.[45] In the last year for which data were collected, providers sent 1.3 million warnings, a trivial fraction of what Tru Optik estimates to be 400 million illegal downloads in the United States each month.[46]

A more promising approach has been adaptation by developing new business models, such as user-friendly online stores and flat-fee streaming and downloading services.[47] For example, Spotify allows users to pay a monthly subscription fee or get access free with an ad every few songs. It now has 12-and-a-half million paying subscribers and has turned over more than $2 billion to the record labels, distributors, and musicians who own the rights to the songs.[48] One record executive calls Spotify "the best thing the industry has ever done to fight piracy."[49] In 2015, Apple introduced Apple Music, which allows subscribers the right to listen to all they want for $9.99 a month.[50] The potential of streaming to cut illegal use is clearly apparent in Norway. There, over the past five years, the number of people admitting to illegally downloading files online has gone from 80 percent to 4 percent. Fewer than 1 percent of young people use illegal downloads as their main source of music. The reason is the rise of streaming services, which account for 65 percent of the country's music market. No one has been prosecuted for illegally downloading music, and no piracy sites have been blocked by Internet service providers.[51] The transformation in norms has come as a result of services that are more "user friendly" than illegal platforms.

So too, the film and television industries have come to realize that "they were fighting the wrong fight all along."[52] They have now recognized that "while piracy is appealing because it's free, it's also appealing because it's easy. The best way to fight piracy isn't with laws and lawsuits attempting to kill the immortal hydra, it's by offering your product as cheaply as you can, as easily as you can."[53] Pirates used to download eight pixelated seasons of *The X-Files* instead of buying a $200 series box set, but now, as one commentator observed,

> all they have to do is have a $8 a month subscription in order to be able to access not only that series, but countless others. Adding up the

> totality of what's offered via Netflix, you're paying practically pennies for each piece of entertainment. The system is easy to use, high quality and dirt cheap, exactly what [is necessary] . . . to fight piracy. And it's working for many shows.[54]

## Persuasion

A third approach to combating piracy is persuasion.[55] Commentators advocating this strategy argue that people need a better understanding of the reasons underlying intellectual property rules so that "a positive moral climate [regarding compliance] can be created."[56] Accordingly, the Motion Picture Association of America is focusing on educating consumers about legal streaming options and "getting young people to understand the importance and value of copyright protection."[57] But, as an industry spokesperson conceded, "it is difficult to compete with free."[58] One effort has involved working with the Los Angeles Boy Scouts to create a "Respect Copyrights" merit badge. Earning the badge requires completing a curriculum designed by the movie industry. That curriculum has been subject to criticism for failing to mention the limited duration of copyright protection or fair use exceptions.[59]

Another strategy is to build on norms of reciprocity to encourage loyalty among users. Magnatune lets customers choose from a given price range, typically $5 to $18, for an album, with a recommended price of $8.00. Consumers also get pre-purchase access ("try before buy"), which allows potential buyers to make an informed purchase decision. In one study, the average payment per album under this system was $8.20.[60] So too, Radiohead's "name your own price" for its album, *In Rainbows*, worked "awfully damn well."[61] The physical CD sold 1.75 million units worldwide, a much higher figure than previous Radiohead releases.

The United Kingdom is also trying a persuasive strategy that involves plastering ads across piracy websites in an attempt to make users think twice. This initiative, called "Operation Creative," tells potential users that "This website has been reported to the police. Please close the browser page containing this website." Authorities partnered with local creative and advertising industries to design the warnings.[62]

## Surrender

A final strategy is surrender. Some commentators have advocated this approach to noncommercial file-sharing. In effect, this strategy would expand fair use to include such sharing.[63] Users would be allowed to download recordings freely and copyright owners would be compensated from money collected through taxes or levies on recording media or equipment.[64] Another option, proposed by the Electronic Frontier Foundation, is for the law to shift its focus "to making sure that copyright holders are paid for their work, rather than trying to stymie how people gain access to it."[65] This alternative framework would replace the " 'exclusive rights' aspect of copyright law that requires permission to publish and allows copyright holders to seek exorbitant damages from infringers, and [would] move toward a system that requires sites and people who make money from another's work to share any profits."[66] For example, under a voluntary licensing model, the music industry could form a society that offered file-sharing in exchange for a monthly payment, such as $5. That payment would permit access to an unlimited selection of works and the proceeds from the licensing fees would be distributed among artists or copyright holders.[67] Other commentators have advocated enhancing the perceived fairness of copyright law by curbing statutory damages that are now in wild excess of actual damages.[68]

There is reason to believe that such systems would not substantially diminish incentives for creativity. Artists have non-economic motives to create, as history amply demonstrates. Prehistoric man drew on cave walls, and Nazi death camp prisoners created works to help alleviate suffering.[69] Despite the concern that the rise in file-sharing would diminish musicians' incentives to produce, Lemley notes that "people are creating more content than ever before, by at least an order of magnitude . . . . There are more songs being released than ever before, more new artists than ever before, and more purchases of music than ever before . . . "[70] A broader range of music is now available to more people than in any time in the nation's history.[71] People made more music purchases in 2010 than they did before the Internet, "whether because it is more convenient, because it is legal, or because people actually like supporting musicians they like."[72]

This is not to suggest that we can dispense with copyright protection entirely without a sacrifice in the quality of art that it encourages. But it is to argue that we should rethink the extent of protection. We need ways to reconcile legal and social norms. And the most effective strategy may be reforms that make compliance more attractive and bring the law more in line with what people believe it should be.

# 7

# Cheating in Insurance and Mortgages

Insurance fraud is the second most frequent white-collar crime in the United States, exceeded only by income tax evasion.[1] Cheating in insurance contexts is a large but elusive target; no national agency gathers comprehensive statistics. Because only a small fraction of such fraud is detected, estimates of frequency and costs are inherently imprecise. Yet what data are available paint a sobering picture. According to the FBI, healthcare fraud accounts for between 3 and 10 percent of total healthcare expenditures, or between $81 billion and $270 billion a year. Other insurance fraud costs between $40 and $80 billion a year, 10 percent of every claims dollar.[2]

Reports of suspected fraud to the National Insurance Crime Bureau have been rising since 2010.[3] The average American family pays between $400 and $700 per year in the form of increased insurance premiums resulting from fraud.[4] Around 30 percent of a policyholder's premium is due to charges necessary to cover losses attributable to cheating.[5] Over a quarter of Americans say they know someone who committed insurance fraud; four-fifths did not report the behavior.[6]

Data concerning cheating on mortgages is similarly imprecise but sobering. Estimates of the annual amount of housing loans originated with fraudulent application data range from $10 to 22 billion.[7] And dishonest behavior among mortgage brokers and customers contributed to the immeasurable misery resulting from the financial crisis of 2008.

## Types of Cheating

The Insurance Information Institute distinguishes "hard" and "soft" insurance fraud. Hard fraud involves the deliberate fabrication of claims or fake accidents.

Soft fraud, also known as "opportunistic fraud," involves padding legitimate claims, or misrepresenting facts to pay lower premiums.[8] Perpetrators include organized criminals, who steal large amounts through fraudulent business activities and insurance claims mills; professionals and service providers who fabricate or inflate charges; and ordinary consumers who want to cover their deductible or make a little money on the side. Many members of this last group don't consider their actions fraudulent. To these consumers, "it's like fudging a bit on the speed limits," says Donald Segraves, Executive Director of the Insurance Research Council.[9]

Most insurance fraud involves the soft variety by ordinary Americans, and the vast majority goes unpunished. The number of suspected fraudulent claims is at least 10 times greater than the number prosecuted.[10] The most common types of soft and hard cheating include:

- Padded claims (e.g., inflated value of home entertainment systems after burglaries or fires);
- Staged accidents;
- Arson;
- Contractor fraud following accidents and natural disasters;
- False disability claims.[11]

So, for example, in the aftermath of Hurricane Katrina, policyholders made claims for expensive home appliances that were never purchased, and inflated claims for items actually destroyed. Contractors, particularly unlicensed "storm chasers," also fleeced insurers out of billions of dollars for unnecessary or excessive repairs. Some of the fires that broke out following the storm were arson, committed by flood victims who did not have flood coverage. Cheating was so pervasive that the Department of Justice created what is now known as the National Center for Disaster Fraud.[12]

Disability cons are often so flagrant that it is hard to imagine how anyone thought it was possible to get away with them. A common script involves an employee who retires with purportedly severe pain while gripping and bending. Surveillance then catches him playing golf or tennis several times a week.[13] A Chicago police officer claimed he couldn't safely fire a gun after falling while chasing suspected criminals; he then went on safari where he shot and killed a hippo.[14] A Newark policeman who claimed that he was blind was caught on video while driving on the Garden State Parkway.[15] Many con artists take up different employment while on disability. In one notorious case, a tree trimmer who climbed up several trees to clear away storm debris asked his customer, "Could you make the check out to my mom? I'm on disability." The customer was Senator Tom Coburn of Oklahoma, a leading critic of such scams.[16]

The areas most vulnerable to cheating are auto insurance, workers' compensation, and healthcare, all of which receive closer scrutiny in the discussion below.

## Causes of Fraud

Primary drivers of insurance fraud are the low likelihood of detection, the widespread acceptability of padding, and the negative perception of insurance companies. More than two-thirds of consumers think insurance fraud happens because people believe that they can get away with it.[17] According to surveys by Accenture and the Insurance Research Council, about a quarter of Americans think that it is acceptable to inflate an insurance claim.[18] Young men are more likely to condone cheating to make up for their earlier premium payments (23 percent) than women of the same age (8 percent) or older men (5 percent). Eighty-six percent of Americans think that "insurance fraud leads to higher rates for everyone;" only 10 percent think that "insurance fraud doesn't hurt anyone."[19] Yet despite the pervasive perception of harm, most consumers fail to report cheating.[20] One study found that less than a quarter of those who knew about insurance fraud reported the crime to law enforcement or an insurer.[21] Age, attitudes toward misconduct, and perceptions of the industry were the most powerful predictors of reporting.[22]

A major cause of insurance fraud is retaliation for a transaction or course of conduct that perpetrators believe is unfair.[23] As Chapter 1 noted, a sense of resentment or entitlement makes cheating seem justified. Over a third of Americans do not have a positive view of the insurance industry, and negative perceptions make fraud more likely.[24] In Allen Wolfe's study of Americans' moral attitudes, one participant acknowledged her willingness to lie to her insurance company concerning her disability claim. When asked if she felt guilty about cheating, her response was "Not really." From her perspective, company employees "try to play games with her and [so] she plays games with them."[25]

However, not all characteristics of insurers appear relevant. In one study, ethical judgments concerning padding behavior did not vary based on key attributes of the policyholder, the insurance agent, or the insurance company. Filing a fraudulent claim was not deemed more justifiable if the policyholder was working class rather than rich, if the insurance agent was inefficient and uncaring, or if the company had a reputation for treating its employees badly and being a poor corporate citizen.[26] What did influence willingness to cheat was a company's seemingly unreasonable policies on what losses qualified for reimbursement. Under such circumstances, study participants awarded claimants nearly double their actual loss. Participants' reasoning appeared to be that the policyholders had been inconvenienced, had suffered emotional stress, and had lost articles of sentimental value, none of which was reimbursable, so padding was justifiable.[27]

## Auto Insurance Fraud

According to the Insurance Research Council, auto insurance fraud adds between $4.8 and $6.8 billion to annual claim payments.[28] That translates into 13 to 18 percent increases in premiums under private passenger automobile policies.[29] To obtain lower rates, cheaters misrepresent facts on their insurance application. For example, they lie about the major use of a vehicle, the number of miles driven, the identity of drivers, or the address where the vehicle is kept.[30] Some owners abandon or damage their cars, stage bogus accidents, or make burglary claims for items never taken. Body repair shops sometimes substitute shoddy counterfeit parts, and bill insurance companies for legitimate products.[31] Vehicles damaged by storm flooding later appear in used car lots and auction sales, with fraudulent vehicle identification numbers and misrepresentations about the vehicle's condition.

Phantom injuries are estimated to cost insurance companies over $6 billion a year.[32] Usually these involve soft-tissue injuries such as sore backs or whiplash, which are difficult to disprove.[33] One study of such injuries found that nearly half (42 percent) were for nonexistent or preexistent conditions.[34] An Insurance Research Council survey estimated that a fifth of all third-party bodily injury auto accident claims that are paid involve the deliberate inflation of damages.[35] In a study of New York City claims, one in three appeared inflated, and one in five had more serious elements of fraud.[36] Even well- off individuals, including a former Pennsylvania superior court judge, have been convicted for padding auto insurance claims.[37]

Organized scams are also a significant problem. In 2013, a Russian-run ring sought more than $400 million through phony crash-injury claims.[38] In a South Florida scam, participants lightly bumped their own cars into each other at low speed. Many further damaged their cars with sledgehammers to mimic crash damage. Dishonest doctors, chiropractors, and other medical providers then billed insurers for millions of dollars for unnecessary or phantom treatments.[39] In another particularly disturbing case, a mother maneuvered her car into crashes with innocent motorists in order to collect inflated damages for injuries to her children.[40] A California family of three burned to death when a staged accident went awry and their car was hit by two large trucks on a California freeway.[41]

Mass disasters or product safety problems often attract what is euphemistically termed "oversubscription." Here serious injuries have occurred and many claimants are genuinely entitled to relief. But others are attracted by the possibility of an undeserved payday. The phenomenon has plagued many prominent disasters. Following the collapse of a Hyatt Hotel skywalk, "more people filed claims than there were people who could possibly have been in virtually every hotel in Kansas City."[42]

## Worker's Compensation Fraud

Worker's compensation fraud takes multiple forms. Some employers get lower premium rates by misrepresenting their number of workers or the types of work they do. Business owners, particularly in the construction industry, hide employees in shell companies, or label them independent contractors. Another scheme involves misclassifying employees and underrepresenting those in high-risk jobs that are expensive to insure. One estimate suggests that 10 percent of the New York workforce, and 15 percent of its construction workers, are misclassified.[43] Some employers simply do not buy state-required insurance, hoping that regulators won't notice. The effect is to cheat workers out of benefits that they assume they will have in case of injury.[44] Employees are also shortchanged by employers who purchase cut-rate worker's compensation insurance; these insurers then misappropriate premiums without ever establishing coverage.[45]

Individual employees can themselves cheat by falsely claiming that they are too injured to work. While receiving benefits, they then secretly take a second job, open a side business, or pursue hobbies, sports, or other activities inconsistent with their asserted injuries. The category of "What were they thinking" includes a postal worker who claimed a disabling shoulder condition and then posted a Facebook photo that showed her riding a zipline.[46] A grocery store employee who asserted that she was unable to put any weight on her foot or wear shoes due to a fractured toe was caught competing in a beauty pageant in high heels.[47] A California construction worker who claimed "excruciating pain" from an arm injury was seen using it with no apparent difficulty while skydiving.[48] As noted earlier, soft tissue injuries such as back and neck problems are hard to disprove so they are ever-popular worker's compensation scams. Sometimes employees are genuinely injured, just not while working. A person who sprains an ankle in a softball game might pretend that it happened at the loading dock.[49] An old injury that never properly healed prompts some individuals to claim that they suffered job-related accidents. Malingering is even more common. Workers get paid for time off by pretending that they are still too disabled to return to work.[50]

Lawyers and healthcare providers ("medical mills") also cheat. Clinics may, for example, inflate the seriousness of workers' injuries and then charge insurers for costly and unnecessary treatments and tests. Some clinics also bill for phantom injuries or bill more than one carrier for the same services. Dishonest lawyers and healthcare providers encourage workers to feign injuries, seek useless treatments, and then threaten to sue unless the insurance company promptly settles the phony claims.[51] Crooked lawyers and clinics also hire "runners" to recruit workers as participants in scams. The runners receive illegal kickbacks for referring these workers. Some of these employees are knowing participants in this cheating; others don't realize it is occurring and are also victims.[52] Occasionally, the clinics are themselves bogus. They have no licensed doctors and give almost no helpful treatments. They are merely a "staging ground" for fabricated worker's compensation claims.[53]

The price of all this fraud is paid by honest employers, employees, and the public. Employers bear the cost of higher premiums necessary to compensate for fraud, and pass those costs on to consumers. Employees who are injured lack benefits if their employer has avoided buying insurance from honest providers. Colleagues of malingering employees have to shoulder additional work. And taxpayers bear the burden of fraud in programs that are run by the government.

## Health Insurance Fraud

Health insurance fraud is big business. One recent Florida scam submitted over a billion dollars worth of false claims to Medicare and Medicaid. The scheme involved doctors, nursing homes, hospitals, and assisted living facilities. They paid kickbacks, provided unnecessary services, and even prescribed narcotic drugs for addicts in order to entice their participation.[54] In diet drug litigation involving fen-phen, the lead lawyer for the class estimated that 70 percent of claimants had diagnoses that were "medically unfounded and unjustified."[55] A federal judge overseeing the case noted that a cardiologist who had ostensibly reviewed more than 15,000 echocardiograms to make diagnoses, had a "mass production operation [that] would have been the envy of Henry Ford."[56]

These scams were unusual only in scale. Their business plans were depressingly common. According to the FBI, the most prevalent types of healthcare fraud involve:

- Billing for services not provided;
- Filing duplicate claims;
- Offering kickbacks;
- Performing unnecessary or excessive services;
- Unbundling (billing in a fragmented fashion for tests or procedures that are required to be billed together at reduced cost);

- Upcoding services and purchases (billing with a code that yields a higher reimbursement than for the service or item actually provided).[57]

Other forms of cheating are also common. Older Americans covered by Medicare have been vulnerable to marketers peddling false claims that supplemental coverage is necessary.[58] Forged prescriptions permit the abuse and resale of narcotics and other high-demand drugs.[59] Identity thieves steal victims' names and personal data in order to make false claims. This form of fraud is rapidly increasing, and takes the average victim 200 hours to resolve.[60] Other swindlers sell fake health plans that promise generous benefits at low prices, often through bogus websites that resemble sites of legitimate providers.[61] Perpetrators are not just fly-by-night operations: some of the nation's leading companies have been implicated. Johnson and Johnson and its subsidiaries paid over $2 billion to resolve allegations of false claims and kickbacks to physicians and nursing care facilities.[62] Pfizer paid an equivalent amount in civil and criminal fines after pleading guilty to similar charges.[63]

In some cases, patients' health and welfare have been at risk. Doctors and other medical service providers have billed for unnecessary coronary procedures and catheterizations.[64] One orthopedic surgeon filed claims for operations performed by his assistant who had never attended medical school; many patients required additional corrective surgeries as a result.[65] A Los Angeles ophthalmologist subjected poor, mostly Hispanic patients, to needless and careless cataract surgery; one woman lost her sight.[66] A Louisiana cardiologist inserted hundreds of stents into healthy patients who didn't need the often painful and risky procedure to open clogged heart valves. The operations generated millions of dollars in health insurance reimbursement. Patients paid an even greater price. Some had heart attacks and strokes. Others needed remedial surgery. The physician ultimately received a 10-year sentence in federal prison.[67] A scam involving sales of bogus insurance plans to high school athletic programs left catastrophically injured students without financial support.[68]

Yet for every scam prosecuted, countless others go undetected. According to the Coalition Against Insurance Fraud, the inadequacy of enforcement is attracting former organized crime drug dealers because "they perceive the risk of getting caught is lower and [the] income potential is much higher."[69] In the view of one expert, the only cheaters who are caught are those who are reckless and stupid: "the fish who jump into the boat."[70] One such example came from New York investigators. They targeted a cluster of luxury condos with a garage full of Porsches and Aston Martins, and 500 residents claiming Medicaid, a program for the poor and disabled. After six residents were charged with fraud, another 150 stopped claiming payments.[71] Yet such successes haven't translated into increased funding for antifraud efforts. Although those efforts bring in eight times more than they cost, budget cuts have forced a reduction in federal enforcement efforts.[72]

## Mortgage Fraud

Another persistent and pervasive problem involves mortgage fraud, which the Federal Bureau of Investigation defines as a "material misstatement, misrepresentation, or omission relied on by an underwriter or lender to fund, purchase, or insure a loan."[73] Over the past 15 years, such fraud has dramatically increased. Reports of these offenses to the federal government rose by over 18 times between 2000 and 2008.[74] Fraud was a key contributor to the "unprecedented growth of toxic mortgage assets, which led to the implosion of the subprime lending market" during the 2008 recession.[75] One study, which compared buyers' incomes reported on tax returns to those reported on mortgage applications during the housing bubble, found a substantial proportion of misstatements.[76] Readily accessible Internet sites make the creation of fake W2 statements and pay stubs relatively easy.[77] Appraisers who earn $300 for a standard appraisal have charged $5000 for a grossly inflated one.[78] In many cases, lenders have been complicit in fraud. One bank during the boom pasted the names of low-earning borrowers onto W-2 forms belonging to higher-earning borrowers in order to make bad loan prospects look better. The bank's break room had all the necessary equipment; workers dubbed it the "Art Department."[79]

Mortgage fraud takes many forms. Two of the most common are fraud for property and fraud for profit. Fraud for property involves misrepresentations by a loan applicant for the purpose of buying a primary residence. Although applicants lie on their forms, they intend to repay the loans. Misrepresentations include:

- Misstating the applicant's position, employment status (full or part time), income, or length of job tenure;
- Misrepresenting the amount and source of a down payment;
- Failing to disclose existing mortgage or debt obligations;
- Misrepresenting property details or omitting information in order to inflate property values;
- Listing co-borrowers who do not intend to take responsibility for the mortgage.[80]

By contrast, fraud for profit involves more elaborate schemes to gain proceeds from property sales. These applicants have no intention to repay their loans.

Gross misrepresentations concerning appraisals and loan documents are common.[81]

Other schemes involve professionals. "Rescue attorneys" lure vulnerable clients with promises to reduce their mortgages or avoid foreclosure and then do neither. A study by the Center for Public Integrity identified more than 1000 lawyers whose scams resulted in law enforcement actions or disciplinary proceedings. [82] For example, one firm hired telemarketers to hawk loan modifications costing $4000; they claimed that its lawyers had over a 90 percent success rate in obtaining such modifications and "would not accept a case they could not win." Their success rate was in fact no more than 20 percent and prosecutors have charged them with cheating homeowners out of $33 million. [83] Other professionals have been indicted for bid rigging of foreclosure auctions, which suppressed prices and cheated banks and would-be homeowners. [84]

Some fraud that starts small can morph into more substantial crimes without individuals fully appreciating the magnitude of their wrongdoing. Chapter 1 describes the psychological processes that facilitate such misconduct. National Public Radio's *Planet Money* profiled such a case in the mortgage context. Toby Groves tried to keep his previously successful business from going bankrupt by taking out a home equity loan. To obtain the loan, he lied about his income, which was essentially nothing. As he explained to reporters, "There wasn't much of a thought process . . . I felt at that point, that was a small price to pay and almost like a cost of doing business . . . . I didn't think I was going to be losing money forever or anything like that."[85] However, the business continued to falter, and to cover the losses, Groves fraudulently documented a loan for a house that did not exist for a buyer who also did not exist. That transaction required help from people who knew how to fabricate the necessary documents. Everyone Groves asked agreed to help him out. To explain how the scheme could be completed so easily, the *Planet Money* reporters interviewed two psychologists. One explained that Groves's ability to frame the original decision to falsify his home loan as a "business" rather than "ethical" decision made his fraud seem more justifiable. Another attributed the complicity of Groves's colleagues to the natural human desire to assist someone who seems like them, particularly when any adverse consequences seem abstract and distant. So "without focusing on the ethics, they helped out a person who was not focusing on the ethics either. And altogether, they perpetrated a $7 million fraud."[86]

Although Groves was convicted, prosecutions of home purchasers are uncommon. In one of the rare exceptions, federal, state, and local investigators joined in a task force to investigate 11,000 San Francisco Bay Area buyers who may have committed fraud during a recent residential real estate frenzy. Some estimates suggested that from a third to a half of home loans written in the East Bay at the height of the housing bubble were based on fraudulent documentation.[87] What local brokers called "liars' loans" were often accepted without verification. As one broker put it, "people would do whatever it took to get the loans approved."[88] Although some commentators criticized the task force for going after the "low-hanging fruit" rather than bank executives, such initiatives are essential to combat the culture of cheating that has grown up around mortgage loan applications.[89] These initiatives are too often lacking. A report by the Inspector General of the Justice Department found that although federal officials declared mortgage fraud to be a high priority, that was not the case at the FBI field offices that were audited.[90]

## Strategies

As the preceding examples suggest, effective measures to combat fraud will require greater enforcement efforts. Forty-one states have insurance fraud bureaus. Most are funded by assessments on insurance companies licensed by the state. Others receive general funds.[91] Almost all need more resources. Four-fifths of Americans agree that persons who commit insurance fraud should be prosecuted to the fullest extent of the law.[92] To make that happen, federal, state, and local enforcement agencies need to step up their efforts.

Anti-fraud efforts have a high rate of return. Blue Cross and Blue Shield estimate that its antifraud investigations saved or recovered an average of $7 for every $1 spent. The federal government reports similar results ($7.90 for every dollar spent).[93] Every dollar devoted to reviewing federal disability claims for fraud saves an even greater amount ($11) in erroneous payments.[94]

Several recent anti-fraud initiatives are a step in the right direction and a model for other efforts. For example, under the Affordable Care Act of 2010, the U.S. Department of Health and Services Secretary may exclude providers who lie on their applications from enrolling in Medicare and Medicaid. A federal Medicare Fraud Strike Task Force also works with other enforcement groups in nine locations across the country.[95] In 2012, the Department of Health and Human Services and the Department of Justice formed the National Fraud Prevention Partnership. The Partnership includes healthcare companies, the National Association of Insurance Commissioners, the National Insurance Crime Bureau, and the National Health Care Fraud Association. The groups share claims information and work together on other initiatives. More such coalitions at the state and local level are needed.

Such efforts should use particularly egregious examples of cheating to galvanize further action. For example in Massachusetts, 13 communities established multiagency taskforces after a 65-year-old grandmother died in a staged car crash. The effort saved taxpayers an estimated half-billion dollars in premiums.[96]

Moral reminders can also be useful in discouraging fraud. As with tax returns, insurance forms that ask for signed statements saying that the information provided is truthful are much likelier to reduce cheating when they require signatures at the top rather than the bottom of forms.[97] Reminding people of their obligation to be honest before they act helps trigger ethical behavior.

Employers and insurance companies can also reduce the chance of fraud by treating individuals fairly. As Chapter 1 noted, retaliatory cheating is particularly likely when individuals believe that they have been victims of injustice. So, for example, to minimize workers' compensation fraud, employers should listen to employees' safety complaints and take prompt and appropriate corrective actions. They should also communicate zero tolerance for fraud, and publicize whistle-blower hotlines for reports of suspicious activity.[98] Health service providers and insurance companies should more clearly communicate with consumers to enlist them in billing oversight. Nearly 40 percent of Americans do not understand their own medical bills or explanations of benefits well enough to know what services they are paying for and whether that amount is correct. Most do not contact their providers to get clarification.[99] Greater transparency would enhance consumers' trust and assist them in detecting inflated bills.

Whistle-blowing might be greater if the public had more confidence in its effectiveness. To that end, courts, prosecutors, and disciplinary authorities should ensure more adequate penalties. For example, most of the Florida lawyers involved in mortgage scams received only reprimands or brief suspensions; only 15 percent were disbarred.[100] When individuals who have engaged in fraud receive only probation and a requirement that they reimburse ill-gotten gains, it sends the wrong message.[101] Because so much cheating goes undetected, when it is discovered, the sanction should be sufficient to serve as an effective deterrent.

Reported cases also can be hooks for better public relations campaigns. A five-year outreach initiative by a Pennsylvania antifraud agency increased awareness and willingness to report insurance misconduct and decreased the number of people who reportedly would consider engaging in it.[102] Such campaigns should assume greater priority. More Americans need to see insurance scams as unfair not simply to deep-pocket defendants such as insurance companies and the government, but also to consumers and taxpayers who are paying the ultimate price. These individuals need to become more active partners in prevention.

# 8

# Cheating in Marriage

"Life is short. Have an affair," suggests Ashley Madison, an Internet site that facilitates discreet extramarital relationships. As that ad suggests, although adultery is as old as marriage, it has gotten easier. According to the president of the American Academy of Matrimonial Lawyers, "If there's dissatisfaction in the existing relationship, the Internet is an easy way for people to scratch the itch."[1] So too, in contemporary society, couples can more readily disappear for a few hours in crowded, anonymous cities or travel quickly to other places. Contraception and abortion limit the possibility of complications. The increasing availability of pornography also has raised expectations of how "good sex should be."[2] Greater sexual expectations have fed desires for experimentation: sexual boredom is considered unacceptable, the sign of a failing relationship, and extramarital relationships are one solution.[3]

However, although cheating in marriage has become easier, it has not become more acceptable. In fact, as subsequent discussion notes, public disapproval of infidelity has increased in recent years. One reason is that the increasing accessibility of divorce has made adultery seem less necessary. And to many Americans, the harms associated with marital infidelity seem greater than those associated with other forms of cheating. Yet as my previous book, *Adultery*, argued, those harms do not justify the archaic criminal, civil, and military sanctions that current laws impose.[4]

## The Frequency of Cheating in Marriage

A threshold question is what exactly constitutes cheating. Traditionally the term meant adultery, sexual relations between a married person and someone who is not his or her spouse. The term "cheating" seems applicable because, as philosopher Bernard Gert notes, adultery involves gaining the goal of marriage, an exclusive sexual partner, without abiding by the standards of that practice, being an exclusive sexual partner.[5] To some individuals, marital cheating has broader connotations than adultery, and includes emotional infidelity, such as online relationships. And to individuals in committed non-marital relationships, affairs with third parties can also seem like cheating.[6] The discussion here focuses on adultery because it is what most individuals consider cheating and it is the kind for which most research is available. And because infidelity in same-sex marriage is a relatively recent and unstudied phenomenon, the findings analyzed below generally involve only heterosexual couples.

How often adultery occurs, and how it has changed over time, are difficult to pin down. One of the most reliable recent studies is the 2010 General Social Survey sponsored by the National Science Foundation. Among its participants, 19 percent of men and 14 percent of women said that they had been unfaithful at some point during their marriage.[7] A 2011 survey cosponsored by the Kinsey Institute found slightly higher rates; 23 percent of men and 19 percent of women reported extramarital affairs.[8] However, such statistics are not entirely reliable.[9] Most researchers believe that self-reports understate the actual amount of infidelity.[10] According to one expert, "You have to realize that if someone is going to lie to their husband or wife, they sure as hell are going to lie to a polltaker. You're asking them to expose the worst thing they ever did."[11]

The demographics of adultery paint an interesting picture. Cheating does not consistently correlate with religion or education, although some studies find that those who attend religious services frequently are less likely to have extramarital affairs.[12] Adultery does correlate with age, class, gender, and power. Those who cheat are more likely to be middle or upper class than poor, and more likely to be employed than unemployed.[13] Separated and divorced individuals have higher rates of affairs with married partners.[14] So do individuals in positions of power.[15] Men are more likely to be unfaithful than women and to have a greater number of partners.[16] However, most evidence suggests that the gender gap in adultery has narrowed as women have more workplace opportunities involving travel and interaction with men, and the feminist movement has made a double standard less acceptable.[17] For example, women seem to be more likely to have one-night stands, and men less likely, than in prior eras.[18] As wives' paid labor force participation has increased, they may be less economically vulnerable and therefore more willing to risk an affair. Changing attitudes toward older women have also had an influence. Wives' chances of having an affair used to be practically nil after they reached their fifties, but recent evidence suggests a significant uptick.[19] Still, as one expert notes, chronic philandering is still primarily a male activity, and when women attempt to follow suit, they often "mess it up by falling in love."[20]

## Causes of Cheating

In *Heartburn*, Nora Ephron's searing autobiographical novel, the heroine tearfully tells her father about her husband's infidelity, only to be advised, "You want monogamy? Marry a swan." But it now appears that not even swans are monogamous.[21] Evolutionary psychologists see sociobiological reasons for promiscuity among humans as well as animals. For men, infidelity is rooted in the desire to mate with as many different women as possible to ensure that their bloodline survives. For women, infidelity may ensure extra resources from an additional partner and a kind of "mate insurance" if their primary partner dies or deserts them. Also, women who have sex with different men can produce more genetically diverse children, which allows for adaptation to a changing environment.[22] Recent research also suggests that some individuals may be genetically predisposed to infidelity.[23]

Like other forms of cheating, adultery in contemporary societies reflects not just values but situational factors. Opportunities and the quality of the marital relationship are critical.[24] Some cheating is a response to problems in marriage or personal life; it arises out of boredom, loneliness, depression, anger, or revenge. Affairs can give people a sense of achievement, adventure, romance, and sexual variety.[25] Part of the appeal of extramarital relationships is that they take place in settings removed from the repetitive routines of daily existence.[26] Adulterers have opportunities to reinvent themselves and their lives.[27] As one woman explained, "I was curious about other men. I was curious about who I had become. And I was angry with [my husband] and I'm afraid there was a certain revenge to this."[28] A desire for growth and self-fulfillment can also encourage infidelity. Another woman noted, "I was breaking out of years of being the Brownie Scout mother and the cookie baker and the Sunday School teacher."[29] Status frequently plays a role. For some individuals, self-esteem is tied to attracting members of the other sex.[30] In subcultures such as those surrounding professional athletes, being seen with a groupie is a measure of achievement.[31] So, too, some individuals use affairs as a way to get out of a marriage; others use them as a catalyst to change the marriage or to satisfy needs that enable them to keep the marriage intact despite its limitations.[32]

Unsurprisingly, most studies find that those who cheat are less likely to have satisfying marriages.[33] In one large national survey, participants who reported that they were "not too happy" with their marriage were almost four times more likely to report extramarital affairs than participants who responded that they were "very happy" in their marriages.[34] A decline in the frequency of sexual activity in a marriage leads to a higher incidence of infidelity, especially for men.[35] Many therapists view adultery more as a symptom of a troubled relationship than its source.[36] Rather than work through their problems, parties seek escape from them.

Not all cheating, however, is attributable to marital unhappiness; it sometimes reflects opportunity structures and is more the cause of marital difficulties than the effect.[37] In one survey, over half of the men and a third of the women who engaged in extramarital affairs rated their marriage as happy or very happy.[38] In a famous scene from the film *When Harry Met Sally*, Harry tells his best friend, Jess, that his wife has just left him for a tax attorney. Jess responds, "Marriages don't break up on account of infidelity. It's just a symptom that something else is wrong." Harry responds, "Oh really? Well that 'symptom' is fucking my wife."[39] Even strong relationships can experience infidelity if the right opportunities come along.[40] So, for example, individuals who engage in sex with co-workers, or one-night stands while traveling, are not necessarily dissatisfied with their marriages.[41] As one man explained, "I really don't see what's so bad about having a few affairs every now and then . . . I just do it for the fun of it. . . . It doesn't mean I don't love [my wife] anymore."[42] Like other forms of cheating described in Chapter 1, cheating in marriage sometimes reflects an incremental process that participants do not intend to initiate. One husband in his forties described his affair with a co-worker in those terms: "I actually really enjoyed just kind of talking with her. I didn't really want the relationship to move beyond where it was." He didn't envision his weekly lunches with the woman evolving into "this sexual thing."[43]

Most research reveals gender differences in the motivations for adultery. For example, in one study, 56 percent of men who entered into affairs said that they had happy or very happy marriages, compared with 30 percent of women.[44] Men's dominant explanation for cheating was that it developed through sexual attraction that was relatively independent of the marriage. Many reported that their sexual relationship with another woman did not reduce their love for their wives.[45] For men, the strongest predictor for having an affair was their attitude toward monogamy. For women, it was marital unhappiness.[46] When asked what would justify affairs, women were more likely to list emotional factors, such as love, intimacy, sharing, and companionship. Men were more likely to cite sexual reasons, such as novelty, change, experimentation, and curiosity.[47] For some husbands, the "other woman" functioned as a "trophy."[48] That was less common among wives. Women characterized their affairs as more emotional than sexual, and men characterized their affairs as more sexual than emotional.[49] Women more often than men saw affairs as a path to independence. As one woman put it, "This is the one thing I know I am not doing for anyone else. I am not taking care of anyone, this is for me."[50]

## The Consequences of Cheating

The consequences of cheating vary widely. Many adulterers report considerable satisfaction, at least in the short term. In one study, 80 percent felt some or a lot of happiness.[51] Affairs offered a sense of validation and "being alive" that was missing in some marriages.[52] As one woman explained, "My husband was pompous, heavily involved in his career [and] didn't think a wife had a life beyond the Hoover. So this affair . . . was a boost to my ego and appearance."[53] Another woman, also the wife of a workaholic uninterested in sex, regained a sense of herself as someone others might desire. Her lover made her "feel pretty and wanted again."[54] Some research suggests that long-term adulterous relationships are, on average, more psychologically fulfilling than marriage. With none of the social and legal supports that buttress marriage, adulterous relationships that endure do so because they have significant benefits for the couple.[55] Participants feel pressure to be on their "best behavior." In one survey, 42 percent of women in extramarital affairs reported better sex than in their marriage; their extramarital partners engaged in more extensive courting.[56] The "other woman" also may "ben[d] over backwards trying to please" on the theory that "no man would want to leave his wife for yet another 'nag.' "[57] She may also be particularly conscious of the need to accommodate her partner's sexual desires. As one study noted, "If the other woman won't allow him to be sexually adventurous, then what the hell does he need her for? He can be bored at home."[58]

For a small percentage of couples, affairs can strengthen their marital relationship.[59] Henry Gauthier Villars, a nineteenth-century Parisian rake, explained why in a famous quip: "adultery is the foundation of society, because in making marriage tolerable, it assures the perpetuation of the family."[60] A contemporary researcher similarly notes that sometimes the "escape valve of a little romping is all that one of the pair needs to shake them back into the sanity of reality and what they could lose in the way of history, family, friends, and financial well being."[61] An affair can also be a catalyst to necessary change. One wife viewed the day that she found out about her husband's infidelity as "the best and worst day of my life."[62] Some couples have found that their relationships were stronger "than a lot of other marriages that haven't been tested in this way."[63] Marriage therapists agree. Somewhat surprisingly, many do not view infidelity as one of the worst things that can happen to a relationship. In one survey, therapists ranked having an affair only ninth in terms of damage done to a marriage, after issues such as poor communication and unrealistic expectations.[64] If couples decide to stay together, honest dialogue about affairs makes their relationships more likely to last.[65] If they decide to separate, their next relationship may have a greater chance of survival because of what they have learned about themselves and their behavior in their previous relationship.[66]

For most couples, however, the long-term outcomes are less positive. Pamela Druckerman's cross-cultural study of adultery found that "when Americans do cheat, it gets very messy . . . . [A]dultery crises in America last longer, cost more and seem to inflict more emotional torture than they do in anyplace else

I visited."[67] Infidelity diverts time and energy away from the marital relationship and often causes considerable guilt and anxiety. Some studies find that in about two-thirds of cases, the innocent spouse finds out about the affair.[68] The results can be devastating. For many of these spouses, adultery undermines their self-esteem and trust. As one woman put it, "The hardest part to deal with was not the infidelity itself but the fact that he had lied to me for two years. I still cannot forget this . . . . Since that day I have loved my husband a little less."[69] Obsession with the affair can leave spouses "bitter and often alone. Some become lifelong victims."[70] Many spouses experience "inner mortification and social ridicule."[71] Such humiliation can be compounded by a sense that their competitors are inadequate. As one husband put it, "I wouldn't mind so much but he seemed so dull and stupid. Why did she have to choose him, for God's sake?"[72]

Some spouses respond by being hyper-vigilant and monitoring their partner's every move. For one wife, "the worst aspect of the whole experience was becoming a suspicious person. I hated the woman I had become, going through the rubbish, the computer, his mobile phone."[73] To be on the receiving end of such suspicion can be even worse. One woman described the aftermath of her affair as "suburban purdah." Her husband checked her phone bills, searched her purse, and installed a tape recorder in her car.[74] Some implications of the traditional double standard still linger, and influence both cultural and legal reactions to infidelity. Women caught having an affair suffer more guilt and more damage to their reputations than men.[75]

So too, adultery is the strongest predictor of divorce.[76] In some studies, infidelity increases the likelihood of divorce approximately two to three times.[77] In one survey, more than half of individuals who engaged in extramarital affairs left their spouse.[78] Of course, correlation should not be confused with causation. As noted earlier, adultery is often more a symptom than a source of marital difficulties. But in many cases, it may be the final straw that terminates a troubled relationship.

Moreover, divorce is not the worst outcome of adultery. Adultery or suspicion of adultery is a frequent cause of domestic violence and the principal motivating factor for husbands who murder their wives.[79] On average, men are more jealous than women and more likely to respond with violence.[80] Women retaliate in other ways. One wife packed her husband's belongings into crates and had them delivered to his office with the word "adulterer" scrawled across the top.[81] Women's jealousy is greater when their rivals are more physically attractive; men's jealousy is greater when their rivals are higher in social dominance, status, and resources.[82] Evolutionary psychologists have suggested that men are more concerned with sexual infidelity than women because it jeopardizes their reproductive success. Women are more concerned with emotional infidelity, and the risk of having to share their partners' resources with another woman. Many studies have found that jealous men focus more on the sexual aspects of their spouse's affairs and that jealous women focus more on the emotional aspects.[83] As one woman put it, "I don't mind if he fucks them as long as he doesn't talk to them."[84]

Innocent spouses are not the only casualties of cheating. Children also suffer. Of all the lies associated with affairs, those that parents tell themselves about children are among the most disturbing. In one study, only about a quarter of the parents said that their decision about starting an affair had been inhibited by the possibility of hurting their children. Even fewer said that such worries had influenced their decision to continue the affair once it had started.[85] Parents want to believe that their children are too young to understand what is happening. Common rationalizations are that "they cannot see what is going on" or that "it doesn't concern them." Research suggests otherwise.[86] Parental infidelity can have a profound impact on children. When an affair is discovered, "the emotional explosion ripples through the house. Both parents are likely to be preoccupied, . . . and have limited resources for dealing with yet more stress from their children who may be more demanding than usual."[87] Children's reactions vary with age. Young children need more time and attention, so they are particularly vulnerable to neglect. Older children are more likely to learn more about the affair and to be forced to take sides or to be drawn into parental conflicts.[88] Even adult children may find it difficult to trust and respect parents who lied to them about adultery.[89]

The "other woman" may suffer too. In one study, over a third of single women involved in an affair with married man reported that they were "sad and lonely." Many worried that their relationships were "going nowhere" or felt short-changed by how things turned out.[90] As one woman put it, "I was fooling myself. I thought he could be depended upon for the big things—that he would be there if I really needed him. He wasn't."[91] Another woman candidly acknowledged, "I wanted so desperately to be a wife. His wife. God, anybody's wife. I began to feel ashamed and useless and used. Damn it, *used*."[92] Many of these women rejected the idea of having another affair. One put it bluntly: "Too much denial. Too much repression. Too much pitying yourself."[93] In *Never Satisfied: How and Why Men Cheat*, Michael Baisden's advice to the "other woman " is to "pack her emotional and sexual suitcase and find a man of her own . . . In the ruthless game of cheating, there are no romantic conclusions or happy endings, only rude awakenings and hard lessons."[94]

Given these consequences, society has a strong stake in discouraging adultery. But how best to accomplish it remains an issue on which Americans are divided. The main options are public disapproval and legal sanctions.

## Public Disapproval

Popular opinion polls show striking consensus on cheating in marriage. Over 90 percent of Americans consider it wrong.[95] At the same time that disapproval of premarital sex and gay sex has diminished, disapproval of infidelity has increased.[96] Eighty percent of Americans say adultery is "always wrong" compared with 70 percent in 1970.[97] Among college-educated individuals, the rates of disapproval have grown from half in the mid-1970s to three-quarters in 2010.[98] As noted earlier, because divorce has become easier and more acceptable, the justification for adultery has weakened.[99] Ninety-nine percent of married Americans say that they expect sexual exclusivity from their spouse.[100] Close to half of these individuals say that they would leave their spouses if they committed adultery.[101]

A majority of Americans also view adultery as one of the most serious moral offenses. In a Pew Research Center poll, adultery ranked worse than cheating on taxes and alcoholism.[102] In a *TIME*/CNN poll, it finished higher than prostitution.[103] An Angus Reid survey found only pedophilia to be more widely condemned.[104] When asked if adultery is an unavoidable part of married life, 72 percent said no.[105] In a survey of 24 countries, disapproval of adultery was stronger in the United States than anywhere else except Ireland and the Philippines.[106]

Americans have a variety of ways to express that disapproval. Shunning and shaming are the traditional methods. Sanctions involving employment are more problematic. In general, most Americans do not think that such sanctions are appropriate except in special circumstances involving religious leaders or potential abuse of power. When asked if adultery should be grounds for dismissal from a variety of positions, Americans said yes if the person was a member of the clergy (73 percent), a professor whose affair was with a student (73 percent), a military officer with someone of lower rank (55 percent), and a boss whose affair was with an employee (55 percent).[107] Most Americans did not think that adultery should be grounds for dismissal for coworkers (61 percent) or for a married military member whose affair was with a civilian (63 percent).[108]

Such attitudes call into question the practices that still prevail in some workplaces. Police departments have demoted or sanctioned adulterous officers on the ground that their cheating has brought the department into "disrepute."[109] For example, in a 2008 Utah case, the department reprimanded a married police officer for having sex while she was at an out-of-town training seminar. The case arose after an inquiry triggered by her estranged husband.[110] The city alleged that her personal life interfered with her duties as an officer, although there was no evidence of what exactly the interference involved. Nonetheless, a court upheld the reprimand on the theory that it could "further internal discipline or the public's respect for its police officers and the department they represent."[111] Similarly, in 2013, two individuals who had committed curfew violations in connection with an extramarital affair were terminated from a residential FBI training program. Again a court upheld the dismissal without a showing that the affair interfered with their job performance.[112] Given the arbitrary, intrusive, and inconsistent nature of such employment sanctions, society should look for other ways to express disapproval of cheating in marriage.

## Legal Sanctions

The same is true for legal sanctions. Twenty-one states have criminal prohibitions on adultery.[113] Enforcement of such statutes is rare, but it should be rarer still, given its arbitrary nature and lack of public support. In opinion polls, between two-thirds and three-quarters of Americans agree that adultery should not be a crime.[114] The reasons for those attitudes are illustrated by the cases in which charges are brought or threatened. One well-publicized example arose in 2010 when an aggrieved Arizona man Dave Banks, complained that his wife of 17 years had cheated on him at least seven or eight times. As he explained to a national news network reporter, if prosecutors routinely brought adultery charges, "maybe women or men would think twice about going and jumping in the sack and throwing away their marriage."[115] The police were not sympathetic. Banks claimed that it took two years for the department even to take his report, and a detective then told him that "It's about time she got on with her life and you get on with yours." Banks was unconvinced. "How do they get to pick and choose which laws they can and can't enforce? They got somebody readily admitting guilt. Seems to me that's a rubber stamp right through the court system," he told a reporter.[116] Prosecutors apparently did not agree; there is no record of a case being filed. Another notorious case involved the 2010 arrest of a 41-year-old New York woman for having sex on a park picnic table. Although there were witnesses to the act, she denied that it was in plain sight or that any children were around. It is not clear why the woman was charged with adultery rather than some other offense such as public exposure. She vowed to fight the constitutionality of the charge, but it does not appear that the case ever got that far.[117]

Military sanctions are much more common, although we lack systematic evidence about their frequency.[118] Members of the armed forces can be disciplined or discharged for adultery that is "directly prejudicial to good order and discipline", that is "of a nature to bring discredit upon the armed forces;" or that is "unbecoming an officer and a gentleman."[119] Enforcement has been plagued with difficulties. Critics charge that it is inconsistent, intrusive, and biased against women. Kelly Flinn, the first woman to pilot a B-52 bomber, was court martialed for having an affair with a married civilian, lying about it, and disobeying orders to end it. She faced a sentence of nine-and-a-half years in prison. Only after public outcry did the military relent and grant her a general discharge.[120] Another common complaint is that the system imposes "different spanks for different ranks," and favors upper-level officers.[121] The response to such concerns has occasionally been to overreact by imposing excessive punishments on these officers even though their conduct posed little threat to good order. Over the last decade, several generals or commanders have resigned or been removed because of adultery.[122]

The most celebrated case involved David Petraeus, the director of the Central Intelligence Agency and one of America's most decorated four-star generals. He resigned after revelations that he was having an affair with the coauthor of his biography.[123] Many Americans were more disturbed by his stupidity than his infidelity. Petraeus had posted sexually explicit messages in a Gmail folder. As one journalist put it, "The head of the Central Intellligence Agency thinks Gmail accounts are secure and untracaeable. What, he couldn't have checked with a tech-savvy 12-year-old first?"[124]

Such cases make clear the need for reform. Sixty-two percent of Americans think that adultery should not be a military crime, and many experts agree.[125] If those prohibitions were removed, the military could still prosecute conduct that posed a threat to good order under other rules. The punishment would stem not from the fact that soldiers or their partners were married, but from the potential for sexual coercion and danger to unit cohesion.[126] Military life is challenging enough without inconsistent enforcement of rules that are out of step with prevailing cultural norms.

The public's lack of enthusiasm for adultery prosecutions in civilian contexts is apparent from all the prominent cases in which charges are not brought. For example, in 2008, New York governor David Paterson announced at a news conference that he had had several extramarital relationships but "didn't break the law." The *New York Times* followed up with a report that began "Well, actually . . . ."[127] Adultery is a misdemeanor in New York, punishable by a fine of $500 or 90 days in jail. Rarely has it been invoked since the 1970s, and when it has, any charges are usually dropped. When asked about the prospect of a criminal prosecution of Paterson, a New York divorce attorney responded, "Absent a Christian fundamentalist replacing [the local district attorney], I doubt it."[128]

So, too, a celebrated affair between two Idaho state legislators in 2016 triggered ethics inquiries but no prosecution. Legislative rules prohibit "conduct unbecoming" a representative or senator, and violation of any state law that "brings discredit" to the body.[129] Adultery is a felony in Idaho, punishable by up to three years in prison. Although both legislators have admitted the affair, no prosecutor appears interested in pursuing charges.

Adultery plays a similarly declining role in divorce cases, and that trend should be encouraged. In some jurisdictions, however, infidelity can be a factor in alimony and custody decisions.[130] Although courts occasionally have talked about adultery as evidence of a mother's moral values, the focus generally has been on whether a child has been exposed to, or harmed by, the mother's illicit conduct.[131] It is no accident that these courts have used the term "mother." Although the doctrine governing parental fitness is gender neutral, sanctions for infidelity in family cases are applied disproportionately to women.[132] That fact, along with the reality that marital infidelity does not necessarily affect parenting abilities or the need for spousal support, argues against punitive treatment of unfaithful spouses in divorce cases.

There is also no justification for allowing civil liability actions against adulterers for "criminal conversation" or alienation of affection. Criminal conversation is an oddly named offense that involves neither crimes nor conversation; it refers to a civil proceeding in which aggrieved spouses seek damages from their partners' lovers. Six states recognize such claims, along with the related action of alienation of affection, which permits judgments against paramours who have destroyed a marriage.[133] Lawsuits on these grounds, although rare, can be expensive; million-dollar awards are not uncommon.[134] The amount of awards seems exceptionally idiosyncratic. A wrestling coach recovered $910,000 in compensatory damages and $500,000 in punitive damages from a man who had sex with his wife in a hotel room.[135] By contrast, a husband who learned during a marital counseling session of his wife's affair with one of his employees received less than a quarter of that amount. But he still recovered $100,001 in actual damages and $250,000 in punitive damages, based on his testimony that the affair caused him severe emotional distress, eroded his self-respect, and "broke [his] heart very badly."[136]

The highest verdict on record came in 2010, in an award of $9 million to Cynthia Shackelford against the woman she sued for breaking up her 33-year marriage. Shackelford told reporters that she hoped the verdict would send a simple message to "would be homewreckers:" "Lay off."[137]

Most states however, have concluded that it is aggrieved spouses who should lay off. The vast majority have abolished actions for criminal conversation and alienation of affection, either by statute or judicial decision. One reason is that these actions may be vexatious or extortionate.[138] Another is that they are too infrequent and idiosyncratic to deter cheating behavior. The response of one 61-year-old man, surprised by such a suit against him, was typical. "You've got to be kidding me. Is this thing for real?"[139] He had a point. Aggrieved spouses need to get a life, not a lawsuit.

## Political Sanctions

A final way for the public to express disapproval of cheating in marriage is by withholding support for unfaithful politicians. Popular opinion has been mixed, but the trend is toward greater permissiveness. One of the curiosities of America's 2016 presidential campaign was that Donald Trump is a self-confessed serial adulterer, yet few conservative voters seemed to care. His relationship with Marla Maples while he was married to his first wife was widely publicized.[140] And in *The Art of the Comeback,* Trump bragged about his sexual experiences with "seemingly very happily married and important women."[141] The public's tolerance of such behavior appears to signal a change in views. In 2009 polls, 61 percent of Americans thought voters should know about a politician's infidelity, and they were almost exactly split on whether adulterers lacked the "personal character and integrity" to hold a political office.[142] In 2013, half of those surveyed would definitely or probably not vote for a congressman who was unfaithful to his wife.[143] But by 2016, 6 in 10 Americans agreed that elected officials can perform their public duties in an ethical manner even if they have committed immoral personal acts. Seven out of 10 white evangelical Protestants also agreed, a jump from 3 in 10 who thought so in 2011.[144]

Those who find adultery relevant generally believe that character cannot be compartmentalized and that the qualities that politicians display in their personal lives spill over to their professional lives. In an age in which divorce is readily available and acceptable, a politician's choice to remain married, while repeatedly violating marital commitments, raises questions of moral values. That was the basis for conservative commentator William Bennett's claim that "[s]omeone who lies in private is going to lie in public and you can't trust someone who does that."[145] A further reason for caring about politicians' cheating in marriage involves public trust and credibility. Leaders charged with making or enforcing the law should abide by it in their own lives. In order to maintain respect and serve as appropriate role models, politicians should behave responsibly in their personal as well as professional lives.

Yet to suggest that adultery is always disqualifying is problematic on several grounds. A threshold difficulty involves the assumption that cheating reflects consistent character traits, and that individuals who exhibit dishonesty or disrespect for ethical standards in marriage will do so in politics. As Chapter 1 indicated, context is critical in shaping moral behavior, and even slight changes in situational factors can substantially affect tendencies toward deceit.[146] Whatever else one may say about infidelity in marriage, history does not disclose it to be an accurate predictor of ethics or effectiveness in office. Compare, for example, Richard Nixon, who was reportedly faithful, and Franklin Delano Roosevelt, who was not.[147]

Society also suffers when its choices for leadership narrow to those willing to put their entire sexual histories on public display. Our nation has a limited supply of gifted leaders, and many who might serve are either unwilling or unable to withstand inquiries into intimate conduct. So, too, as my previous book on adultery argued, focusing on the sexual conduct of politicians encourages a kind of Gresham's law of journalism.[148] All it takes is one reporter with a peephole perspective. As soon as a scandal breaks in any major media outlet, it becomes difficult for other members of the press to remain above the fray. The prevailing philosophy of "let the public decide" often encourages the media to pander to our worst instincts, and to divert its attention from more substantive issues. Details about politicians' sex lives can distract, distort, and destroy a career in public service. Excessive attention demeans not only politicians but ourselves.[149]

The point is not that adultery should never be considered in assessing qualifications for leadership. It is rather that context matters. Much depends on the nature and consequences of the cheating and what other issues are at stake. Did the affair involve abuse of office, other illegal conduct such as prostitution, exceptionally poor judgment, or unduly reckless behavior? Is the position one such as president, which necessarily entails moral leadership? What will happen in terms of other policy concerns if the politician is defeated or forced to resign?[150] Four examples of political leaders implicated in marital scandals suggest the kind of inquiry that is necessary. Two, Gary Hart and John Edwards, were derailed by adultery. Two others, Bill Clinton and Mark Sanford, survived, and the reasons illumine the strengths and limitations of public disapproval as a sanction for cheating in marriage.

Gary Hart's adultery shattered the boundaries of discretion that had previously marked media coverage of marital cheating. For the first time, reporters asked a candidate about infidelity. And the answer doomed the candidacy of a man who had been the front runner in the 1988 presidential race.[151] Charges of philandering surfaced early in his political career, but Hart's initial response to press inquiries was simply that "adultery was a matter between himself and God" and he didn't have to answer to anyone else.[152] Later, with unparalleled recklessness, Hart not only denied charges of infidelity, but also invited the media to prove him wrong: "Follow me around. I'm serious. If anybody wants to put a tail on me, go ahead. They'll be bored."[153]

They weren't. Acting on an anonymous tip even before Hart issued his challenge, *Miami Herald* reporters staked out his Washington townhouse.[154] When confronted there with a young blond woman not his wife, Hart denied being involved in any sexual relationship.[155] As a *New York Times* editorial wryly inquired, "would 'political' or 'business' relationship better describe it?"[156] When *Herald* reporters asked if Hart had taken the woman on a yachting trip in

Florida, Hart implausibly responded, "I don't remember."[157] When asked point blank if he had ever committed adultery, Hart responded, "I don't think that's a fair question . . . . I'm not going to get into a theological definition of what constitutes adultery."[158]

When reports of other affairs resurfaced, Hart was forced to suspend his campaign. In the final analysis, what doomed Hart's candidacy had less to do with sex than with judgment. For a position such as the presidency, which involves moral leadership, appearances matter. Hart's reckless self-indulgence was not what the public wanted in a leader of the free world. Yet at the same time, the price Hart paid after the campaign seems excessive. He became the "iconic adulterer," a perpetual political pariah who never gained another meaningful opportunity for public service.[159] As he told a *New York Times* reporter in 2009, "I made a mistake . . . " It was "a single incident fifteen years ago. I think I've paid my dues . . . I'm not even asking for forgiveness, but fairness . . . . This whole business of '87 is flypaper to me. It's so frustrating. It's like being in a time warp. I want to get unstuck."[160] Because he never did, the public lost out on a potentially gifted public servant.

John Edwards also doomed his presidential candidacy by cheating in marriage. It began in 2006 with Rielle Hunter, who joined Edwards's presidential campaign to produce a series of webisodes that portrayed life behind the scenes on the campaign trail. The affair soon became obvious to staff, and Edwards's wife, Elizabeth, discovered it through a cell phone in her husband's luggage. Edwards told her it was a "one night stand." Hunter's contract was terminated and she disappeared. But not for long.

By all accounts, the Edwards had an unhappy marriage, but neither of them wanted a divorce. Elizabeth's ambitions were tied to her husband's presidential aspirations. John believed that his wife was more popular than he was, and that a divorce would torpedo his political career.[161] The risks of separation became even greater when Elizabeth learned that she had incurable cancer. She insisted that John remain in the race. He did, and rumors circulated that Hunter had reappeared at hotels where he was staying. Elizabeth began closely monitoring his movements and the tabloids were sniffing at his door. But according to campaign aide Andrew Young, Edwards

> never seemed to grasp the magnitude of the trouble he faced. Instead he would tell me that if the truth ever came out it would be, at worst, a one day news story because "everyone knows" that politicians screw around on their wives. What this position denied was the fact that his wife had cancer and he had sold himself to the American public as a devoted husband and family man who talked about his faith in order to appeal to Christian voters.[162]

In October 2007, the *National Enquirer* published an expose of Edwards's affair with an unnamed campaign worker and followed it up in December with a piece titled "Update: John Edwards Love Child Scandal." The article featured a photo of Hunter six months pregnant, and identified Edwards as the father.[163] Edwards dismissed the story as "lies" and "tabloid trash," but it took on new legs when *Enquirer* reporters confronted him after he met with Hunter and the baby in a Beverly Hills hotel room.[164] Claiming he was "dogged by tabloids," Edwards tried to put the matter to rest by appearing on ABC's *Nightline*.[165] There he acknowledged the affair but in a way that was strikingly tone deaf. As *New York Times* columnist Maureen Dowd noted, the "creepiest part of his creepy confession was when he stressed . . . that he cheated on Elizabeth in 2006 when her cancer was in remission. His infidelity was oncologically correct."[166] In 2010, Edwards finally admitted he was the father of Hunter's child and separated from his wife. She died shortly thereafter. A survey that year by Public Policy Polling revealed that he was the "most unpopular person we've polled anywhere at any time."[167]

Edwards's troubles were compounded in 2011 when he was prosecuted on six felony charges. They concerned payments made to Hunter and Young that allegedly violated campaign finance laws. After a mistrial on one charge and an acquittal on five others, the Justice Department chose not to retry the case.[168] Edwards then struggled to rebuild his career as a trial lawyer.[169] As one friend put it, "He doesn't want his legacy to be he had a toot with this gal from nowhere and that's the sum of his life."[170] As was true of Hart, Edwards's conduct over the course of the political campaign raised serious questions of integrity, judgment, and ability to lead. His carefully cultivated public image as a devoted husband was simply too far from the truth to make him a viable candidate.

By contrast, Bill Clinton came through his scandals with substantial public support. He set the tone for his relationship with his future wife Hillary Rodham when she followed him to Arkansas to act as his campaign manager in the 1974 congressional election and he slept with another of his campaign workers.[171] However, they married in 1975 and she stood beside him while he served six terms as governor despite what one aide labeled constant "bimbo eruptions."[172] Clinton strayed so often and so flagrantly from his marriage that his advisor Betsy Wright talked him out of a run for the presidency in 1988. She compiled a list of women with whom he had had sexual relationships and suggested that he would suffer the same fate as Gary Hart, whose campaign had imploded just months earlier.[173]

Four years later, Clinton launched his campaign for the 1992 presidential nomination and publicly confessed that he had caused "problems" in his marriage. This did not, however, avoid scandal once Gennifer Flowers sold her story of their 12-year affair to a tabloid and began appearing on talk shows.[174] Four state troopers confirmed that they regularly took Clinton to Flowers's apartment and that they overheard him using his influence to find her a state job.[175] The scandal was later compounded by other claims of Arkansas state troopers that they had facilitated Clinton's extramarital involvements. They asserted that they had bought gifts of lingerie for his partners and had been offered employment in exchange for their silence.[176]

What salvaged Clinton's political career was his national television appearance on *60 Minutes.* There, he denied the affair with Flowers and Hillary was stoically supportive. According to Bill, Flowers was a "friendly acquaintance" whose claims were motivated by payments from the tabloid. He acknowledged causing "pain in my marriage" but was not prepared to say more. No married couple, he asserted, should have to discuss the details with anyone other than each other. Hillary agreed, and emphasized the dangers for the country if a "zone of privacy was lost."[177]

Despite the scandal, Clinton won the nomination and the election as president. During his first term, he continued to be dogged by allegations of infidelity. The one that almost proved his undoing involved Monica Lewinsky, a 22-year-old White House intern. While passing by Clinton, she flashed her thong underwear at him.[178] Days later, when he invited her into his office, she blurted out, "You know, I have a really big crush on you."[179] One thing led to another, and ultimately to an inquiry by special prosecutor Kenneth Starr. He had been investigating the Clintons for alleged corruption involving Whitewater, a series of Arkansas land deals.[180] Starr then broadened his inquiry to include possible perjury and obstruction of justice in connection with a sexual harassment case in which Clinton denied having sexual relations with Lewinsky.

Two years into the relationship, Clinton finally broke it off, telling Lewinsky that "It was wrong for me, wrong for my family, and wrong for her."[181] In the aftermath of the breakup, Clinton reminded her that "You told me when this affair started that when it was over you would not give me any trouble." With unintended prescience, Lewinsky responded, "Trouble? You think I have been trouble? You don't know trouble."[182]

The trouble came in several forms. On national television, Clinton falsely claimed that "I did not have sexual relations with that woman, Miss Lewinsky."[183] His decision to lie was partly driven by poll numbers. His advisor Dick Morris had run some surveys and had told Clinton that a majority of voters would not support an adulterer as president. [184] But denials of a sexual relationship were short-lived. Starr pressured Lewinsky into cooperating with his investigation and answering questions under oath about who touched whom when and where and whether orgasm resulted.[185] Starr also had physical evidence of the affair, including a semen-stained dress that Lewinsky had worn during sex with Clinton. On the day before being called by Starr to testify before a grand jury, Clinton disclosed his relationship with Lewinsky to his wife. Then, following his grand jury testimony, he went on television and acknowledged his infidelity to the nation. Sounding more combative than contrite, he admitted engaging in a relationship that was "not appropriate. In fact it was wrong. It constituted a critical lapse in judgment and a personal failure on my part for which I am solely and completely responsible." However, the president also lashed out at the independent counsel, and claimed that the investigation of Whitewater land deals had spiraled into intensely private matters; it had "gone on too long, cost too much and hurt too many innocent people. Now, this matter is between me, the two people I love most—my wife and our daughter—and our God . . . . It's nobody's business but ours. Even presidents have private lives. It is time to stop . . . the prying into private lives and get on with our national life."[186]

Although the speech functioned more as an attack than an apology, subsequent polls found that 62 percent of Americans gave Clinton a favorable job performance rating, and around two-thirds thought that his relationship with Lewinsky was a private matter and had nothing to do with his effectiveness in office. By a margin of 65 to 31 percent, Americans also thought Clinton's testimony and subsequent apology should have ended the matter.[187] Part of the reason is that although Clinton had an abysmal record on personal fidelity, he had a strong one on gender equality, and the national economy flourished under his administration. Even after the House of Representatives voted to impeach him, Clinton's national approval rating jumped 10 points to 73 percent, one of the highest levels ever.[188] A 2014 poll showed that Clinton was, by a wide margin, the most admired president of the last quarter century.[189]

Another political leader who survived an adultery scandal is former South Carolina governor Mark Sanford. In June 2009, Sanford vanished for six days. His wife, staff, and security detail all had no idea where he was. A spokesperson issued a statement that he was hiking the Appalachian Trail.[190] On his return, Sanford was confronted by a reporter who had received a tip that he had been visiting a mistress in Argentina. Several hours later, Sanford held a press conference where he tearfully admitted that he had been "unfaithful to my wife," but said that he would die "knowing that I had met my soulmate."[191] And in what was widely viewed as an excess of candor, he confessed spending the past five days "crying in Argentina."[192] Adding to his humiliation, the local newspaper published copies of steamy emails he had written to the woman.

The *New York Times* called for Sanford to resign and a majority of voters (54 percent) agreed that he should.[193] As the *Times* noted, he had failed to transfer emergency powers to the lieutenant governor, lied to the state and his staff, and tapped taxpayer funds to drum up a trade mission to Argentina that allowed him to see his lover.[194] But Sanford vowed to stay on, and the Judiciary

Committee of the South Carolina House of Representatives rejected a resolution to impeach him.[195] Sanford's wife then filed for divorce on grounds of adultery, and published a book detailing her husband's deception.[196] Sanford subsequently became engaged to the woman from Argentina, broke off the engagement, and then resumed the relationship.[197]

His political career was far from over. After finishing his term as governor, Sanford successfully ran for his original congressional seat.[198] Some conservatives withheld support. As one commentator put it:

> Let me say upfront: I would rather we lived in a society where adultery had a higher cost. That's not to say people shouldn't be forgiving or that there should be no such thing as second chances. But ideally, I'd like it if things were less loosey-goosey. Cheat on your wife, and maybe you don't get to run for public office anymore . . . . Or if that's too much to ask, maybe the interval between scandal and rehabilitation could last a little longer than the maturation time of a fruit fly.[199]

Most voters disagreed; ideology trumped sex.[200] Nate Silver crunched the numbers and, after extrapolating from the congressional district's past Republican electoral record, estimated that the scandal had cost Sanford 13 percentage points. Voters in South Carolina may not like infidelity, he concluded, "but they appear to like Democrats even less."[201] The same appeared to be true with Trump voters in 2016.

In the final analysis, that is a defensible position. As journalist Matt Bai notes, American history is rife with examples of people who were "crappy husbands . . . but great stewards of the state, just as we had thoroughly decent men who couldn't summon the executive skills to run a bake sale."[202] To be sure, there may be some politicians such as John Edwards whose conduct was so egregious as to make them unfit for positions of moral leadership. And there are reasons to discourage and deplore the collateral consequences that often accompany adultery by politicians. Leadership scholar Joanne Ciulla chronicles the costs of presidential infidelity: blackmail, hush money, security threats, abuse of office (to obtain jobs for mistresses), and diversion of staff time and energy.[203] And when affairs become public, they can tarnish the office and undermine public respect for those who hold it. But these costs need to be balanced against the risks of journalistic voyeurism and the other traits and contributions that a candidate offers. For most politicians, most of the time, what makes for personal goodness in marriage is less critical than what makes for the common good in public life. It often makes sense to hate the sin, but vote for the sinner.

The same is true in other contexts. A time-honored nightclub joke recounts how Moses came down from the mountain and announced, "I have some good news and some bad news. The good news is that I bargained him down to only ten commandments. The bad news is that adultery stays in." There are reasons why it should; the adverse consequences for innocent spouses and children are substantial. But legal, employment, and political sanctions are generally ill-suited to shore up the values of marital fidelity. Public disapproval remains the last, but generally the best, resort against cheating in marriage.

# 9

# Conclusion

Writing about cheating is a perilous project. It is difficult to avoid seeming platitudinous, hypocritical, or both. Authors risk being called out for some minor, long-forgotten, or unintended act of the very sort they are condemning. The fear of a response such as "Where does *she* get off writing about cheating" may be one reason that the subject has attracted inadequate attention from serious scholars.

But the price of that neglect is substantial. As Chapter 1 noted, a crude estimate is that losses attributable to cheating total somewhere in the neighborhood of a trillion dollars annually. And the costs are not simply financial. Cheating in marriage is one of the major causes of divorce, domestic violence, and personal pain. Staged auto accidents can result in severe injuries. Cutting corners on car safety tests costs lives. Students and athletes pay the price when cheating creates an uneven playing field.

Equally disturbing are the attitudes toward cheating among American youth. According to a survey of some 23,000 students by the Josephson Institute of Ethics, 57 percent agreed that "in the real world, successful people do what they have to do to win even if others consider it cheating."[1] Although half of students acknowledged cheating on a test and three-quarters had copied another student's homework, 93 percent were satisfied with their own character and ethics.[2] A national study of ethical attitudes among young adults age 18 to 23 found that 60 percent had an "individualist" approach toward morality; in their view, what was right and wrong were "essentially matters of individual opinion."[3] Typifying this attitude, one student at an Ivy League university explained that although she didn't cheat, she also didn't judge classmates who did. As she put it, "I guess that's a decision everyone is entitled to make for themselves. I'm sort of a proponent of not telling other people what to do."[4] "Who am I to judge" was the prevailing view, which helps explain why the vast majority of cheating goes unreported.[5] A third of the sample also were prepared to do things they thought were morally wrong if they thought they could get away with it. As one young adult put it, "People cheat. That's how a lot of people have gotten ahead, especially in this country. It's like a cutthroat world out there . . . I will do what I can to get ahead."[6]

Although people often believe that the personal benefits of their cheating outweigh the risks, they rarely take into account the social costs. Psychologists William Damon and Ann Colby note that "each instance of dishonesty contributes to cultures that stimulate and justify further dishonesty. The power and destructiveness of this vicious cycle may be the best argument against cheating as well as the most compelling explanation for its prevalence."[7]

The preceding chapters have drilled down on the causes and consequences of various forms of cheating in everyday life. The discussion that follows draws some general lessons from that analysis, and identifies the most promising responses.

## Causes of Cheating

One explanation for some forms of cheating lies in the lack of individual awareness or social consensus about what exactly it is. Definitions blur at the margins, and large percentages of the public are unclear about what constitutes copyright infringement or plagiarism. The vast majority of cheating, however, reflects no such ambiguities and is heavily influenced by situational factors. Although individuals vary in their vulnerability to temptation, and small minorities almost always or almost never cheat, for most of us, most of the time, context is critical.

That point emerged clearly in sociologist Alan Wolfe's study of moral attitudes in America. As one interviewee put it, "Cheating is not so much good or bad; it depends on what you're cheating about."[8] Another noted, "I consider myself to be really honest. However there are times when I keep my mouth shut. I will cheat the IRS if I have a chance. And insurance companies, I would cheat them too."[9] Most Americans viewed honesty as "something we ought to approximate, a virtue that remains important as an ideal, but that always needs to be tempered by reality."[10]

Wolf's study, like the research summarized in earlier chapters, makes clear that cheating is heavily dependent on the social norms, rewards, and penalties applicable in a given context. Most of us are at least sometimes willing to cut corners if the likely payoffs sufficiently outweigh the risks and we can find a plausible rationalization. Part of the reason cheating is so common is that people's moral reasoning is so easily skewed by self-interest. From an ethical perspective, relatively little cheating is justifiable under the standard set forth in Chapter 1. It requires that a disinterested decision-maker could conclude that the benefits to cheating outweigh the harms, that no alternatives to cheating are available, and that if everyone in similar circumstances acted similarly, society would be no worse off. Cheaters rarely subject their own conduct to that test. Rather, they fall back on the techniques described in preceding chapters to neutralize the harms of their misconduct. "Everybody does it" is a common position, particularly in contexts such as evading taxes, downloading music and videos, and plagiarizing academic work. Rationalization becomes still easier when people feel that they have been unfairly treated or that the victims of cheating are unsympathetic. As one individual in the young adult sample reasoned, large companies "have money," and "if it's not hurting an individual, its not really wrong."[11] Many Americans are willing to retaliate against ostensibly greedy record and insurance companies, ineffective teachers, unfeeling spouses, and the Internal Revenue Service.

## Responses to Cheating

### Families

Our responses to cheating need to start early because so does cheating. This point came through clearly in a *Wall Street Journal* article with a headline asking "How Could a Sweet Third-Grader Just Cheat on That School Exam?"[12] The answer, it turned out, had much to do with parents. Some overscheduled their children and left them too little time for study. Others exerted undue pressure for good grades and provided too much assistance in orchestrating science projects, composing, or typing, and correcting essays. As one expert put it, "not only does this send the message that presenting someone else's work as your own is ok, but it suggests that grades are more important than learning—an attitude linked in research to higher rates of cheating."[13] Parents need to actively promote integrity, and to make clear by word and example that cheating is inconsistent with their family's fundamental values.[14]

A large literature addresses other parental strategies for encouraging ethical behavior in children. As Chapter 1 noted, authoritative parenting styles, which combine authority with reasoning and fairness, can reinforce ethical responsibility.[15] Among the most common suggestions are to treat children equitably and respectfully, and to talk through the reasons for discipline or other interventions to prevent dishonesty.[16] Setting realistic goals, providing support for meeting them, and monitoring their achievement are also critical.[17] Equally important is to model behaviors that children can observe and imitate. Those behaviors include not just how parents treat their children but also how they relate to others, and how much priority they place on honesty and integrity. As psychologists note, parental examples shape beliefs about appropriate conduct and the "fact that these 'lessons' are often unintended makes them no less powerful."[18]

## Schools

Values education is another way to reinforce integrity. Gallup polls have found that 84 percent of parents of public school students want schools to teach moral values, and that most believe that schools aren't doing enough along these lines.[19] The federal government responded in the 1990s with a major push for such education. In his 1996 State of the Union address, President Clinton "challenge[d] all our schools to teach character education, to teach good values and good citizenship."[20] Since the early 1990s, almost half the states have passed legislation dealing with character education.[21] So, too, in the 1998 amendment to the Higher Education Act, Congress announced its commitment to "support and encourage character building initiatives in schools across America and urge colleges and universities to affirm that the development of character is one of the primary goals of higher education."[22] However, that rhetorical commitment has not been matched by financial resources. As one commentator wryly observed, a per pupil expenditure of under a dollar a year "may not buy a lot of practical virtue."[23] A study by the National Center for Education Statistics found that only a third of public schools provided character education as part of their curriculum.[24]

What doomed the effort was a lack of consensus on what and whose values should be taught. Skeptics on the right worried that "character education initiatives were a cloak for breeding political correctness, and [skeptics on] the [l]eft suspected the initiatives were hidden attempts at Christian indoctrination."[25] Many of the programs that emerged from this standoff were vague, superficial, and ineffective. The messages regarding cheating were no exception. For example, one common text, *Growing Up Caring,* shows a picture of a girl looking over the shoulder of another student while taking a test. The caption reads, "Cheating, in any form, is bad for your self esteem," as if that were its only harm.[26] One of the few studies available, sponsored by the U.S. Department of Education, found that of seven typical character education programs, none produced measurable improvement in students' behavior or perceptions of their schools' ethical climate.[27]

That is not to suggest that all efforts at values education are doomed. The Character Counts Coalition, a group of leaders from a range of backgrounds, has identified six pillars of character that can be the basis for educational initiatives: trustworthiness, responsibility, caring, respect for others, fairness, and citizenship.[28] Ninety percent of American adults agree on the need to stress core values such as fairness and respect for others.[29] Cheating is inconsistent with those values, and needs to be presented as such. Moreover, as law professor Anita Allen notes, "there is no way to avoid teaching values." Teachers, like other adults, "do it by example," whether intended or not; "The question before us is only whether we choose to do it deliberately or by happenstance."[30] For children to take morality seriously, "they must be in the presence of adults who take morality seriously."[31]

Promoting ethical behavior also requires strategies that enhance ethical reasoning capacities. Such strategies should encompass role modeling, guided reflection, and collective problem solving concerning actual dilemmas, such as those that arise in the school or community.[32] Best practices for moral education should include:

- Promoting a moral atmosphere in the school and/or classroom;
- Modelling of good character by teachers, administrators, and community members;
- Guiding student discussions of moral issues;
- Including student participation in school governance;
- Involving families in moral education initiatives;
- Providing a practical experience in addressing a moral issue.[33]

Every school should have its own vision of a character education program so that all stakeholders have ownership in its success.[34] Educators also need to be sure that the hidden curriculum is consistent with the formal one, and that their own conduct reflects the values that they hope to instill.[35]

To address cheating specifically, schools should strengthen sanctions and enforcement, as well as provide more support services for at-risk students, particularly college athletes. Assessment of such strategies is equally critical. As psychologists Christopher Peterson and Martin Seligman note, "millions of young people participate in school programs and after-school programs intended to cultivate good character. The almost total absence of program evaluation . . . is remarkable."[36] The same is true in higher education. Traditionally, colleges and universities have been reluctant to assess the extent of academic misconduct on their campuses and the effectiveness of strategies to address it. [37] All educational institutions should take a harder look at how well they are doing.

## Organizations

Other organizations should do the same. They need to be better informed about the dynamics of cheating and the adequacy of responses. More workplaces need ethical infrastructures that effectively integrate concerns about honesty into official policies and reward systems. Ethical leadership is critical, both in providing role models and institutionalizing practices such as ethics training programs, hotlines, and ombudspersons. To assess their cultures, workplaces should conduct ethical climate surveys and track the effectiveness of training programs and whistle-blower protections.

Regulatory bodies need similar enforcement and assessment initiatives, as well as additional resources that will make them possible. Increasing the audit rate for tax returns and the investigation of insurance claims would be highly cost effective. Doubling the funding for tax audits is projected to increase revenues by as much as 60 times the cost of the additional oversight.[38] Investigations of insurance fraud have saved or recovered an estimated average of $7 for every $1 spent.[39] Both governmental and private organizations also need further experimentation, innovation, and evaluation of efforts to reduce cheating.

The psychological research summarized in earlier chapters should inform these strategies. For example, we know that more moral reminders could be helpful in discouraging cheating. Individuals are more truthful when they are required to sign statements at the top rather than the bottom of documents attesting to the validity of information they are about to provide.[40] Ethical codes can also promote honesty in academic and workplace contexts, but only if they are widely accepted and enforced.

Sanctions should also be strengthened. Because so much cheating goes undetected, the penalties need to be significant when it is in fact discovered. White-collar offenses should receive more stringent punishments, and enforcement resources should be increased. Sports fans, coaches, and owners should take rule violations more seriously. Good sportsmanship should not just receive lip service at annual sports banquets; it should affect athletes' reputations and rewards. Shunning and shaming tax evaders and plagiarists should be the norm. We need less tolerance for first, and particularly repeat, offenders.

Media coverage and public relations campaigns can also help. Cheating scandals should become teachable moments, which remind Americans of the costs paid by honest individuals if dishonest peers gain a competitive advantage. Ethics columns can do the same. For example, the *New York Times Magazine* publishes a weekly column in which commentators weigh in on dilemmas sent by readers. One former commentator, Randy Cohen, invoked the social costs of cheating in response to a reader who lost a $15 MetroCard that had nine rides remaining. He asked if he could use his brother's card for unlimited use in order to take the rides he had already paid for. Cohen said no, and reasoned, "Part of what makes civility possible is a sense that one is part of a community of honest people. Your proposed act of petty deception would undermine that sense, much as the spectacle of turnstile jumpers discourages other riders from paying their fare." The act would also drag his brother into a "web of deceit . . . . While you're certainly entitled to the nine rides you paid for, you're not entitled to commit fraud to get them."[41] Yet Cohen also told a teenager who was too young to be admitted to R-rated movies that it was all right to lie about his age or to buy a ticket to another movie and then sneak in if his parents didn't object to his seeing the film. Cohen acknowledged that

> a case could be made that when you engage in a voluntary act like going to the movies, you ought to obey the rules. However, rules ought to be reasonable, hardly the case with this capricious and arbitrary rating system (No to sex but yes to violence, vulgarity, and Chevy Chase) . . . . To lie here is regrettable, but it is the less regrettable path. Your alternative is to truckle to an overreaching authority that imposes an unreasonable stricture simply to keep the wheels of commerce turning. Obedience to such rules isn't honesty; it is docility.[42]

What that reasoning ignores is the corrosive effect of telling adolescents that cheating is permissible when they disagree with a rule. Cheating here violates the test set forth earlier. There is an alternative to cheating; indulgent parents could accompany their son to the R-rated movie or rent it and let their son watch it without lying about his age.

However, as Cohen's latter example suggests, in some circumstances, it would make sense to adjust formal rules in light of social norms. Most Americans believe that current copyright laws are too broad, and increased penalties have done little to curb widespread defiance. The best way to reduce cheating is likely to require a system for paying copyright holders that is cheaper and more convenient for consumers. So, too, legal sanctions for adultery are simply too idiosyncratic and intrusive to serve a socially defensible function. Criminal prohibitions should be repealed, and infidelity should generally cease to be a factor in employment and divorce contexts. Although society clearly has an interest in discouraging extramarital affairs, current legal sanctions are an ineffective means to that end.

Finally, all of us must take more responsibility for fostering ethical behavior in contexts where pressures to cheat arise. That requires subjecting our own conduct to more demanding standards, as well as assuming a greater obligation to prevent and report cheating. For too many Americans, willful blindness is the most convenient response to such misconduct. Employees and educators who suspect fraud should assume responsibility for coming forward, and they need more support for doing so. We all need to build moral muscle by cultivating habits of integrity and avoiding the situational pressures that erode it.[43]

Over a century ago, Mark Twain quipped that "virtue has never been as respectable as money."[44] Proving him wrong should be a greater personal and professional priority. Sustaining a culture that actively discourages cheating is a collective obligation, and one in which we all have a substantial stake.

# NOTES

## *Chapter 1*

1. See the text accompanying notes 25–28 below.
2. David A. Graham, "The Many Scandals of Donald Trump: A Cheat Sheet," *Atlantic*, November 22, 2016; Emily Futter, " Trump's Art of the Deal—Dispute Your Bills," *Reuters*, November 13, 2015; Steve Reilly, "Hundreds Allege Donald Trump Doesn't Pay His Bills," *USA Today*, June 9, 2016 (reporting at least 60 lawsuits and hundreds of liens, judgments, and other government filings against Trump organizations for failure to pay bills).
3. Graham, "Many Scandals;" Michael Barbaro and Steve Eder, "Former Trump University Workers Call the School a 'Lie' and a 'Scheme' in Testimony," *New York Times*, May 31, 2016; Steve Eder, "Would Trump Have Won Trump University Cases? Evidence Says He Faced Hard Fight," *New York Times*, November 23, 2016.
4. *New York Times*, "CBS Poll" (May 19, 2016), https://www.nytimes.com/interactive/2016/05/19/us/politics/poll-presidential-race.html.
5. Stuart P. Green, *Lying, Cheating, and Stealing: A Moral Theory of White-Collar Crime* (New York: Oxford University Press, 2006), 54. *See also* Michael Lewis and Carolyn Saarni, eds., *Lying and Deception in Everyday Life* (New York: Guilford Press, 1993) (cheating is discussed on only four pages).
6. David Callahan, *The Cheating Culture: Why More Americans Are Doing Wrong to Get Ahead* (New York: Harcourt, 2004), 13.
7. Oxford English Dictionary Online (New York: Oxford University Press, 2015), http://www.oed.com/view/Entry/31071?rskey=HWRjNT&result=2.
8. Bernard Gert, *Morality: Its Nature and Justification* (New York: Oxford University Press, 2005), 192.
9. Immanuel Kant, *On a Supposed Right to Lie from Altruistic Motives, reprinted in* Sissela Bok, *Lying: Moral Choice in Public and Private Life* (New York: Vintage Books, 1978), 285–290.
10. William Damon and Anne Colby, *The Power of Ideals: The Real Story of Moral Choice* (New York: Oxford University Press, 2015), 98.
11. Robert C. Solomon, "What a Tangled Web: Deception and Self-Deception in Philosophy," in Lewis and Saarni, eds., *Lying and Deception in Everyday Life*, 34.
12. Emma E. Levine and Maurice E. Schweitzer, "Prosocial Lies: When Deception Breeds Trust," *Organizational Behavior and Human Decision Processes* 126 (2015):88, 102.
13. Emma E. Levine and Maurice E. Schweitzer, "Are Liars Ethical? On the Tension between Benevolence and Honesty," *Journal of Experimental Social Psychology* 53 (2014):107; Levine and Schweitzer, "Prosocial Lies," 89. *See also* Thomas I. Carson, *Lying and Deception: Theory and Practice* (New York: Oxford University Press, 2010).

14. Plato, *Republic,* Volume I, Books 1–5, edited and translated by Christopher Emlyn-Jones and William Preddy (Cambridge, MA: Harvard University Press, 2013), 485.
15. Bella M. DePaulo, Deborah A Kashy, Susan E. Kirkendol, Melissa M. Wyer, and Jennifer M. Epstein, "Lying in Everyday Life," *Journal of Personality and Social Psychology* 70 (1996): 979, 991.
16. DePaulo et al., "Lying in Everyday Life," 979, 986, 991.
17. Bok, *Lying,* 31.
18. John Rawls, *A Theory of Justice* (Cambridge, MA: Harvard University Press, 1971), 133.
19. Ife Floyd and Liz Schott, *TANF Cash Benefits Have Fallen by More than 20 Percent in Most States and Continue to Erode* (Washington, DC: Center on Budget and Policy Priorities, 2015), 1.
20. Gert, *Morality,* 209.
21. Sissela Bok makes an analogous point about lying. Bok, *Lying.*
22. Francesco Gino, *Sidetracked: Why Our Decisions Get Derailed and How We Can Stick to the Plan* (Cambridge, MA: Harvard Business Press, 2013), 215.
23. Bok, *Lying,* 26–27.
24. Walter James Bate, ed., Samuel Johnson, *Selected Essays from the Rambler, Adventurer, and Idler* (New Haven: Yale University Press, 1968).
25. Tax Gap for Tax Year 2006, Internal Revenue Service (2006), http://www.irs.gov/pub/newsroom/overview_tax_gap_2006.pdf. For higher estimates, see Edgar L. Feige and Richard Cebula, *America's Underground Economy: Measuring the Size, Growth and Determinants of Income Tax Evasion in the U.S.* (University of Wisconsin–Madison, 2011).
26. United States Department of Justice, Prosecuting Intellectual Property Crimes (2006); Progress Report of the Department of Justice's Task Force on Intellectual Property (June 2006), https://www.justice.gov/archive/opa/docs/ipreport61906.pdf.
27. *See* Chapter 8.
28. Yoav Vardi and Ely Weitz, *Misbehavior in Organizations: A Dynamic Approach* (New York: Routledge, 2d ed. 2016), 5, 14. *See also* Association of Certified Fraud Examiners, *ACFE Report to the Nation on Occupational Fraud and Abuse* (2014).
29. Felicia R. Lee, "Are More People Cheating?: Despite Ample Accounts of Dishonesty, a Moral Decline Is Hard to Calculate," *New York Times,* October 4, 2003, B7. *See also* Anita L. Allen, *The New Ethics: A Guided Tour of the Twenty-First Century Moral Landscape* (New York: Miramax Books, 2004), xxiii.
30. For the 21 states where adultery is illegal, see Deborah L. Rhode, *Adultery: Infidelity and the Law* (Cambridge, MA: Harvard University Press, 2016), 60, 62.
31. Joel Slemrod and Jon Bakija, *Taxing Ourselves: A Citizen's Guide to the Great Debate over Tax Reform* (Cambridge, MA: MIT Press, 2006), 178.
32. John S. Carroll, "How Taxpayers Think about Their Taxes: Frames and Values," in Joel Slemrod, ed., *Why People Pay Taxes: Tax Compliance and Enforcement* (Ann Arbor: University of Michigan Press, 1992), 55.
33. Jenna Wortham, "The Unrepentant Bootlegger," *New York Times,* September 28, 2014, B1.
34. Ethics Research Center, *National Business Ethics Survey* (Arlington, VA: Ethics Research Center, 2013); David Shulman, *From Hire to Liar: The Role of Deception in the Workplace* (Ithaca, NY: ILR, 2007), 163.
35. Muel Kaptein, "The Ethics of Organizations: A Longitudinal Study of the U.S. Working Population," *Journal of Business Ethics* 92 (2010):601, 609.
36. Bernard E. Whitley, "Factors Associated with Cheating among College Students: A Review," *Research in Higher Education* 39 (1998):235, 238.
37. Donald L. McCabe, Kenneth D. Butterfield, and Linda K. Treviño, *Cheating in College: Why Students Do It and What Educators Can Do about It* (Baltimore: John Hopkins University Press, 2012), 24–25; Josephson Institute, *Report Card on the Ethics of American Youth* (2008).
38. Brian C. Gunia, Long Wang, Li Huang Insead, Jiunwen Wang, and J. Keith Murnighan, "Contemplation and Conversation: Subtle Influences on Moral Decision Making," *Academy of Management Journal* 55 (2012):13, 27.

39. Peggy Drexler, "The New Face of Infidelity," *Wall Street Journal*, October 19, 2012; Edward O. Laumann, John H. Gagnon, Robert T. Michael, and Stuart Michaels, *The Social Organization of Sexuality: Sexual Practices in the United States* (Chicago: University of Chicago Press, 1994), 216.
40. Jon M. Doris, *Lack of Character: Personality and Moral Behavior* (Cambridge: Cambridge University Press, 2002), 93; Philip E. Tetllock, "Accountability: A Social Check on the Fundamental Attribution Error," *Social Psychology Quarterly* 48 (1985); Lee Ross, "The Intuitive Psychologist and His Shortcomings: Distortions in the Attribution Process," in Leonard Berkowitz, ed., *Advances in Experimental Social Psychology* (Orlando: Academic Press, 1967), 10. *See also* William Fleeson and Erik Noftle, "The End of the Person-Situation Debate: An Emerging Synthesis in the Answer to the Consistency Question," *Social and Personality Psychology Compass* 2 (2008):1667, 1669.
41. The phrase comes from David L. Rosenhan, "Moral Character," *Stanford Law Review* 27 (1975):925–926. For an analysis of the importance of context, see Lisa L. Shu, Francesca Gino, and Max H. Bazerman, "Ethical Discrepancy: Changing Our Attitudes to Resolve Moral Dissonance," in David De Cremer and Ann E. Tenbrunsel, eds., *Behavioral Business Ethics: Shaping an Emerging Field* (New York: Routledge, 2002), 223–225.
42. Thomas Gabor, *Everybody Does It!: Crime by the Public* (Toronto: University of Toronto Press, 1994), 58.
43. Roger V. Burton, "Generality of Honesty Reconsidered," *Psychological Review* 70 (1963):481; Walter Mischel and Yuichi Shoda, "A Cognitive-Affective System Theory of Personality: Reconceptualizing Situations, Dispositions, Dynamics, and Invariance in Personality Structure," *Psychological Review* 102 (1995):246.
44. Gabor, *Everybody Does It!*, 58.
45. Callahan, *Cheating Culture*, 138.
46. Donald Palmer, *Normal Organizational Wrongdoing: A Critical Analysis of Theories of Misconduct in and by Organizations* (New York: Oxford University Press, 2012), 275.
47. Lisa G. Lerman, "The Slippery Slope from Ambition to Greed to Dishonesty: Lawyers Money, and Professional Integrity," *Hofstra Law Review* 30 (2002):883, 893.
48. David DeSteno and Piercarlo Valdesolo, *Out of Character: Surprising Truths about the Liar, Cheat, Sinner (and Saint) Lurking in All of Us* (New York: Three Rivers Press, 2011), 57.
49. For the stability of personality traits, see Fleeson and Noftle, "End of the Person-Situation Debate," 1670.
50. DeSteno and Valdesolo, *Out of Character*, 12.
51. James R. Rest, ed., *Moral Development: Advances in Research and Theory* (New York: Praeger, 1994), 26–39. For the influence of Rest's model on behavioral ethics, see Jennifer L. Kish-Gephart, David A. Harrison, and Linda K. Treviño, "Bad Apples, Bad Cases, and Bad Barrels: Meta-analytic Evidence about Sources of Unethical Decisions at Work," *Journal of Applied Psychology* 95 (2010):1.
52. Lawrence Kohlberg, "Stage and Sequence: The Cognitive Developmental Approach to Socialization," in David A. Goslin, ed., *Handbook of Socialization Theory and Research* (Chicago: Rand McNally, 1969), 347; Lawrence Kohlberg, *The Psychology of Moral Development: The Nature and Validity of Moral Stages* (New York: Harper and Row, 1984); Lawrence Kohlberg, "Moral Stages and Moralization: The Cognitive Developmental Approach," in Lawrence Kohlberg, ed., *The Psychology of Moral Development: The Nature and Validity of Moral Stages*, Volume 2 (San Francisco: Harper and Row, 1984):170.
53. For discussion of Kohlberg's framework, see Linda Klebe Treviño, Gary R. Weaver, and Scott J. Reynolds, "Behavioral Ethics in Organizations: A Review," *Journal of Management* 32 (2006):951, 955; James R. Rest, Darcia Narvez, Muriel H. Bebeau, and Stephen J. Thoma, *Postconventional Moral Thinking: A Neo-Kohlbergian Approach* (Mahwah, NJ: Lawrence Erlbaum, 1999).
54. Kish-Gebhart et al., "Bad Apples, Bad Cases and Bad Barrels," 1, 3; Treviño et al., "Behavioral Ethics in Organizations," 951, 960.

55. Augusto Blasi, "Bridging Moral Cognition and Moral Action: A Critical Review of the Literature," *Psychological Bulletin* 88 (1980):1, 37–41; Kish-Gephart et al., "Bad Apples, Bad Cases and Bad Barrels," 18; Cecilia Moore, James R. Detert, Linda Klebe Treviño, Vicki L. Baker, and David M. Mayer, "Why Employees Do Bad Things: Moral Disengagement and Unethical Organizational Behavior," *Personnel Psychology* 65 (2012):1, 9.
56. Ruodan Shao, Karl Aquino, and Dan Freeman, "Beyond Moral Reasoning: A Review of Moral Identity Research and Its Implications for Business Ethics," *Business Ethics Quarterly* 18 (2008):513, 516; Darcia Narvaez and Daniel K. Lapsley, "The Psychological Foundations of Everyday Morality and Moral Expertise," in Daniel K. Lapsley and F. Clark Power, eds., *Character Psychology and Character Education* (Notre Dame, IN: University of Notre Dame Press), 140, 142; David Eagelman, *Incognito: The Secret Lives of the Brain* (New York: Pantheon, 2011), 4; Jonathan Haidt, "The Emotional Dog and Its Rational Tail: A Social Intuitionist Approach to Moral Judgment," 108 *Psychology Review* 814, 822–888 (2001). *See also* Daniel K. Lapsley and Darcia Narvaez, "A Social Cognitive Approach to the Moral Personality," in Daniel K. Lapsley and Darcia Naraez, eds., *Moral Development, Self and Identity* (Mahwah, NJ: Lawrence Erlbaum, 2004),189.
57. Gary R. Weaver and Michael E. Brown, "Moral Foundations at Work: New Factors to Consider in Understanding the Nature and Role of Ethics in Organizations," in De Cremer and Tenbrunsel, *Behavioral Business Ethics*, 144; Haidt, "Emotional Dog;" Scott J. Reynolds, "A Neurocognitive Model of the Ethical Decision-Making Process: Implications for Study and Practice," *Journal of Applied Psychology* 91 (2006):736.
58. Daniel Kahneman, *Thinking Fast and Slow* (New York: Farrar, Straus, and Giroux, 2011); Max H. Bazerman and Francesca Gino, "Behavioral Ethics: Toward a Deeper Understanding of Moral Judgment and Dishonesty," *Annual Review of Law and Social Science* 8 (2012):85, 99; Daniel Kahneman and Shane Frederick, "Representativeness Revisited: Attribute Substitution in Intuitive Judgment," in Thomas Gilovich, Dale Griffin, and Daniel Kahneman, eds., *Heuristics and Biases: The Psychology of Intuitive Judgment* (New York: Cambridge University Press, 2002), 49.
59. Max H. Bazerman and Ann E. Tenbrunsel, *Blind Spots: Why We Fail to Do What's Right and What to Do about It* (Princeton: NJ: Princeton University Press, 2011), 93, 154; Don A. Moore and George F. Loewenstein, "Self-Interest, Automaticity, and the Psychology of Conflict of Interest," *Social Justice Research* 17 (2004): 189.
60. Kahneman, *Thinking Fast and Slow*; Bazerman and Gino, "Behavioral Ethics," 99.
61. Max Bazerman, Ann E. Tenbrunsel, and Kimberly Wade-Benzoni, "Negotiating with Yourself and Losing: Making Decisions with Competing Internal Preferences," *Academy of Management Review* 23 (1998):235; Ann Tenbrunsel, Kristina A. Diekmann, Kimberly A. Wade-Benzoni, and Max H. Bazerman, "The Ethical Mirage: A Temporal Explanation as to Why We Are Not as Ethical as We Think We Are," *Research in Organizational Behavior* 30 (2010):153, 156–157. For an earlier account, see E. Tory Higgins, "Self-Discrepancy: A Theory Relating Self and Affect," *Psychological Review* 94 (1987):319, 321.
62. Bazerman et al., "Negotiating with Yourself and Losing;" Tenbrunsel, Diekmann, Wade-Benzoni and Bazerman, "Ethical Mirage," 156–157.
63. DeSteno and Valdesolo, *Out of Character*, 33–35. *See also* Bazerman and Tenbrunsel, *Blind Spots*, 36. For examples, see Chen-Bo Zhong, "The Ethical Dangers of Deliberative Decision Making," *Administrative Science Quarterly* 56 (2011):1.
64. Dolly Chugh, Mahzarin R. Banajai, and Max Bazerman, "Bounded Ethicality as a Psychological Barrier to Recognizing Conflicts of Interest," in Don A. Moore, Daylian M. Caine, George Lowenstein, and Max Bazerman, eds., *Conflicts of Interest: Problems and Solutions from Law, Medicine and Organizational Settings* (Cambridge: Cambridge University Press, 2005), 74.
65. Francesca Gino, Maurice E. Schweitzer, Nicole L. Mead, and Dan Ariely, "Unable to Resist Temptation: How Self-Control Depletion Promotes Unethical Behavior," *Organizational Behavior and Human Decision Processes* 115 (2011):191, 199; Mark Muraven and Roy F.

Baumeister, "Self-Regulation and Depletion of Limited Resources," *Psychological Bulletin* 126 (2000); Martin S. Hagger, Chantelle Wood, Chris Stiff, and Nikos L. D. Chatzisarantis, "Ego Depletion and the Strength Model of Self-Control: A Meta-analysis," *Psychological Bulletin* 136 (2010):495; Nicole L. Mead, Roy F. Baumeister, Francesca Gino, Maurice E. Schweitzer, and Dan Ariely, "Too Tired to Tell the Truth: Self-Control Resource Depletion and Dishonesty," *Journal of Experimental Social Psychology* 45 (2009):594; William D.S. Killgore, Desiree B. Killgore, Lisa M. Day, Christopher Li, Gary H. Kamimori, and Thomas J. Balkin, "The Effects of 53 Hours of Sleep Deprivation on Moral Judgment," *Sleep* 30 (2007):345.

66. Bazerman and Tenbrunsel, *Blind Spots*; Ann E. Tenbrunsel, "Misrepresentation and Expectations of Misrepresentation in an Ethical Dilemma: The Role of Incentives and Temptation," *Academy of Management Journal* 41 (198):330.
67. Francesca Gino, *Sidetracked: Why Our Decisions Get Derailed and How We Can Stick to the Plan* (Cambridge, MA: Harvard Business Press, 2013), 121.
68. The study is discussed in Gino, *Sidetracked*, 198.
69. Bazerman and Tenbrunsel, *Blind Spots*, 84.
70. Ann E. Tenbrunsel and David M. Messick, "Ethical Fading: The Role of Self-Deception in Unethical Behavior," *Social Justice Research* 17 (2004):223. *See also* Tenbrunsel, Diekmann, Wade-Benzoni, and Bazerman, "Ethical Mirage," 159–162.
71. Scott J. Reynolds, "Moral Attentiveness: Who Pays Attention to the Moral Aspects of Life," *Journal of Applied Psychology* 93 (2008):1027, 1028.
72. See Chapter 6 below. For discussion of how categorization of behaviors affects ethical conduct, see Nina Mazar and Dan Ariely, "The Dishonesty of Honest People: A Theory of Self-Concept Maintenance," *Journal of Marketing Research* 45 (2008):633, 634.
73. Stephen M. Rosoff, Henry N. Pontell, and Robert Tillman, *Profit without Honor: White Collar Crime and the Looting of America* (Upper Saddle River, NJ.: Prentice Hall, 1998), 140.
74. Ben J. Heineman Jr., *Inside the Counsel Revolution: Resolving the Partner-Guardian Tension* (Chicago: American Bar Association, 2016), 99.
75. Donald Cressey, *Other People's Money* (Belmont, CA: Wadsworth, 1972).
76. Eugene Soltes, *Why They Do It: Inside the Mind of the White-Collar Criminal* (New York: Public Affairs, 2016), 257.
77. Tenbrunsel and Messick, "Ethical Fading," 228.
78. Palmer, *Normal Organizational Wrongdoing*, 104–105.
79. Donald N.M. Horning, "Blue-Collar Theft: Conceptions of Property, Attitudes toward Pilfering, and Work Group Norms in a Modern Industrial Plant," in Erwin O. Smigel and H. Laurence Ross, eds., *Crimes against Bureaucracy* (New York: Van Nostrand Reinhold, 1970), 61.
80. Horning, "Blue-Collar Theft," 62.
81. Blake E. Ashforth and Vikas Anand, "The Normalization of Corruption in Organizations," *Research in Organizational Behavior* 25 (2003):1, 14.
82. Francesca Gino and Max H. Bazerman, "When Misconduct Goes Unnoticed: The Acceptability of Gradual Erosion in Others' Unethical Behavior," *Journal of Experimental Social Psychology* 45 (2009):708.
83. For internal reward mechanisms, see Nina Mazar and Dan Ariely, "Dishonesty in Everyday Life and Its Policy Implications," *Journal of Public Policy and Marketing* 25 (2006):1, 8. For the incremental slide into greater misconduct, see David T. Welsh, Lisa D. Ordonez, Deirdre G. Snyder, and Michael S. Christian, "The Slippery Slope: How Small Ethical Transgressions Pave the Way for Larger Future Transgressions," *Journal of Applied Psychology* 100 (2015):114: Cecilia Moore and Francesca Gino, "Ethically Adrift: How Others Pull Our Moral Compass from True North, and How We Can Fix It," *Research in Organizational Behavior* 33 (2013):64.
84. Patrick J. Schiltz, "On Being a Happy, Healthy, and Ethical Member of an Unhappy, Unhealthy, and Unethical Profession," *Vanderbilt Law Review* 52 (1999):871, 917–918.

85. For other examples, see Blake E. Ashforth and Vikas Anand, "The Normalization of Corruption in Organizations," *Research in Organizational Behavior* 25 (2003):1, 30.
86. Palmer, *Normal Organizational Wrongdoing*, 122–123.
87. Soltes, *Why They Do It*, 257, 265.
88. Francesca Gino and Max Bazerman, "When Misconduct Goes Unnoticed: The Acceptability of Gradual Erosion in Others' Unethical Behavior," 708.
89. Dolly Chugh, Mahzarin R. Banaji, and Max H. Bazerman, "Bounded Ethicality as a Psychological Barrier to Recognizing Conflicts of Interest," in Don A. Moore, Daylian M. Cain, George Loewenstein, and Max H. Bazerman, eds., *Conflicts of Interest: Problems and Solutions from Law, Medicine, and Organizational Settings* (New York: Cambridge University Press, 2005).
90. Kenneth D. Butterfield et al., "Moral Awareness in Business Organizations: Influences of Issue-Related and Social Context Factors," *Human Relations* 53 (2000):981–982; Thomas M. Jones, "Ethical Decision Making by Individuals in Organizations: An Issue-Contingent Model," *Academy of Management Review* 16 (1991):366, 368, 379; Linda Klebe Treviño and Gary R. Weaver, *Managing Ethics in Business Organizations: Social Scientific Perspectives* (Stanford, CA: Stanford University Press, 2003), 171.
91. Lynn Sharp Paine, *Value Shift: Why Companies Must Merge Social and Financial Imperatives to Achieve Superior Performance* (New York: McGraw Hill, 2002), 45–46; Kim S. Cameron, David Bright, and Arran Caza, "Organizational Virtuousness and Performance," *American Behavioral Scientist* 47 (2004):766, 773; Brian Mullin, Carolyn Copper, and James E. Driskell, "Jaywalking as Function of Model Behavior," *Personality and Social Psychology Bulletin* 16 (1990):320.
92. Scott J. Reynolds and Tara L. Ceranic, "The Effects of Moral Judgment and Moral Identity on Moral Behavior: An Empirical Examination of the Moral Individual," *Journal of Applied Psychology* 92 (2007):1610, 1611; Kenneth D. Butterfield et al., "Moral Awareness in Business Organizations: Influences of Issue-Related and Social Contextual Factors," *Human Relations* 53 (2000): 981, 1001.
93. Gabor, *Everybody Does It!*, 183.
94. Francesca Gino, Shahar Ayal, and Dan Ariely, "Contagion and Differentiation in Unethical Behavior: The Effect of One Bad Apple on the Barrel," *Psychological Science* 20 (2009):393.
95. Soltes, *Why They Do It*, 287, 303.
96. Soltes, *Why They Do It*, 302–303.
97. John Cassidy, "The Investigation: How Eliot Spitzer Humbled Wall Street," *New Yorker*, April 7, 2003, 54.
98. Callahan, *Cheating Culture*, 4.
99. The classic account of cognitive dissonance appears in Leon Festinger, *A Theory of Cognitive Dissonance* (Stanford, CA: Stanford University Press, 1957), 128–134. For more recent accounts, see Eddie Harmon-Jones and Judson Mills, eds., *Cognitive Dissonance: Progress on a Pivotal Theory in Social Psychology* (Washington, DC: American Psychological Association, 1999). For an application in contexts of ethical behavior such as cheating, see Shahar Ayal and Francesca Gino, "Honest Rationales for Dishonest Behavior," in Mario Mikulincer and Phillip R. Shaver, *The Social Psychology of Morality: Exploring the Causes of Good and Evil* (Washington, DC: American Psychological Association, 2012):149–150; Elizabeth E. Umphress and John B. Bingham, "When Employees Do Bad Things for Good Reasons: Examining Unethical Pro-organizational Behaviors," *Organization Science* 22 (2011): 621, 632.
100. Lisa L. Shu, Francesca Gino, and Max H. Bazerman, "Dishonest Deed, Clear Conscience: When Cheating Leads to Moral Disengagement and Motivated Forgetting," *Personality and Social Psychology Bulletin* 37 (2011):330; Karl Aquino and Americus Reed II, "The Self-Importance of Moral Identity," *Journal of Personality and Social Psychology* 83 (2002):1443; Mazar et al., "Dishonesty of Honest People," 633, 634.

101. Dan Ariely, *The (Honest) Truth about Dishonesty: How We Lie to Everyone—Especially Ourselves* (New York: HarperCollins, 2012), 27.
102. Mazar et al., "Dishonesty of Honest People," 633, 642.
103. C. Daniel Batson et al., "In a Very Different Voice: Unmasking Moral Hypocrisy," *Journal of Personality and Social Psychology* 72 (1997):1335; C. Daniel Batson, Elizabeth R. Thompson, Greg Sueferling, Heather Whitney, and Jon A. Strongman, "Moral Hypocrisy: Appearing Moral to Oneself Without Being So," *Journal of Personality and Social Psychology* 77 (1999):523; Daniel Batson, "What's Wrong with Morality?", *Emotion Review* 3 (2011):230, 231; Moore and Gino, "Ethically Adrift," 53, 64.
104. Dan Ariely, *Predictably Irrational: The Hidden Forces That Shape Our Decisions* (New York: Harper Perennial, 2010), 295–296, 299–300; Mazar et al., "Dishonesty of Honest People," 637–638.
105. Ariely, *Predictably Irrational*, 295–296.
106. Ariely, *Predictably Irrational*, 305.
107. Soltes, *Why They Do It*, 273.
108. Soltes, *Why They Do It*, 273.
109. Ann E. Tenbrunsel, Kristina A. Diekmann, Kimberly A. Wade-Benzoni, and Max H. Bazerman, "Ethical Mirage: A Temporal Explanation as to Why We Are Not as Ethical as We Think We Are," *Research in Organizational Behavior* 30 (2010):153, 154.
110. Michael Ross, Cathy McFarland, Michael Conway, and Mark P. Zanna, "Reciprocal Relation between Attitudes and Behavior Recall: Committing People to Newly Formed Attitudes," *Journal of Personality and Social Psychology* 45 (1983):257. *See also* Tenbrunsel et al., "Ethical Mirage," 163.
111. Shu et al., "Dishonest Deed," 330, 332; Moore and Gino, "Ethically Adrift," 55.
112. Lisa L. Shu and Francesca Gino, "Sweeping Dishonesty under the Rug: How Unethical Actions Lead to Moral Rules," *Journal of Personality and Social Science* 102 (2012):1164, discussed in Lisa L. Shu et al., "Ethical Discrepancy," 231.
113. For unfairness, see Benedict Carey, "The Psychology of Cheating," *New York Times*, April 16, 2011. For envy, see Francesca Gino and Lamar Pierce, "The Abundance Effect: Unethical Behavior in the Presence of Wealth," *Organizational Behavior and Human Decision Processes* 109 (2009):142. For inequity, see Francesca Gino and Lamar Pierce, "Dishonesty in the Name of Equity," *Psychological Science* 20 (2009):1153; Francesca Gino and Lamar Pierce, "Lying to Level the Playing Field: Why People May Dishonestly Help or Hurt Others to Create Equity," *Journal of Business Ethics* 95 (2010):89.
114. Elizabeth Landau, "Morality: It's Not Just for Humans," http://www.cnn.com/2013/01/19/health/chimpanzee-fairness-morality; TED Talk, https://www.ted.com/talks/frans_de_waal_do_animals_have_morals?language=en#t-5752, (November 2011). Footage of Frans de Waal's experiment is available at https://www.youtube.com/watch?v=meiU6TxysCg.
115. Gabor, *Everybody Does It!*, 184; Treviño and Weaver, *Managing Ethics in Business Organizations*, 233; Gwen E. Jones and Michael J. Kavanagh, "An Experimental Examination of the Effects of Individual and Situational Factors on Unethical Behavioral Intentions in the Workplace," *Journal of Business Ethics* 15 (196):511, 520.
116. Gabor, *Everybody Does It!*, 84.
117. Ariely, *(Honest) Truth about Dishonesty*, 177–178.
118. Gresham M. Sykes and David Matza, "Techniques of Neutralization: A Theory of Delinquency," *American Sociological Review* 22 (1957):667. For more recent prominent accounts, see Albert Bandura, "Moral Disengagement in the Perpetuation of Inhumanities," *Personal and Social Psychological Review* 3 (1999):193; Richard C. Hollinger, "Neutralizing in the Workplace: An Empirical Analysis of Property Theft and Production Deviance," *Deviant Behavior: An Interdisciplinary Journal* 12 (1991):169; and Moore et al., "Why Employees Do Bad Things," *Personal Psychology* 1; William A. Stadler and Michael L. Benson, "Revisiting the Guilty Mind: The Neutralization of White-Collar Crime," *Criminal Justice Review* 37 (2012):1.

119. Christian Smith with Kari Christoffersen, Hillary Davidson and Patricia Snell Herzog, *Lost in Transition* (New York: Oxford University Press, 2011), 41, 48.
120. Stadler and Benson, "Revisiting the Guilty Mind," 12.
121. Soltes, *Why They Do It*, 269.
122. Steve Fishman, "Bernie Madoff: Free at Last," *New York Magazine*, June 6, 2010.
123. A classic article is W.W. Minor, "Techniques of Neutralization: A Reconceptualization and Empirical Examination," *Journal of Research in Crime and Delinquency* 18 (1981):295, 298.
124. Smith with Christoffersen, Davidson and Herzog, *Lost in Transition*, 48.
125. Anna C. Merrit, Daniel A. Effron, and Benoit Monin, "Moral Self-Licensing: When Being Good Frees Us to Be Bad," *Social and Personality Psychology Compass* 4 (2010):344; Moore and Gino, "Ethically Adrift," 55. *See also* Hollinger, "Neutralizing in the Workplace," *Deviant Behavior*, 169.
126. Vivian K.G. Lim, "The IT Way of Loafing on the Job: Cyberloafing, Neutralizing, and Organizational Justice," *Journal of Organizational Behavior* 23 (2002):675.
127. Patrick McGeehan, "Listing Perks, But Not as an Endangered Species," *New York Times*, April 3, 2005; Andrew Ross Sorkin, "Tyco's Ex-chief Is Humbled but Unbowed," *New York Times*, January 16, 2005, A21 (quoting Dennis Kozlowski).
128. Palmer, *Normal Organizational Wrongdoing*, 119; Moore et al., "Why Employees Do Bad Things," 15, 146.
129. Charles R. Snyder, "Excuses, Excuses: They Sometimes Actually Work—To Relieve the Burden of Blame," *Psychology Today* 18 (September 1984):50–55.
130. Soltes, *Why They Do It*, 321 (quoting David Solomon).
131. *See* sources cited in Deborah L. Rhode, "Where Is the Leadership in Moral Leadership?," in Deborah L. Rhode, ed., *Moral Leadership: The Theory and Practice of Power, Judgment and Policy* (San Francisco: Jossey-Bass, 2006), 23.
132. Susan D. Blum, *My Word!: Plagiarism and College Culture* (New York: Cornell University Press, 2010), 162.
133. Deborah L. Rhode, David Luban, and Scott L. Cummings, *Legal Ethics* (New York: Foundation Press, 7th ed., 2016), 811.
134. Rhode et al., *Legal Ethics*, 812; Helen Coster, "The Inflation Temptation," *American Lawyer*, October 2004, 129.
135. William G. Ross, "The Ethics of Hourly Billing by Attorneys," *Rutgers Law Review* 44 (1991):1, 92.
136. Claudia MacLachlan and Harvey Berkman, "Little Rock's Bar Shaken to Its Core: Local Lawyers Are Reeling as Washington Woes Come Home to Roost," *National Law Journal*, April 11, 1994, 18.
137. Donald L. Bartlett and James B. Steele, *The Great American Tax Dodge: How Spiraling Fraud and Avoidance Are Killing Fairness, Destroying the Income Tax, and Costing You* (Oakland: University of California Press, 2002), 219.
138. Deborah L. Rhode, *In the Interests of Justice* (New York: Oxford University Press, 2000), 171–172. *See* Lisa G. Lerman, "Blue-Chip Bilking: Regulation of Billing and Expense Fraud by Lawyers," *Georgetown Journal of Legal Ethics* 12 (1999):205; Lerman, "The Slippery Slope," 897.
139. Rest, *Moral Development*, 32–33.
140. Batson, "What's Wrong with Morality?," 231.
141. Nicole E. Ruedy, Celia Moore, Francesca Gino, and Maurice E. Schweitzer, "The Cheater's High: The Unexpected Affective Benefits of Unethical Behaviors," *Journal of Personality and Social Psychology* 105 (2013):531–532. *See also* Robert Weiss, "The Cheater's High: New Research May Explain Why So Many Couples Experience Infidelity," *Psychology Today*, October 2, 2014, https://www.psychologytoday.com/blog/love-and-sex-in-the-digital-age/201410/the-cheaters-high.
142. Gabor, *Everybody Does It!*, 241.
143. Jones, "Ethical Decision Making by Individuals in Organizations," 366; Kish-Gephart et al., "Bad Apples, Bad Cases, and Bad Barrels," 1, 5, 20; Treviño et al., "Behavioral Ethics

in Organizations," 953–954, 956; J. Weber, "Influences upon Managerial Moral Decision Making: Nature of the Harm and Magnitude of Consequences," *Human Relations* 49 (1996):1.

144. Gabor, *Everybody Does It!*, 229; Gwynn Nettler, *Lying, Cheating and Stealing* (Cincinnati, OH: Anderson, 1982).
145. Maurice E. Schweitzer, Lisa Ordoñez, and Bambi Douma, "Goal Setting as a Motivator of Unethical Behavior," *Academy of Management Journal* 47 (2004):422, 430.
146. Paine, *Value Shift*, 168–169; Julia Flynn, Christina Del Valle, and Russell Mitchell, "Did Sears Take Other Customers for a Ride?," *Business Week*, August 3, 1992; Rhode, "Where Is the Leadership in Moral Leadership?," 31.
147. Treviño and Weaver, *Managing Ethics in Business Organizations*, 181; Treviño et al., "Behavioral Ethics in Organizations: A Review," *Journal of Management* 32 (2006): 951, 965.
148. Nancy Eisenberg, "Emotion, Regulation, and Moral Development," *Annual Review of Psychology* 51 (2000):665; Treviño et al., "Behavioral Ethics in Organizations," 965.
149. Kevin Ryan, *Building Character in Schools* (San Francisco: Jossey-Bass, 1999); Wolfgang Althof and Marvin W. Berkowitz, "Moral Education and Character Education: Their Relationship and Roles in Citizenship Education," *Journal of Moral Education* 35 (2006):495; David N. Aspin and Judith D. Chapman, *Values Education and Lifelong Learning: Principles, Policies, Programs* (Dordrecht, Netherlands: Springer, 2007); William J. Bennett and Edwin J. Delattre, "Moral Education in the Schools," *Public Interest* 50 (1978):81.
150. Diana Baumrind, "Early Socialization and Adolescent Competence," in Sigmund E. Dragastin and Glen H. Elder, eds., *Adolescence in the Life Cycle* (New York: Wiley, 1975); Diane Baumrind, "Parenting Styles and Adolescent Development," in Richard M. Lerner, Ann C. Peterson, and Jeanne Brooks-Gunn, eds., *The Encyclopedia of Adolescence* (New York: Garland, 1989). *See also* Lawrence Steinberg, Nina S. Mounts, Susie D. Lamborn, and Sanford M. Dornbusch, "Authoritative Parenting and Adolescent Adjustment across Varied Ecological Niches," *Journal of Research on Adolescence* 1 (1991):19–36; Eleanor E. Maccoby and John A. Martin, "Socialization in the Context of the Family: Parent-Child Interaction," in Paul Mussen, ed., *Handbook of Child Psychology*, Volume 4 (New York Wiley, 4th ed. 1983), 1.
151. C.F. Hemphill, "Cutting Pilferage and Petty Cash Losses," *Administrative Management* 30 (February 1969):40.
152. Thomas Likona, "Character Education: Seven Crucial Issues," *Action in Teacher Education* 20 (1998):77.
153. Marilyn Watson, "Developmental Discipline and Moral Education," in Larry Nucci, Darcia Narvaez, and Tobias Krettenauer, eds., *Handbook of Moral and Character Education* (New York: Routledge, 2014):159, 170.
154. Elizabeth Campbell, "Teaching Ethically as a Moral Condition of Professionalism," in Nucci et al., *Handbook of Moral and Character Education*, 107; Darcia Narvaez and Tonia Black, "Developing Ethical Expertise and Moral Personalities," in Nucci et al., *Handbook of Moral and Character Education*, 150.
155. Tenbrunsel et al., "Ethical Mirage."
156. Bazerman and Tenbrunsel, *Blind Spots*, 36; Robert B. Cialdini, *Influence: Science and Practice* (Boston: Allyn and Bacon, 2001).
157. Tenbrunsel and Messick, "Ethical Fading," 234; Ann E. Tenbrunsel, Kristin Smith-Crowe, and Elizabeth E. Umphress, "Building Houses on Rocks: The Role of the Ethical Infrastructure in Organizations," *Social Justice Research* 16 (2003):285.
158. For role modeling and reward structures, see Kish-Gephart et al., "Bad Apples, Bad Cases, and Bad Barrels," 21. For open and honest discourse, *see* Arthur P. Brief, Robert T. Buttram, and Janet M. Dukerich, "Collective Corruption in the Corporate World: Toward a Process Model," in Marlene E. Turner, ed., *Groups at Work: Theory and Research* (Mahwah, NJ: Lawrence Erlbaum, 2001): 471, 493; Brian C. Gunia, Long Wang, Li Huang Insead, Jiunwen Wang, and J. Keith Murnighan, "Contemplation and Conversation: Subtle Influences on Moral Decision Making," *Academy of Management Journal* 55 (2010):13, 27.

159. See Chapter 3 and Michael E. Brown and Marie S. Mitchell, "Ethical and Unethical Leadership: Exploring New Avenues for Future Research," *Business Ethics Quarterly* 20 (2010):583, 585.
160. Marshall Schmninke and Manuela Priesemuth, "Behavioral Business Ethics: Taking Context Seriously," in De Cremer and Tenbrunsel, *Behavioral Business Ethics*, 50; Mark John Somers, "Ethical Codes of Conduct and Organizational Context: A Study of the Relationship between Codes of Conduct, Employee Behavior and Organizational Values," *Journal of Business Ethics* 30 (2001):185. The presence of a code alone was not significant in a meta-analysis. Enforcement is key. Kish-Gephart et al., "Bad Apples, Bad Cases, and Bad Barrels," 21.
161. For an example, see Shu et al., "Dishonest Deed," 344.
162. Ariely, *(Honest) Truth about Dishonesty*, 42.
163. The phrase comes from Jason Dana, Roberto A. Weber, and Jason Xi Kuang, "Exploiting Moral Wiggle Room: Behavior Inconsistent with a Preference for Fair Outcomes," *Economic Theory* 1 (2007):67.
164. Callahan, *Cheating Culture*, 282.
165. Rhode, "Where Is the Leadership in Moral Leadership?," 35; Callahan, *Cheating Culture*, 283; Leah Nathans Spiro, "Ethics and Andersen Didn't Add Up," *Wall Street Journal*, March 20, 2003, D8.
166. Moore and Gino, "Ethically Adrift," 53, 69.
167. Ariely, *(Honest) Truth about Dishonesty*, 39–40.
168. Ariely, *(Honest) Truth about Dishonesty*, 50; Gino, *Sidetracked*, 220–221.
169. Shu et al., "Ethical Discrepancy," 233.
170. Shu et al., "Ethical Discrepancy," 234.
171. Roberta Ann Johnson, *Whistleblowing: When It Works—and Why* (Boulder, CO: Lynne Riennner, 2002), 93; C. Fred Alford, *Whistleblowers: Broken Lives and Organizational Power* (Ithaca, NY: Cornell University Press, 2001), 1, 19–20.
172. Myron P. Glazer and Penina M. Glazer, *Whistleblowers: Exposing Corruption in Government and Industry* (New York: Basic Books, 1991), 207 (quoting Hugh Kaufman).
173. *See* Rhode, "Where Is the Leadership in Moral Leadership?," 43.
174. Richard Lacayo and Amanda Ripley, "Persons of the Year 2002: The Whistleblowers," *TIME*, December 30, 2002, 30.
175. Welsh et al., "Slippery Slope," 125.
176. Soltes, *Why They Do It*, 325.
177. Editorial: "Wells Fargo Needs to Change More than Just Its CEO," *New York Times*, October 14, 2016.
178. Melissa Bateson, Daniel Nettle, and Gilbert Roberts, "Cues of Being Watched Enhance Cooperation in a Real-World Setting," *Biology Letters* 2 (2006):412.
179. Ann E. Tenbrunsel and David M. Messick, "Sanctioning Systems, Decision Frames, and Cooperation," *Administrative Science Quarterly* 44 (1999):684, 685; Robert B. Cialdini, "Social Influence and the Triple Tumor Structure of Organizational Dishonesty," in David M. Messick and Ann E. Tenbrunsel, eds., *Codes of Conduct: Behavioral Research into Business Ethics* (New York: Russell Sage, 1996), 4.
180. Cialdini, "Social Influence and the Triple Tumor," 57.
181. Tenbrunsel and Messick, "Sanctioning Systems," 697, 704.
182. Callahan, *Cheating Culture*, 238; Jenni Bergal, "White-Collar Crime Costs Firms Millions," *SunSentinel*, April 5, 2002.
183. Clifton Leaf, "Enough Is Enough: They Lie They Cheat They Steal and They've Been Getting Away with It for Too Long," *Fortune*, March 18, 2002, 60.
184. http://www.biography.com/people/michael-milken-234612; Callahan, *Cheating Culture*, 253–254; Cynthia Dockrell, "The Insider Milken's Circuitous Route," *Boston Globe*, January 23, 2001, 3E.
185. Garry Trudeau, "Doonesbury," *Houston Post*, November 15, 1993, A12, quoted in Stephen M. Rosoff, Henry N. Pontell, and Robert Tillman, *Profit without Honor: White-Collar Crime and the Looting of America* (Upper Saddle River, NJ: Prentice Hall, 1998), 159.
186. Peter Marks, "Ethics and the Bottom Line," *Chicago Tribune Magazine*, May 6, 1990, SM26.

## *Chapter 2*

1. Paul Anthony, *Sex & Drugs & Sport & Cheating* (Nottingham, UK: DB Publishing, 2014), 9–23.
2. Alex Hutchinson, "When Doping Isn't Cheating," *New York Times*, November 30, 2014.
3. Anthony, *Sex & Drugs*, 35.
4. Anthony, *Sex & Drugs*, 36.
5. David Callahan, *The Cheating Culture: Why More Americans Are Doing Wrong to Get Ahead* (New York: Harcourt, 2004), 12.
6. Stephen Ambrose, "Eisenhower," *Miller Center Journal* 4 (Spring 1997):12. Don Van Natta, *First Off the Tee* (New York: Public Affairs, 2004), 74.
7. Bob Woodward, *Shadow: Five Presidents and the Legacy of Watergate* (New York: Simon and Schuster, 2000), 498; Shepherd Campbell and Peter Landau, *Presidential Lies: The Illustrated History of White House Golf* (New York: Macmillan, 1996), 218.
8. Michael Kranish and Marc Fisher, *Trump Revealed: An American Journey of Ambition, Ego, Money, and Power* (New York: Scribner, 2016), 181.
9. Ben Terris, "Does Donald Trump Cheat at Golf?: A Washington Post Investigation," *Washington Post*, September 7, 2015 (quoting Rick Reilly).
10. Terris, "Does Donald Trump Cheat at Golf?" (quoting Rick Reilly).
11. Terris, "Does Donald Trump Cheat at Golf?" (quoting Mark Mulvoy).
12. Terris, "Donald Trump Cheat at Golf ?" (quoting Donald Trump).
13. Dan Ariely, *The (Honest) Truth about Dishonesty: How We Lie to Everyone—Especially Ourselves* (New York: HarperCollins, 2012), 59.
14. Ariely, *(Honest) Truth about Dishonesty*, 60–61.
15. Ariely, *(Honest) Truth about Dishonesty*, 62 (quoting Donald Palmer).
16. Randolph Feezell, "Celebrated Athletes, Moral Exemplars, and Lusory Objects," *Journal of the Philosophy of Sport* 32 (2005):20.
17. David Light Shields and Brenda Light Bredemeier, "Can Sports Build Character?," in Daniel K. Lapsley and F. Clark Power, eds., *Character Psychology and Character Education* (Notre Dame, IN: University of Notre Dame Press, 2005):121, 124–125.
18. Matthew Karnitschnig, Sports: "FIFA's Match-Fixing Problem: A Convicted Fixer Says Soccer Isn't Doing Enough to Fight Corruption," *Wall Street Journal*, August 21, 2014.
19. David E. Sumner, "Cheating in College Sports," *Saturday Evening Post*, November/ December 2013; Albert J. Figone, *Cheating the Spread: Gamblers, Point Shavers and Game Fixers in College Football and Basketball* (Champaign: University of Illinois Press, 2012).
20. Sumner, "Cheating in College Sports" (quoting Brian Tuohy).
21. Sumner, "Cheating in College Sports."
22. Sumner, "Cheating in College Sports" (quoting David Schwartz, director of the Center for Gaming Research at the University of Nevada).
23. Thomas Boswell, *How Life Imitates the World Series: An Inquiry into the Game* (New York: Doubleday, 1982), 198.
24. Garrett R. Broshuis, "Restoring Integrity to America's Pastime: Moving Towards a More Normative Approach to Cheating in Baseball," *Texas Review of Entertainment and Sports Law* 14 (2013):119, 122–123.
25. Jonathan Fraser Light, *The Cultural Encyclopedia of Baseball* (Jefferson, North Carolina: McFarland, 2005), 457.
26. Broshuis, "Restoring Integrity to America's Pastime," 122.
27. Andrew Beyer, "A Problem That Is Bigger than One Man," *Washington Post*, April 28, 2014, D3.
28. "49ers Hall of Famer Jerry Rice Admits Using Banned 'Stickum' on Gloves during His Playing Days," February 6, 2015, http://sanfrancisco.cbslocal.com/2015/02/06/49ers-hall-of-famer-jerry-rice-admits-using-banned-stickum-on-gloves-during-his-playing-days/.
29. Mark Maske, "NFL's Season-Long Turbulence Makes for Bumpy Ride," *Washington Post*, January 26, 2015, D1.

30. John Branch, "Tom Brady Probably Knew Footballs Were Doctored, N.F.L. Finds," *New York Times*, May 6, 2015. For a critique of the investigation, see Kevin A. Hassett and Stan A. Veuger, "Deflating 'Deflategate,'" *New York Times*, June 12, 2015.
31. National Football Management Council v. National Football Players Association, 125 F. Supp. 3d 449 (S.D.N.Y. 2015), *reversed*, National Football Management Council v. National Football League Players Association, 820 F. 3d 527 (2d Cir. 2016).
32. William C. Rhoden, "Tom Brady's Punishment Is a Matter of Perspective," *New York Times*, May 11, 2015 (quoting Ron Katz).
33. William C. Rhoden, "In Deflation Case, Seeking a Penalty That Restores Credibility," *New York Times*, May 8, 2015, B10 (quoting Ron Katz).
34. Chris Chase, "Joe Montana Says He'd Have Thought about Doctoring Footballs Like Tom Brady," *USA Today*, June 9, 2015 (quoting Montana).
35. Ryan Wilson, "Joe Montana on Patriots: 'If You Ain't Cheating, You Ain't Trying,'" CBS Sports, October 16, 2015, http://www.cbssports.com/nfl/news/joe-montana-on-patriots-if-you-aint-cheating-you-aint-trying.
36. Barry Svrluga, "Little League Champs Lose Their Title," *Washington Post*, February 12, 2015, A1.
37. Glyn C. Roberts, Yngvar Ommundsen, Pierre-Nicolas Lemyre, and Blake W. Miller, "Cheating in Sport," in Charles D. Spielberger, ed., *Encyclopedia of Applied Psychology: A–E*, Volume 1 (Amsterdam and New York: Elsevier Academic Press, 2004).
38. Anita L. Allen, *The New Ethics: A Guided Tour of the Twenty-First Century Moral Landscape* (New York: Miramax, 2004), 36.
39. Svrluga, "Little League Champs," A1. *See also* Herb Appenzeller, *Ethical Behavior in Sport* (Durham, NC: Carolina Academic Press, 2011), 76.
40. Robert C. Schneider, *Ethics of Sport & Athletics: Theory, Issues, and Application* (New York: Lippincott Williams & Wilkins, 2009), 105.
41. Svrluga, "Little League Champs," A1.
42. Christian Smith, with Kari Christoffersen, Hillary Davidson, and Patricia Snell Herzog, *Lost in Transition* (New York: Oxford University Press, 2011), 48.
43. Phil Sheridan, "Ethicist Advises Falcons to Go for McNabb's Ankle," *Philadelphia Inquirer*, January 8, 2003.
44. Robert L. Simon, Cesar R. Torres, and Peter F. Hager, *Fair Play: The Ethics of Sports* (Boulder, CO: Westview Press, 2015), 238–239.
45. Jay Coakley, *Sports in Society: Issues and Controversies* (New York: McGraw Hill, 9th ed. 2007), 207–210.
46. Maria Kavussanu, "Why World Cup Soccer Players Hit, Kick, and Bite Each Other," *Washington Post*, June 28, 2014.
47. Anthony, *Sex & Drugs*, 41.
48. Geoff Foster, "The World Cup Flopping Rankings," *Wall Street Journal*, June 27, 2014.
49. Stephen L. Carter, *Integrity* (New York: Perseus Basic Books, 1996), 4.
50. Carter, *Integrity*, 5.
51. Carter, *Integrity*, 4.
52. Appenzeller, *Ethical Behavior in Sport*, 45.
53. "Belick Draws $500,000 Fine, but Avoids Suspension," ESPN.com, September 14, 2007.
54. Anthony, *Sex & Drugs*, 91–93, 96; Norman R. Augustine et al., *Harvard Business Review on Crisis Management* (Boston: MA: Harvard Business School Press, 2000), 88.
55. Mary Pilon, "Judges of a Graceful Sport, Caught in a Clumsy Cheating Scandal," *New York Times*, July 17, 2013, A1.
56. Stephanie Clifford and Matt Apuzzo, "U.S. Vows to Rid Global Soccer of Corruption," sports.ndtv.com, May 28, 2015, A1.
57. Sam Borden and Andrew Das, "FIFA Officials Took Big Raises amid Scandal," *New York Times*, June 4, 2016; Joshua Robinson and Matthew Futterman, "FIFA Reveals Millions Paid to Ex-leaders," *Wall Street Journal*, June 4, 2016.

58. Simon Romero, "A Region's Soccer Strongmen Are Facing a Hard Fall," *New York Times*, May 28, 2015, B10.
59. Bill Dwyre, Crossing the Line, Commentary: "Unfair Way in Which U.S. Women's Team Won World Cup Raises Morality Issue in Sports," *Los Angeles Times*, July 15, 1999.
60. Dwyre, Crossing the Line.
61. Dwyre, Crossing the Line.
62. Hutchinson, "When Doping Isn't Cheating."
63. Verner Moller, *The Ethics of Doping and Anti-doping: Redeeming the Soul of Sport?* (New York: Routledge, 2010), 4.
64. World Anti-Doping Agency (WADA), *World Anti-doping Code* (Montreal: WADA, 2003), 8.
65. Moller, *Ethics of Doping*, 6.
66. Simon et al., *Fair Play*, 85.
67. Simon et al., *Fair Play*, 97.
68. Moller, *Ethics of Doping*, 8–9.
69. WADA, *World Anti-doping Code.*
70. WADA, *World Anti-doping Code.*
71. Robert Voy and Kirk D. Deeter, *Drugs, Sport, and Politics* (Champaign IL: Leisure Press, 1991), 5.
72. Robert Smith, "A Different Kind of Performance Enhancer," NPR (March 31, 2006), http://www.npr.org/templates/story/story.php?storyID=5314753.
73. Moller, *Ethics of Doping*, 35; Les Woodland, *Dope: The Use of Drugs in Sport* (London: David and Charles, 1980), 16.
74. Patrick Mignon, "The Tour de France and the Doping Issue," *The International Journal of the History of Sport* 20 (2003):227, 230.
75. Anthony, *Sex & Drugs*, 57.
76. Mark Fainaru-Wada and Lance Williams, *Game of Shadows: Barry Bonds, BALCO, and the Steroids Scandal That Rocked Professional Sports* (New York: Gotham Books, 2006), 19; Michael J. Diacin, Janet B. Parks, and Pamela C. Allison, "Voices of Male Athletes on Drug Use, Drug Testing, and the Existing Order in Intercollegiate Athletics," *Journal of Sport Behavior* 26 (March 2003):1–2; Dionne L. Koller, "From Medals to Morality: Sportive Nationalism and the Problem of Doping in Sports," *Marquette Sports Law Review* 19 (2008):91.
77. Voy and Deeter, *Drugs, Sport, and Politics*, 6; "Olympic Trainer Admits Giving Drug to Danish Cyclist Who Died," *New York Times*, August 29, 1960. For an account of disputed facts, see Moller, *Ethics of Doping*, 37–39.
78. Woodland, *Dope*, 116.
79. Proper and Improper Use of Drugs by Athletes, Hearing Before the Senate Subcommittee to Investigate Juvenile Delinquency, Committee on the Judiciary, 93rd Congress (1973), 274 (Statement of Harold Connolly).
80. Moller, *Ethics of Doping*, 42–43; Woodland, *Dope*, 125.
81. Fainaru-Wada and Williams, *Game of Shadows*, 20.
82. Ivan Waddington, *Sport, Health and Drugs: A Critical Sociological Perspective* (New York: Routledge, 2000), 180.
83. Moller, *Ethics of Doping*, 108 (quoting Danish cyclist Brian Holm).
84. Anabolic Steroid Restriction Act of 1989, Hearing Before the Subcommittee on Crime of the House Committee on the Judiciary, 101st Congress (1989), 49, 46 (Statement of Dr. Charles Yesalis).
85. Diacin et al., "Voices of Male Athletes," 2.
86. George J. Mitchell, Report to the Commissioner of Baseball of an Independent Investigation into the Illegal Use of Steroids and Other Performance Enhancing Substances by Players in Major League Baseball (2007), 70–71.
87. Waddington, *Sport, Health and Drugs*, 163.

88. Nick Zaccardi, "World's Top-Ranked Badminton Player Fails Drug Test," NBC Sports, November 8, 2014; Greg Beacham, "Sponsors Ditch Sharapova, World's Top Earning Female Athlete," *New York Times*, March 8, 2016; International Tennis Federation, Decision in the Case of Maria Sharapova, June 8, 2016.
89. Liz Clarke, "Proposed Legislation Calls for USADA to Set and Enforce Standards," *Washington Post*, November 21, 2013, D5. For abuses, see Beyer, "A Problem That Is Bigger than One Man," D3.
90. For a general account, see Lindsey J. Mean, "On Track, Off Track on Oprah: The Framing of Marion Jones as Golden Girl and American Fraud," in Lawrence A. Wenner, ed., *Fallen Sports Heroes, Media, & Celebrity Culture* (New York: Peter Lang, 2013), 84.
91. Duff Wilson and Michal S. Schmidt, "Olympic Champion Acknowledges Use of Steroids," *New York Times*, October 5, 2007.
92. Koller, "From Medals to Morality," 91 (quoting Kenneth Karas).
93. Matt Hart, "'This Doesn't Sound Legal': Inside Nike's Oregon Project," *New York Times*, May 19, 2017.
94. Hart, "'This Doesn't Sound Legal,'" (quoting report).
95. Glenn Kessler, "Is Lance Armstrong the World's Biggest Liar?," *Washington Post* Blogs, January 18, 2013.
96. Dan Roan and Matt Slater, "Lance Armstrong: I'd Change the Man, Not Decision to Cheat," *BBC Sport*, January 26, 2015.
97. Reed Albergotti and Vanessa O'Connell, "Armstrong Switches Gears in Effort to Fix His Image," *Wall Street Journal*, January 15, 2013, A1.
98. Paul Krimmage, *Rough Ride* (London: Yellow Jersey Press, 2007), 91, 98, 146, 150.
99. Ian Austen, "Report Says Doping Was Ignored to Shield Armstrong," *New York Times*, March 8, 2015.
100. Max H. Bazerman and Ann E. Tenbrunsel, *Blind Spots: Why We Fail to Do What's Right and What to Do about It* (Princeton, NJ: Princeton University Press, 2011), 84.
101. Simon et al., *Fair Play*, 83.
102. Bill James, "Cooperstown and the 'Roids," in *The Bill James Gold Mine* (Chicago, IL: ACTA Sports, 2010).
103. Francesca Gina, *Sidetracked: Why Our Decisions Get Derailed and How We Can Stick to the Plan* (Cambridge, MA: Harvard Business Press, 2013), 211 (quoting Andy Pettitte).
104. Hank Aaron used amphetamines, which are now banned. Ben McGrath, "King of Walks: Barry Bonds and the Doping Scandal," *New Yorker*, March 28, 2011. For other athletes, see Bryan E. Denham, "From Coverage to Recovery: Mediating the Fallen Sports Celebrity," in Wenner, *Fallen Sports Heroes*, 43; Fainaru-Wada and Williams, *Game of Shadows*, xiii; Simon et al., *Fair Play*, 82.
105. Fainaru-Wada and Williams, *Game of Shadows*, 266.
106. Fainaru-Wada and Williams, *Game of Shadows*, 178.
107. United States v. Bonds, 784 F.3d 582 (9th Cir. 2015).
108. Rick Reilly, "Giving Barry His Due," *Sports Illustrated*, July 23, 2007. *See also* Lisa Doris Alexander, "Barry Bonds: Of Passion and Hostility," in David C. Ogden and Joel Nathan Rosen, *Fame to Infamy: Race, Sport, and the Fall from Grace* (Jackson: University Press of Mississippi, 2010), 23.
109. Report to the Commissioner of Baseball of an Independent Investigation into the Illegal Use of Steroids and Other Performance Enhancing Substances by Players in Major League Baseball (December 13, 2003).
110. David Millar, "How to Get Away with Doping," *New York Times*, October 16, 2016, SR5.
111. Millar, "How to Get Away with Doping," SR5.
112. Moller, *Ethics of Doping*, 136.
113. Ron Cook, "Testing Won't Stop Steroid Use," *Pittsburgh Post-Gazette*, June 4, 2002. *See also* Coakley, *Sports in Society*, 185–186.
114. Diacin et al., "Voices of Male Athletes," 1, 3, 8.

115. Moller, *Ethics of Doping*, 128.
116. Moller, *Ethics of Doping*, 129.
117. Moller, *Ethics of Doping*, 133.
118. Michael Power, "In Russian Doping Scandal, Time for a Punishment to Fit the Crime," *New York Times*, June 16, 2016; Rebecca R. Ruiz, Juliet Macur, and Ian Austen, "Even with Confessions of Cheating, World's Doping Watchdog Did Nothing," *New York Times*, June 15, 2016.
119. Rebecca Ruiz, "Russia May Face Olympics Ban as Doping Scheme Is Confirmed," *New York Times*, July 18, 2016.
120. Decision of the IOC Executive Board Concerning the Participation of Russian Athletes in the Olympic Games of Rio 2016 (July 24, 2016), https://www.olympic.org/news/decision-of-the-ioc-executive-board-concerning-the-participation-of-russian-athletes-in-the-olympic-games-rio-2016.
121. Rebecca R. Ruiz, "Olympic Officials Set Russia's Roster: More than 100 Are Barred for Doping," *New York Times.com*, August 4, 2016, http://www.nytimes.com/2016/08/05/sports/olympics/rio-russians-barred-doping.html.
122. Rebecca R. Ruiz, "I.O.C. Expands WADA's Authority to Lead Antidoping Efforts," *New York Times*, October 8, 2016.
123. Broshuis, "Restoring Integrity to America's Pastime," 127.
124. Kavussanu, "Why World Cup Soccer Players, Hit, Kick and Bite Each Other."
125. Boswell, *How Life Imitates the World Series*, 199.
126. Coakley, *Sports in Society*, 167 (quoting Jeremy Shockley).
127. Kevin Baxter, "Cheaters Never Prosper? Well . . . ," *Los Angeles Times*, June 16, 2013.
128. Moller, *Ethics of Doping*, 142–143.
129. David Luban and Daniel Luban, "Cheating in Baseball," in Leonard Cassuto and Stephen Partridge, eds., *The Cambridge Companion to Baseball* (Cambridge: Cambridge University Press, 2011), 186.
130. Luban and Luban, "Cheating in Baseball," 187.
131. Luban and Luban, "Cheating in Baseball," 188.
132. Nico W. Van Yperen, Melvyn R.W. Hamstra, and Marloes van der Klauw, "To Win, or Not to Lose, At Any Cost: The Impact of Achievement Goals on Cheating," *British Journal of Management* 22 (2011):S5.
133. Joseph M. Hoedel, *Role Models: Examples of Character & Leadership* (Williamstown, MI: Character Development Group, 2005), x.
134. Herb Appenzeller, *Ethical Behavior in Sport* (Durham, NC: Carolina Academic Press, 2011), xi.
135. Schneider, *Ethics of Sport & Athletics*, 105.
136. George Dorfman and Thayer Evans, "The Money," *Sports Illustrated*, September 18, 2013.
137. Dorfman and Evans, "The Money."
138. Jay M. Smith and Mary Willingham, *Cheated: The UNC Scandal, The Education of Athletes, and the Future of Big-Time College Sports* (Lincoln: Potomac Books, University of Nebraska Press, 2015), xvi.
139. Smith and Willingham, *Cheated*, xvii.
140. Paul M. Barrett, "Carolina Confronts Classroom Corruption as Athletes Fail to Read," *Bloomberg Business Week*, February 27, 2014.
141. Smith and Willingham, *Cheated*, xvii.
142. Smith and Willingham, *Cheated*, 17.
143. Smith and Willingham, *Cheated*, 23.
144. Smith and Willingham, *Cheated*, 23.
145. Barrett, "Carolina Confronts Classroom Corruption." *See also* Smith and Willingham, *Cheated*, 32.
146. Smith and Willingham, *Cheated*, 29, 45.
147. Barrett, "Carolina Confronts Classroom Corruption."

148. Smith and Willingham, *Cheated*, 194.
149. Barrett, "Carolina Confronts Classroom Corruption."
150. Barrett, "Carolina Confronts Classroom Corruption."
151. Pete Thamel, "Top Grads and No Class Time for Auburn Players," *New York Times*, July 4, 2006.
152. Joe Nocera, "Syracuse, Boeheim and the N.C.A.A.," *New York Times*, March 14, 2015, 19.
153. Ken Armstrong and Nick Perry, *Scoreboard Baby: A Story of College Football, Crime, and Complicity* (Lincoln, NE: Bison Books, 2010); Smith and Willingham, *Cheated*, 215.
154. Derek Bell, *Ethical Ambition: Living a Life of Meaning and Worth* (New York: Bloomsbury Publishing PLC, 2002), 152–153.
155. "Tutor Wrote Papers for Players," *Associated Press*, March 24, 1999, http://juneauempire.com/stories/032499/Spo_tutor.html# (quoting Jan Gangerlhoff).
156. Smith and Willingham, *Cheated*, 229.
157. Justin Rogers, University of Michigan Athletes Steered to Professor, March 19, 2008, http://www.mlive.com/wolverines/academics/stories/index.ssf/2008/03/athletes_steered_to_prof.html.
158. "University of Michigan Athletes Steered to Professor" (quoting Terry McDonald).
159. Academics and Athletics: A Four-Day Ann Arbor News Series on the University of Michigan, March 16–19, 2008, http://www.mlive.com/wolverines/academics; "University of Michigan Athletes Steered to Professor."
160. "University of Michigan Athletes Steered to Professor."
161. Smith and Willingham, *Cheated*, 217–218; Academics and Athletics.
162. Smith and Willingham, *Cheated*, 151.
163. Sara Ganim, CNN Analysis: "Some College Athletes Play Like Adults, Read Like 5th-Graders," January 8, 2014, http://www.cnn.com/2014/01/07/us/ncaa-athletes-reading-scores/index.html.
164. Smith and Willingham, *Cheated*, 156.
165. Smith and Willingham, *Cheated*, 175.
166. Smith and Willingham, *Cheated*, 183.
167. Patricia A. Adler and Peter Adler, *Backboards & Blackboards: College Athletes and Role Engulfment* (New York: Columbia University Press, 1991), 189.
168. Smith and Willingham, *Cheated*, 195.
169. Smith and Willingham, *Cheated*, 243.
170. Smith and Willingham, *Cheated*, 244.
171. Aaron Beard, "NCAA Hits UNC Football with 1-Year Postseason Ban," *USA Today*, March 12, 2012.
172. Schneider, *Ethics of Sport & Athletics*, 101.
173. Angela Lumpkin, Sharon Kay Stoll, and Jennifer Marie Beller, *Sport Ethics: Applications for Fair Play* (New York: MGraw Hill, 2003).
174. Carwyn Jones and Michael John McNamee, "Moral Reasoning, Moral Action, and the Moral Atmosphere of Sport," *Sport, Education and Society* 5 (2000):131.
175. *Peanuts*, November 6, 1967, http://peanuts.wikia.com/wiki/November_1967_comic_strips.
176. Carter, *Integrity*, 158.
177. Feezell, "Celebrated Athletes," 20, 23.
178. Roberts et al., "Cheating in Sport," 319.
179. David Light Shields, Brenda Light Bredemeier, Nicole M. LaVol, and F. Clark Power, "The Sports Behavior of Youth, Parents, and Coaches: The Good, the Bad, and the Ugly," *Journal of Research in Character Education* 2 (2005):43.
180. Shields and Bredemeir, "Can Sports Build Character?," 133–134.
181. http://www.positivecoach.org/our-story/.
182. Murray Sperber, *Onward to Victory: The Crises That Shaped College Sports* (New York: Henry Holt, 1998).

## Chapter 3

1. Association of Certified Fraud Examiners, Report to the Nation on Occupational Fraud and Abuse: 2014 Global Fraud Study (Association of Certified Fraud Examiners, 2014), 4.
2. David Shulman, *From Hire to Liar: The Role of Deception in the Workplace* (Ithaca, NY: ILR, 2007), 163.
3. Shulman, *From Hire to Liar*, 2; Jennifer J. Kish-Gephart, David A. Harrison, and Linda Klebe Treviño, "Bad Apples, Bad Cases, and Bad Barrels: Meta-analytic Evidence about Sources of Unethical Decisions at Work," *Journal of Applied Psychology* 95 (2010):1.
4. Eugene Soltes, *Why They Do It: Inside the Mind of the White-Collar Criminal* (New York: Public Affairs, 2016), 8; Shulman, *From Hire to Liar*; Donald Palmer, *Normal Organizational Wrongdoing: A Critical Analysis of Theories of Misconduct in and by Organizations* (Oxford: Oxford University Press, 2012); Blake E. Ashforth and Vikas Anand, "The Normalization of Corruption in Organizations," *Research in Organizational Behavior* 25 (2003):1.
5. Ben Heineman Jr., *The Inside Counsel Revolution: Resolving the Partner-Guardian Tension* (Chicago: Amercan Bar Association, 2016), 137.
6. James William Coleman, *The Criminal Elite: Understanding White-Collar Crime* (New York: St. Martin's Press, 4th ed. 1998), 178. *See also* Ashforth and Anand, "Normalization of Corruption in Organizations," 5.
7. Vikas Anand, Blake E. Ashforth, and Mahendra Joshi, "Business as Usual: The Acceptance and Perpetuation of Corruption in Organizations," *Academy of Management Executive* 18 (2004):39, 40. *See also* William A. Stadler and Michael L. Benson, "Revisiting the Guilty Mind: The Neutralization of White-Collar Crime," *Criminal Justice Review* 37 (2012):1, 4, 13. For examples, see the embezzlers profiled in Donald R. Cressey, "The Violators' Vocabularies of Adjustment," in Erwin O. Smigel and H. Laurence Ross, eds., *Crimes Against Bureaucracy* (New York: Van Nostrand Reinhold, 1970), 65, 74, 76.
8. Soltes, *Why They Do It*, 257.
9. Palmer, *Normal Organizational Wrongdoing*, 124; James Weber, "Managers' Moral Reasoning: Assessing Their Responses to Three Moral Dilemmas," *Human Relations* 43 (1990):687, 689; Michael Bommer, Clarence Gratto, Jerry Gravander, and Mark Tuttle, "A Behavioral Model of Ethical and Unethical Decision Making," *Journal of Business Ethics* 6 (1987):265, 268.
10. Robert Jackall, *Moral Mazes: The World of Corporate Managers* (New York: Oxford University Press, 1988), 6, 109.
11. Jerald Greenberg, "The Cognitive Geometry of Employee Theft: Negotiating 'the Line' between 'Taking' and 'Stealing,'" in Ricky W. Griffin, Ann O'Leary-Kelly, and Judith M. Collins, eds., *Dysfunctional Behavior in Organizations: Nonviolent Behaviors in Organizations* (Stamford, CT: JAI Press, 1998), 147, 168.
12. Donald N.M. Horning, "Blue Collar Theft: Conceptions of Property, Attitudes Toward Pilfering, and Work Group Norms in a Modern Industrial Plant," in Smigel and Ross, eds., *Crimes Against Bureaucracy*, 58.
13. Horning, "Blue Collar Theft," 55.
14. Michael E. Brown and Marie S. Mitchell, "Ethical and Unethical Leadership: Exploring New Avenues for Future Research," *Business Ethics Quarterly* 20 (2010):583, 600.
15. Shulman, *From Hire to Liar*, 133; Vardi and Weitz, *Misbehavior in Organizations*, 107–108.
16. Vivien K.G. Lim, "The IT Way of Loafing on the Job: Cyberloafing, Neutralizing, and Organizational Justice," *Journal of Organizational Behavior* 23 (2002):675, 676.
17. Shulman, *From Hire to Liar*, 118, 133.
18. "Resume Falsification Statistics," Statistic Brain, October 1, 2015, http://www.statisticbrain.com/resume/falsification/statistic/; Nick Fishman, "Survey Results: 40% of Applicants Distort Information on Resumes," EmployeeScreenIQ, April 4, 2012, http://www.employeescreen.com/iq/blog/resume-fraud-surveyu-results-40-of-applicants-distort-information-on-resumes; Tracy K. and BrightMove Recruiting Software and Onboarding Solutions, "Fact or Fiction? Why Resume Fraud Is a Legitimate Concern,"

January 9, 2011, https://www.brightmove.com/fact-and-fiction-resume-fraud-may-be-a-legitimate-concern-when-screening-candidates//; Jeffrey Kluger, "Pumping Up Your Past," *Time*, June 10, 2002, 45.

19. Shulman, *From Hire to Liar*, 138.
20. Shulman, *From Hire to Liar*, 138.
21. Jordan Belfort, *The Wolf of Wall Street* (New York: Bantam, 2007).
22. Jackall, *Moral Mazes*, 108–109.
23. Stephen M. Rosoff, Henry N. Pontell, and Robert Tillman, *Profit without Honor: White-Collar Crime and the Looting of America* (Upper Saddle River, NJ: Prentice Hall, 1998), 181.
24. Troy Segal, "They Didn't Even Give at the Office," *Business Week*, January 25, 1993, 68–69.
25. Annette Bernhardt et al., Broken Laws, Unprotected Workers: Violations of Employment and Labor Laws in America's Cities (2009), 2, 3, 5, http://www.nelp.org/page/-broken-laws/brokenlawsreport2009.pdf?nocdn=1. *See* Steven Greenhouse, "Low-Wage Workers Are Often Cheated, Study Says," *New York Times*, September 1, 2009.
26. Alice Hines, "Walmart Fined by Labor Department for Denying Workers Overtime Pay, Agrees to Pay $4.8 Million in Back Wages," *Huffington Post*, May 2, 2012, http://www.huffingtonpost.com/2012/05/02/walmart-overtime-labor-department-settlement_n_1470543.html.
27. Nick Penzenstadler and Susan Page, " Trump's 3,500 Lawsuits Unprecedented for a Presidential Nominee," *USA Today*, June 1, 2016.
28. Steve Reilly, "Hundreds Allege Donald Trump Doesn't Pay His Bills," *USA Today*, June 9, 2016.
29. Selwyn Raab, "After 15 Years in Court, Workers' Lawsuit against Trump Faces Yet Another Delay," *New York Times*, June 14, 1998; Tom Robbins, "Deal Sealed in Trump Tower Suit," *New York Daily News*, March 8, 1999.
30. Eunice Hyunhye Cho, "Exploiting Immigrants: Labor Laws Need to Protect Undocumented Workers, Too," *San Jose Mercury News*, April 25, 2013.
31. Michael Lewis, *Liar's Poker* (New York: Penguin, 1990), discussed in Palmer, *Normal Organizational Wrongdoing*, 81–82.
32. Lewis, *Liar's Poker*, 167.
33. John Coffee, "'No Soul to Damn; No Body to Kick': An Unscandalized Inquiry into the Problem of Corporate Punishment," *Michigan Law Review* 79 (1981):386, 398.
34. Richard M. Strassberg, David B. Pitofsky, and Samantha L. Schreiber, "Lawyers on Trial," *New York Law Journal*, July 18, 2005 (quoting Steven M. Cutler).
35. Palmer, *Normal Organizational Wrongdoing*, 189.
36. Marshall B. Clinard and Peter C. Yeager, *Corporate Crime* (New York: Free Press, 1980), 277.
37. Kermit Vandiver, "Why Should My Conscience Bother Me?," in Clinard and Yeager, *Corporate Crime*, 138.
38. Massimo Calabresi, "Wells Fargo Customer Fraud Deals Political Setback to Banks," *Time*, October 2, 2016, 14. *See also* Andrew Ross Sorkin, "Pervasive Sham Deals at Wells Fargo, and No One Noticed?," *New York Times*, September 12, 2016. For Wells Fargo's own internal investigation, see Independent Directors of the Board of Wells Fargo & Co, Sales Practice Investigation Report, April 10, 2017, i, 6–7, https://www.wellsfargo.com/assets/pdf/about/investor-relations/presentations/2017/board-report.pdf.
39. Stacy Cowley, "Lions Hunting Zebras: Ex Wells Fargo Bankers Describe Abuses," *New York Times*, October 20, 2016. *See also* David Lazarus, "Did Wells Fargo Target Seniors with Its Bogus Account Scheme?," *Los Angeles Times*, September 27, 2016.
40. Thomas Lee, "Suit: Wells Fargo Targeted 'Undocumented Immigrants' for Accounts," *San Francisco Chronicle*, April 26, 2017; Gillian B. White, "A Lawsuit Claims Wells Fargo Targeted Undocumented Immigrants to Hit Sales Quotas," *Atlantic*, April 27, 2017.
41. Stacy Cowley, "At Wells Fargo, Complaints about Fraudulent Accounts since 2005," *New York Times*, October 11, 2016; Calabresi, "Wells Fargo Customer Fraud," 14.
42. Sorkin, "Pervasive Sham Deals."

43. Dan Ariely, *Predictably Irrational: The Hidden Forces That Shape Our Decisions* (New York: Harper Perennial, 2010), 305 (quoting Upton Sinclair).
44. Palmer, *Normal Organizational Wrongdoing,* 184–185, 190; Walter Pavlo and Neil Weinberg, *Stolen without a Gun* (Tampa, FL: Etika Books, 2007).
45. Shulman, *From Hire to Liar,* 1.
46. Steven Greenhouse, *The Big Squeeze: Tough Times for American Workers* (New York: Random House, 2008), quoted in Palmer, *Normal Organizational Wrongdoing,* 186.
47. Jackall, *Moral Mazes,* 120.
48. Jackall, *Moral Mazes,* 38 ("reasonable" and "flexible"); Ann E. Tenbrunsel, Kristina A. Diekmann, Kimberly A Wade-Benzoni, and Max Bazerman, "Ethical Mirage: A Temporal Explanation as to Why We Are Not as Ethical as We Think We Are," *Research in Organizational Behavior* 30 (2010):153, 161 ("creative accounting").
49. Anton R. Valukas, Report to Board of Directors of General Motors Company Regarding Ignition Switch Recalls (May 29, 2014), discussed in Michele Benedetto Neitz, "Where Were the Lawyers? The Ethical Implications of the General Motors Recall Scandal in the United States," *Legal Ethics* 18 (2015):93, 94.
50. Leah McGrath Goodman, "Why Volkswagen Cheated," *Newsweek,* December 15, 2015 (quoting Ferdinand Dudenhoffer).
51. Sue Reisinger, "Bad Advice From "'Attorney A,'" *American Lawyer,* March 2017, 10; Jack Ewing, "Inside VW's Campaign of Trickery," *New York Times,* May 7, 2017, B5.
52. Kish-Gephart et al., "Bad Apples, Bad Cases and Bad Barrels," 18; Linda Klebe Treviño and Gary R. Weaver, *Managing Ethics in Business Organizations: Social Scientific Perspectives* (Stanford, CA: Stanford University Press, 2003), 171; Kenneth D. Butterfield et al., "Moral Awareness in Business Organizations: Influences of Issue Related and Social Contextual Factors," *Human Relations* 53 (2000):981, 982; Thomas M. Jones, "Ethical Decision Making by Individuals in Organizations: An Issue-Contingent Model," *Academy of Management Review* 16 (1991):366, 368, 379. For an overview, see Lynn L. Dallas, "A Preliminary Inquiry into the Responsibility of Corporations and Their Officers and Directors for Corporate Climate: The Psychology of Enron's Demise," *Rutgers Law Journal* 35 (2003):1, 10–11.
53. Shulman, *From Hire to Liar,* 146.
54. Kelly D. Martin and John B. Cullen, "Continuities and Extensions of Ethical Climate Theory: A Meta-analytic Review," *Journal of Business Ethics* 69 (2006):175, 177; Kish-Gephardt et al., "Bad Apples, Bad Cases, and Bad Barrels," 6; Tim Barnett and Cheryl Vaicys, "The Moderating Effect of Individuals' Perceptions of Ethical Work Climate on Ethical Judgments and Behavioral Intentions," *Journal of Business Ethics* 27 (2000):351.
55. Kish-Gephardt et al., "Bad Apples, Bad Cases, and Bad Barrels," 6.
56. Kish-Gephardt et al., "Bad Apples, Bad Cases, and Bad Barrels," 21. For the importance of ethical climate in shaping employee behavior, see David M. Mayer, Maribeth Kuenzi, and Rebecca L. Greenbaum, "Examining the Link between Ethical Leadership and Employee Misconduct: The Mediating Role of Ethical Climate," *Journal of Business Ethics* 95 (2010):7, 9, 13.
57. Diane Vaughan, *Controlling Unlawful Organizational Behavior: Social Structure and Corporate Misconduct* (Chicago: University of Chicago Press, 1983), 63; Diane Vaughan, "Toward Understanding Unlawful Organizational Behavior," *Michigan Law Review* 80 (1982):1377, 1334–1385.
58. Elizabeth E. Umphress and John B. Bingham, "When Employees Do Bad Things for Good Reasons: Examining Unethical Pro-organizational Behaviors," *Organization Science* 22 (2011):621, 629; Ashforth and Anand, "Normalization of Corruption in Organizations," 5–6.
59. Dawn L. Keig, Lance Eliot Brouthers, and Victor B. Marshall, "Formal and Informal Corruption Environments and Multinational Enterprise Social Irresponsibility," *Journal of Management Studies* 52 (2015):89, 95.
60. Vaughan, "Toward Understanding Unlawful Organizational Behavior," 1399.
61. Vaughan, *Controlling Unlawful Organizational Behavior,* 12.

62. Palmer, *Normal Organizational Wrongdoing*, 76–77; Bethany McLean and Peter Elkind, *The Smartest Guys in the Room: The Amazing Rise and Scandalous Fall of Enron* (New York: Portfolio Hardcover, 2004), 267.
63. Melissa S. Baucus, "Pressure, Opportunity and Predisposition: A Multivariate Model of Corporate Illegality," *Journal of Management* 20 (1994):699, 704, 707.
64. Rosoff et al., *Profit without Honor: White-Collar Crime*, 405.
65. Jonathan Soble, "Behind Mitsubishi's Faked Data, Fierce Competition," *New York Times*, April 21, 2016; Goodman, "Why Volkswagen Cheated" (describing difficulties company faced in finding technical solutions within its "time frame and budget" to meet U.S. emission standards); "Mitsubishi Motors Admits Falsifying Fuel Economy Tests," BBC. April 20, 2016, http://www.bbc.com/news/business-36089558 (describing automotive scandals).
66. Palmer, *Normal Organizational Wrongdoing*, 49; Kurt Eichenwald, *Conspiracy of Fools: A True Story* (New York: Broadway Books, 2005); Anand et al., "Business as Usual," 44.
67. Mimi Swartz and Sharron Watkins, *Power Failure: The Inside Story of the Collapse of Enron* (New York: Doubleday, 2003), 217. *See also* Anand et al., "Business as Usual," 44; and McLean and Elkind, *The Smartest Guys in the Room.*
68. John C. Coffee Jr., *Gatekeepers: The Professions and Corporate Governance* (New York: Oxford University Press, 2006), 29.
69. Ellen Joan Pollock, "Enron's Lawyers Faulted Deals but Failed to Blow the Whistle," *Wall Street Journal*, May 22, 2002.
70. Rosoff et al., *Profit without Honor*, 205.
71. United States Congress, House Committee on Government Operations, Combatting Fraud, Abuse and Misconduct in the Nation's Financial Institutions: Current Federal Reports Are Inadequate, House Report No 100–1088, 100th Congress, 2d Session (Washington, DC: Government Printing Office, October 13, 1988), 34.
72. U.S. Congress, House Committee on Government Operations, Combatting Fraud, 34. For the costs of the Savings and Loans failures, see Rosoff et al., *Profit without Honor*, 204–205.
73. Kirk O. Hanson, "The Ethical Challenges Facing Entrepreneurs," *Wall Street Journal*, November 23, 2015.
74. Melissa S. Baucas, "Pressure, Opportunity and Predisposition: A Multivariate Model of Corporate Illegality," *Journal of Management* 20 (1994):699, 712. *See also* Arthur P. Brief, Robert T. Buttram, and Janet M. Dukerich, "Collective Corruption in the Corporate World: Toward a Process Model," in Marlene E. Turner, ed., *Groups at Work: Theory and Research* (Mahwah, NJ: Lawrence Erlbaum, 2001):471, 484.
75. Soltes, *Why They Do It*, 272.
76. Shulman, *From Hire to Liar*, 130.
77. Palmer, *Normal Organizational Wrongdoing*, 190.
78. Brief et al., "Collective Corruption in the Corporate World," 471, 474.
79. Andris A. Zoltner, P.K. Sinha, and Sally E. Lorimer, "Wells Fargo and the Slippery Slope of Sales Incentives," *Harvard Business Review*, September 20, 2016; Jim Puzzanghera, "Did Wells Fargo Violate Overtime Laws? Elizabeth Warren among 8 Senators Seeking Labor Investigation," *Los Angeles Times*, September 22, 2016.
80. For an overview of how financial incentives drive unethical behavior, *see* John M. Darly, David M. Messick, and Tom R. Tyler, "Introduction: Social Influence and Ethics in Organizations," in John M. Darly, David M. Messick, and Tom R. Tyler, eds., *Social Influences on Ethical Behavior in Organizations* (Mahwah, NJ: Lawrence Erlbaum, 2001), 202.
81. Ronald R. Sims and Johannes Brinkmann, "Enron Ethics (Or: Culture Matters More than Codes)", *Journal of Business Ethics* 45 (2003):243, 252–253. David Skeel, *Icarus in the Boardroom: The Fundamental Flaws in Corporate America and Where They Came From* (New York: Oxford University Press, 2005), 171.
82. Sims and Brinkmann, "Enron Ethics," 252.
83. Barbara Ley Toffler and Jennifer Reingold, *Final Accounting: Greed, Ambition, and the Fall of Arthur Andersen* (New York: Broadway Business, 2003), 124.

84. Cowley, "At Wells Fargo, Complaints about Fraudulent Acts" (quoting Ricky Hansen).
85. Lisa G. Lerman, "Blue-Chip Bilking: Regulation of Billing and Expense Fraud by Lawyers," *Georgetown Journal of Legal Ethics* 12 (1999):205, 281 (quoting Roy Simon).
86. Linda Klebe Treviño, Niki A. den Nieuwenboer, and Jennifer J. Kish-Gephart, "(Un)Ethical Behavior in Organizations," *Annual Review of Psychology* 65 (2014):635, 645; Vardi and Weitz, *Misbehavior in Organizations,* 42; Treviño and Weaver, *Managing Ethics in Business Organizations,* 275–276, 285–286; James C. Wimbush and Jon M. Shepard, "Toward an Understanding of Ethical Climate: Its Relationship to Ethical Behavior and Supervisory Influence," *Journal of Business Ethics* 13 (1994):637, 641; Tom R. Tyler and Steven I. Blader, "Social Identity and Fairness Judgments," in Stephen Gilliland, Dirk Douglas Steiner, and Daniel Skarlicki, eds., *Emerging Perspectives on Values in Organizations* (Charlotte, NC: Information Age Publishing, 2003), 67, 69–73; Daniel Skarlicki and Robert Folger, "Retaliation in the Workplace: The Roles of Distributive, Procedural, and Interactional Justice," *Journal of Applied Psychology* 82 (1997):434; Robert J. Bies and Thomas M. Tripp, "Revenge in Organizations: The Good, the Bad, and the Ugly," in Ricky W. Griffin, Ann O'Leary-Kelly, and Judith M. Collins, eds., *Dysfunctional Behavior in Organizations: Violent and Deviant Behavior* (Greenwich, CT: Jai Press, 1998), 49, 54.
87. Richard Hollinger and John Clark, *Theft by Employees* (Lexington, MA: Lexington Books, 1983).
88. Cecilia Moore and Francesca Gino, "Ethically Adrift: How Others Pull Our Moral Compass from True North, and How We Can Fix It," *Research in Organizational Behavior* 33 (2013):53, 61.
89. Jerald Greenberg, "Employee Theft as a Reaction to Underpayment Inequality: The Hidden Costs of Pay Cuts," *Journal of Applied Psychology* 75 (190):561. *See also* Greenberg, "Cognitive Geometry of Employee Theft;" Jerald Greenberg and Kimberly Scott, "Why Do Employees Bite the Hands That Feed Them? Employee Theft as a Social Exchange Process," *Research in Organizational Behavior* 18 (1996):111.
90. Palmer, *Normal Organizational Wrongdoing,* 78–79: Kish-Gephart et al., "Bad Apples, Bad Cases, and Bad Barrels," 4; Bies and Tripp, "Revenge in Organizations," 61. For experiments documenting the response, see Francesca Gino and Lamar Pierce, "Dishonesty in the Name of Equity," *Psychological Science* 20 (2009):1153.
91. Lim, "IT Way of Loafing on the Job," 675, 688.
92. Brown and Mitchell, "Ethical and Unethical Leadership," 585.
93. Maria P. Miceli, Janet P. Near, and Terry Morehead Dworkin, *Whistleblowing in Organizations* (New York: Routledge, 2008), 82–83.
94. Umphress and Bingham, "When Employees Do Bad Things for Good Reasons;" Janet M. Dukerich, Roderick Kramer, and Judi McLean Parks, "The Dark Side of Organizational Identification," in David A. Whetten and Paul C. Godfrey, eds., *Identity in Organizations: Building Theory through Conversations* (Thousand Oaks, CA: Sage, 1998), 245; Baucus, "Pressure, Opportunity, and Predisposition," 713.
95. Umphress and Bingham, "When Employees Do Bad Things for Good Reasons," 624–625, 633.
96. Moore and Gino, "Ethically Adrift;" Treviño et al., "(Un)Ethical Behavior in Organizations," 642; Ann E. Tenbrunsel, "Misrepresentation and Expectations of Misrepresentation in an Ethical Dilemma: The Role of Incentives and Temptation," *Academy of Management Journal* 41 (1998):330; Baucas, "Pressure, Opportunity and Predisposition, 699, 712. *See also* Brief et al., "Collective Corruption in the Corporate World," 484.
97. Moore and Gino, "Ethically Adrift," 55, 58.
98. Umphress and Bingham, "When Employees Do Bad Things for Good Reasons," 627; Dolly Chugh, Max H. Bazerman, and Mahzarin R. Banaji, "Bounded Ethicality as Psychological Barrier to Recognizing Conflicts of Interest," in D.A. Moore, D.M. Cain, G. Lowenstein, and Max H. Bazerman, eds., *Conflicts of Interests: Challenges and Solutions from Law, Medicine and Public Policy* (London: Cambridge University Press, 2005), 74; Ashforth and Anand, "Normalization of Corruption," 10.

99. Goodman, "Why Volkswagen Cheated."
100. Scott S. Wiltermuth, "Cheating More When the Spoils Are Split," *Organizational Behavior and Human Decision Processes* 115 (2011):157.
101. Soltes, *Why They Do It*, 126; Steven R.H. Barrett et al., "Impact of the Volkswagen Emissions Control Defeat Device on US Public Health," *Environmental Research Letters* 10 (2014):1.
102. Soltes, *Why They Do It*, 197–199.
103. Soltes, *Why They Do It*, 173 (quoting Paul Bilzerian).
104. Jackall, *Moral Mazes*, 109, 39.
105. Brief et al., "Collective Corruption in the Corporate World," 488.
106. Brief et al., "Collective Corruption in the Corporate World," 479.
107. C.S. Lewis, "The Inner Ring," in C.S. Lewis, *They Asked for a Paper: Papers and Addresses* (London: Geoffrey Bles, 1962), 146–147.
108. David M. Mayer, Samir Nurmohamed, Linda Klebe Treviño, Debra L. Shapiro, and Marshall Schminke, "Encouraging Employees to Report Unethical Conduct Internally: It Takes a Village," *Organizational Behavior and Human Decision Processes* 121 (2013):90.
109. Anand et al., "Business as Usual," 45.
110. Anand et al., "Business as Usual," 45.
111. Mayer et al., "Encouraging Employees to Report Unethical Conduct Internally," 89, 90.
112. Mayer et al., "Examining the Link between Ethical Leadership and Employee Misconduct," 8.
113. Umphress and Bingham, "Why Employees Do Bad Things for Good Reasons," 629; David M. Mayer, Karl Aquino, Rebecca Greenbaum, and Maribeth Kuenzi, "Who Displays Ethical Leadership, and Why Does It Matter? An Examination of Antecedents and Consequences of Ethical Leadership," *Academy of Management Journal* 55 (2012):151, 153–154; Ruodan Shao, Karl Aquino, and Dan Freeman, "Beyond Moral Reasoning: A Review of Moral Identity Research and Its Implications for Business Ethics," *Business Ethics Quarterly* 18 (2008):513, 533; Greenberg, "Cognitive Geometry of Employee Theft," 147, 159.
114. Linda Klebe Treviño, Gary R. Weaver, and Scott J. Reynolds, "Behavioral Ethics in Organizations: A Review," *Journal of Management* 32 (2006):951, 971.
115. Gary R. Weaver, Linda Klebe Treviño, and Bradley Agle, " 'Somebody I Look Up To': Ethical Role Models in Organizations," *Organizational Dynamics* (2005):313, 318, 322.
116. Jackall, *Moral Mazes*, 119.
117. Baucus, "Pressure, Opportunity, and Predisposition," 714; Michael E. Brown, Linda K. Treviño, and David Harrison, "Ethical Leadership: A Social Learning Perspective for Construct Development and Testing," *Organizational Behavior and Human Decision Processes* 97 (2005):117; Linda K. Treviño and Michael Brown, "Ethical Leadership," in David V. Day, ed., *The Oxford Handbook of Leadership and Organizations* (New York: Oxford University Press, 2014), 532.
118. Sims and Brinkmann, "Enron Ethics," 243, 247. *See also* McLean and Elkind, *Smartest Guys in the Room.*
119. Donald C. Langevoort, "The Organizational Psychology of Hyper-Competition: Corporate Irresponsibility and the Lessons of Enron," *George Washington Law Review* 70 (2002): 968, 970.
120. Rebecca Roiphe, "The Ethics of Willful Ignorance," *Georgetown Journal of Legal Ethics* 24 (2011):187.
121. Roderick Kramer, "The Harder They Fall," *Harvard Business Review*, October, 2007.
122. Kramer, "The Harder They Fall."
123. Ronald R. Sims and Johannes Brinkmann, "Leaders as Role Model Models: The Case of John Gutfreund at Salomon Brothers," *Journal of Business Ethics* 35 (2002):327.
124. Linda Grant, "Taming the Bond Buccaneers at Salomon Brothers," *Los Angeles Times Magazine*, February 16, 1992, 22. For the Salomon culture generally, see Lewis, *Liar's Poker* 63–67, 69–70, 73, 75–76, 81–83.
125. Soltes, *Why They Do It*, 138; In re Goldman Sachs Group, Inc. Securities Litigation, Defendant's Memorandum of Law in Support of Their Motion to Dismiss the Consolidated Complaint, United States District Court Southern District of New York October 6, 2011.

126. James B. Stewart, "For John Stumpf, the Buck Stopped Where It Should Have," *New York Times*, October 12, 2016; Testimony of John Stump, Hearing Before the U.S. Senate Committee on Banking, Housing, and Urban Affairs, September 20, 2016.
127. Independent Directors of Wells Fargo & Company, 53, 55.
128. Independent Directors of Wells Fargo & Company, 6.
129. Jerry Useem, "What Was Volkswagen Thinking?," *Atlantic*, January/February 2016.
130. Treviño and Weaver, *Managing Ethics in Business Organizations*, 225.
131. Soltes, *Why They Do It*, 320–330.
132. This discussion of Salomon Brothers draws on Deborah L. Rhode and Amanda Packel, *Leadership for Lawyers* (New York: Wolters Kluwer, 2d ed., forthcoming 2017).
133. Michael Useem, *The Leadership Moment: Nine True Stories of Triumph and Disaster and Their Lessons for Us All* 178 (New York, NY: Three Rivers Press, 1998) (quoting Deryck Maughan).
134. Carol J. Loomis, "Warren Buffet's Wild Ride at Salomon," *Fortune*, October 27, 1997, 118.
135. In re Gutfreund, Securities Exchange Release No. 34–31554 (December 3, 1992).
136. Grant, "Taming the Bond Buccaneers," 22.
137. Useem, *Leadership Moment*, at 197.
138. Hannah Arendt, *On Violence* (New York: Houghton, Mifflin, Harcourt, 1970), 38–39.
139. Moore et al., "Why Employees Do Bad Things," 38; Moore and Gino, "Ethically Adrift," 66.
140. Palmer, *Normal Organizational Wrongdoing*, 171 (quoting Ralph Gretzinger).
141. Anton R. Valukas, Report to Board of Directors of General Motors Company Regarding Ignition Switch Recalls (May 29, 2014), 68–69.
142. Valukas, Report to the Board of Directors, 108.
143. *See* Valukas, Report to the Board of Directors, discussed in Michele Benedtto Neitz, "Where Were the Lawyers? The Ethical Implications of the General Motors Recall Scandal in the United States," *Legal Ethics* 18 (2015):93, 94.
144. Ben W. Heineman Jr., "GC and CEO Responsibility for GM's Dysfunctional Culture," *Corporate Counsel*, June 6, 2014 (quoting Mary Barra). *See also* Michael W. Peregrine, "The Broader Governance Lessons of the Valukas Report," *Columbia Law School Blue Sky Blog*, September 12, 2014.
145. In 2015, GM agreed to a Deferred Prosecution Agreement with the Department of Justice that included a $900 million fine and creation of a $600 million fund for victim compensation. Robert Eli Rosen, "The Sociological Imagination and Legal Ethics," *Legal Ethics* 19 (2016):99, 100.
146. Jennifer J. Kish-Gephart, James R. Detert, Linda Klebe Treviño, and Ann C. Edmondson, "Silenced by Fear: The Nature, Sources, and Consequences of Fear at Work," *Research in Organizational Behavior* 29 (2009):163.
147. Jackall, *Moral Mazes*, 107, 109. *See* Maria P. Miceli and Janet P. Near, "What Makes Whistle-Blowers Effective?: Three Field Studies," *Human Relations* 55 (2002):455, 457.
148. Jean Lipman-Blumen, *The Allure of Toxic Leaders* (New York: Oxford University Press, 2003), 45–46.
149. Ben Heineman Jr., "Who's Responsible for the Walmart Mexico Scandal?," *Harvard Business Review*, May 15, 2014.
150. Cowley, "At Wells Fargo, Complaints about Fraudulent Acts."
151. Heineman, "Inside Counsel Revolution," 117–118.
152. Kish-Gephart et al., "Silenced by Fear," 172, 177.
153. For varying estimates of the frequency of retaliation, see Miceli et al., *Whistleblowing in Organizations*, 23–25. *See also* Jessica Mesmer-Magnus and Chokalingam Viswesvaran, "Whistleblowing in Organizations: An Examination of Correlates of Whistleblowing Intentions, Actions and Retaliation," *Journal of Business Ethics* 62 (2005):277. John Gibeaut, "Telling Secrets: When In-House Lawyers Sue Their Employers, They Find Themselves in the Middle of the Debate on Client Confidentiality," *ABA Journal*, November 2004, 39, 73; Roberta Ann Johnson, *Whistleblowing: When It Works—and Why* (Boulder, CO: Lynne Rienner, 2003), 93; C. Fred Alford, *Whistleblowers: Broken Lives and Organizational Power*

(Ithaca, NY: Cornell University Press, 2001), 1, 19–20; Robert Pack, "Whistleblowers and the Law," *Washington Lawyer Online*, June 2002, 21, 28; Terance Miethe, *Whistleblowing at Work: Tough Choices in Exposing Fraud, Waste, and Abuse on the Job* (Boulder, CO: Westview Press, 1999), 149–208.

154. Mesmer-Magnus and Viswesvaran, "Whistleblowing in Organizations," 282, 288. For the costs of internal whistle-blowing, see Miethe, *Whistleblowing at Work*, 81; Alford, *Whistleblowers*, 20.
155. For a meta-analysis of research on these points, see Mesmer-Magnus and Viswesvaran, "Whistleblowing in Organizations," 276, 291, 297. For the tendency of organizations to ignore reports, see Miceli et al., *Whistleblowing in Organizations*, 151.
156. Johnson, *Whistleblowing*, 50.
157. Alford, *Whistleblowers*, 31–32; Johnson, *Whistleblowing*, 112.
158. Charles Haddad and Amy Barrett, "A Whistleblower Rocks an Industry," *Business Week*, June 24, 2002, 130 (quoting Douglas Durand).
159. Bazerman and Tenbrunsel, *Blind Spots*, 118; Tenbrunsel et al., "Ethical Mirage."
160. William Damon, *The Moral Advantage: How to Succeed in Business by Doing the Right Thing* (San Francisco: Berrett-Koehler, 2004), 3. *See also* Kish-Gephart et al., "Bad Apples, Bad Cases, and Bad Barrels," 7; Anand et al., "Business as Usual," 48 (noting that performance evaluations need to take into account more than numbers).
161. Linda Klebe Treviño, Gary R. Weaver, David C. Gibson, and Barbara Ley Toffler, "Managing Ethics and Legal Compliance: What Works and What Hurts," *California Management Review* 41 (1999):131, 131–132.
162. Brown et al., "Ethical Leadership," 117, 119–120. For the importance of ethical leaders, see Brown and Mitchell, "Ethical and Unethical Leadership."
163. Brown et al., "Ethical Leadership," 120.
164. Bazerman and Tenbrunsel, *Blind Spots*, 127.
165. Weaver et al., "Somebody I Look Up To."
166. Treviño et al., "Behavioral Ethics in Organizations," 971.
167. Daniel P. Skarlicki and Robert Folger, "Retaliation in the Workplace: The Roles of Distributive, Procedural and Interactional Justice," *Journal of Applied Psychology* 82 (1997):434, 435.
168. Treviño et al., "Behavioral Ethics in Organizations," 971; Treviño et al., "(Un)Ethical Behavior in Organizations," 645; Greenberg and Scott, Why Do Employees Bite the Hands That Feed Them?," 148; Greenberg, "Cognitive Geometry of Employee Theft," 176–177; Robert R. Taylor, "Your Role in the Prevention of Employee Theft," *Management Solutions* 31 (1986):20, 24.
169. Winston S. Churchill, *The Grand Alliance* (Boston: Houghton Mifflin, 1950), 611.
170. Vardi and Weitz, *Misbehavior in Organizations*, 41. *See also* Taylor, "Your Role in the Prevention of Employee Theft," 25.
171. Bazerman and Tenbrunsel, *Blind Spots*, 110–111; Treviño et al., "Behavioral Ethics in Organizations," 966; Tenbrunsel et al., "Ethical Mirage," 161; Ann E. Tenbrunsel and David Messick, "Sanctioning Systems, Decision Frames and Cooperation," *Administrative Science Quarterly* 44 (1999):684, 685.
172. Lim, "IT Way of Loafing on the Job," 690.
173. Heineman, "Inside Counsel Revolution," 119.
174. Ashforth and Anand, "Normalization of Corruption in Organizations," 39; Anand et al., "Business as Usual," 49.
175. Bazerman and Tenbrunsel, *Blind Spots*, 164–165; Anand et al., "Business as Usual," 50; Moore and Gino, "Ethically Adrift."
176. Emily Glazer and Christina Rexrode, "As Regulators Focus on Culture, Wall Street Struggles to Define It," *Wall Street Journal*, February 1, 2015 (quoting Susan Ochs of the Better Banking Project at the New America Foundation).
177. Glazer and Rexrode, "As Regulators Focus on Culture" (quoting Kelly King).

178. Sheelah Kolhatkar, "Stickler Status," *New Yorker*, May 15, 2017, 37.
179. Dallas, "Preliminary Inquiry," 40; W. Michael Hoffman, "Integrating Ethics into Business Cultures," in Chris Moon and Clive Bonny, eds., *Business Ethics: Facing Up to the Issues* (London: Profile Books, 2001), 43–44; Chris Moon and Clive Bonny, "Attitudes and Approaches," in Moon and Bonny, eds., *Business Ethics*, 34.
180. Paine, *Value Shift*, 249; Treviño et al., "Managing Ethics and Legal Compliance," 142–143; Christine Parker, The Open Corporation: Effective Self-Regulation and Democracy (Cambridge: Cambridge University Press, 2002), 50, 94, 203.
181. Treviño et al., "Managing Ethics and Legal Compliance," 142; Heesun Wee, Corporate Ethics: Right Makes Might," *Bloomberg*, April 10, 2002, https://www.bloomberg.com/news/articles/2002-04-10/corporate-ethics-right-makes-might (describing findings of Ethics Resource Center 2000 Survey).
182. Treviño et al., "Behavioral Ethics in Organizations," 971.
183. Dennis Thompson, *Restoring Responsibility: Ethics in Government, Business, and Health Care* (New York: Cambridge University Press, 2004), 263. John C. Coffee, "Understanding Enron: 'It's about the Gatekeepers, Stupid,'" *Business Lawyer*, 57 (2002):1403.
184. E. Norman Veasey and Christine T. Di Guglielmo, *Indispensable Counsel: The Chief Legal Officer in the New Reality* (New York: Oxford University Press, 2013), 4, 100 (quoting Dan Cooperman). *See also* Heineman, , *The Inside Counsel Revolution*, 15–16, 193–196.
185. Prashant Dubey and Eva Kripalani, *The Generalist Counsel: How Leading General Counsel Are Shaping Tomorrow's Companies* (New York: Oxford University Press, 2013), 72 (quoting Hillary Krane).
186. Kolhatkar, "Stickler Status," 37.
187. Matthew J. Belvedere, "If Ever There's a Case for Clawbacks, Wells Fargo Is It: Ex-FDIC Chair," CNBC, September 14, 2016.
188. Stephen Gandel, "Wells Fargo Exec Who Headed Phony Accounts Unit Collected $125 Million," *Fortune*, September 12, 2016.
189. Thornton McEnery, "Wells Fargo Is Punishing the Executive Who Oversaw Widespread Fraud with $124.6 M," *Dealbreaker*, September 13, 2016; Susan M. Ochs, "In Wells Fargo Scandal, the Buck Stopped Well Short," *New York Times*, September 15, 2016.
190. Gandel, "Wells Fargo Exec."
191. Michael Corkery and Stacy Cowley, "Wells Fargo Chief Abruptly Steps Down," *New York Times*, October 12, 2016; Robert L. Borosage, "The Lawless Suites," *The Nation*, October 17, 2016, 9.
192. Corkery and Cowley, "Wells Fargo Chief."
193. Matt Egan, "Wells Fargo Stock Sinks to 2 ½ Year Low, "*CNN Money*, September 26, 2016, http://money.cnn.com/2016/09/26/investigation; "Executive Clawbacks," *Time*, April 24, 2017, 19.
194. *See generally* Stuart Albert and David A. Whetten, "Organizational Identity," in Mary Jo Hatch and Majken Shultz, *Organizational Identity: A Reader* (New York: Oxford University Press, 2004), 90; Albert Stuart, "The Definition and Metadefinition of Identity," in David A. Whetten and P.C. Godfrey, eds., *Identity in Organizations* (Thousand Oaks, CA: Sage, 1998), 1.
195. Soltes, *Why They Do It*, 322.
196. Vicky Arnold, James C. Lampe, and George G. Sutton, "Understanding the Factors Underlying Ethical Organizations: Enabling Continuous Ethical Improvement," *Journal of Applied Business Research* 15 (Summer 1999):l, 10; Moon and Bonny, "Attitudes and Approaches," 29–34; Hoffman, "Integrating Ethics into Business Cultures," 50.
197. Ethics Resource Center, *Ethics in American Business: Policies, Programs and Perceptions* (Washington, DC: Ethics Resource Center, 1994).
198. Kish-Gephart et al., "Bad Apples, Bad Cases, and Bad Barrels," 7, 21; Treviño et al., "Managing Ethics and Legal Compliance," 140; Dallas, "Preliminary Inquiry," 32; Mark S. Schwartz, "A Code of Ethics for Corporate Code of Ethics," *Journal of Business Ethics* 41 (2002):27, 27–28; Kimberly D. Krawiec, "Organizational Misconduct: Beyond the

Principal, Agent Model," *Florida State University Law Review* 32 (2005): 571, 593; Kimberly D. Krawiec, "Cosmetic Compliance and the Failure of Negotiated Governance," *Washington University Law Quarterly* 81 (2003):487, 511. *See also* Treviño et al., "Behavioral Ethics in Organizations," 971 (suggesting that impact is minimal in isolation from other efforts).

199. Donald L. McCabe, Linda Klebe Treviño, and Kenneth D. Butterfield, "The Influence of Collegiate and Corporate Codes of Conduct on Ethics-Related Behavior in the Workplace," *Business Ethics Quarterly* 6 (1996):461, 464.
200. Sims and Brinkmann, "Enron Ethics."
201. Treviño and Weaver, *Managing Ethics in Business Organizations*, 128.
202. Treviño et al., "(Un)Ethical Behavior in Organizations," 639.
203. Ronald Berenbeim, "Global Ethics," *Executive Excellence* 17 (2000):7.
204. Linda Klebe Treviño and Katherine A. Nelson, *Managing Business Ethics: Straight Talk About How to Do It Right* (New York: Wiley, 1995); Greenberg, "Cognitive Geometry of Employee Theft," 177–178.
205. Umphress and Binham, "When Employees Do Bad Things for Good Reasons," 634; Heineman, "Inside Counsel Revolution," 123–125.
206. Bazerman and Tenbrunsel, *Blind Spots*, 37, 159; Richard P. Larrick, "Debiasing," in Derek J. Koehler and Nigel Harvey, eds., *Blackwell Handbook of Judgment and Decision Making* (Oxford: Blackwell, 2004), 316.
207. Tenbrunsel et al., "Ethical Mirage," 166; Brian C. Gunia, Long Wang, Li Huang Insead, Jiunwen Wang, and J. Keith Murnighan, "Contemplation and Conversation: Subtle Influences on Moral Decision Making," *Academy of Management Journal* 55 (2012):13, 27.
208. Anand et al., "Business as Usual," 48.
209. Ashforth and Anand, "Normalization of Corruption in Organizations," 39; Moore et al., "Why Employees Do Bad Things," 40.
210. Kish-Gephart et al., "Bad Apples, Bad Cases, and Bad Barrels," 20; Greenberg, "Cognitive Geometry of Employee Theft," 179. *See also* Bies and Tripp, "Revenge in Organizations," 61 (noting that individuals are not always aware of how their actions are harmful).
211. Jean Chatzky, "Meet the Whistle-Blower," *Money*, February 2004 (quoting Noreen Harrington).
212. Greg Farrell, "Ethics Training as Taught by Ex-Cons: Crime Doesn't Pay," *USA Today*, November 16, 2005, B1.
213. Treviño et al., "(Un)Ethical Behavior in Organizations," 640.
214. Rushworth M. Kidder, "White House Ethics Briefings: Do They Deserve Kudos or Catcalls," *Ethics Newsline*, Institute for Global Ethics, November 14, 2005.
215. Treviño and Weaver, *Managing Ethics in Business Organizations*, 339.
216. Michael Corkery and Stacy Cowley, "Wells Fargo Warned Workers against Sham Accounts but 'They Needed a Paycheck,' " *New York Times*, September 16, 2016.
217. Alford, *Whistleblowers*, 21.
218. Mayer et al., "Encouraging Employees to Report Unethical Conduct Internally," 102.
219. Miceli et al., *Whistleblowing in Organizations*, 194–197; Miceli and Near, "What Makes Whistle-Blowers Effective?," 475; Benisa Berry, "Organizational Culture: A Framework and Strategies for Facilitating Employee Whistleblowing," *Employee Responsibilities and Rights Journal* 16 (2004):1, 10 (advocating and describing multiple channels); Greenberg, "Cognitive Geometry of Employee Theft," 180–181 (discussing hotlines).
220. Heineman, "Inside Counsel Revolution," 117, 120.
221. Miceli et al., *Whistleblowing in Organizations*, 151; Leonard M. Baynes, "Just Pucker and Blow? An Analysis of Corporate Whistleblowing and the Duty of Care, the Duty of Loyalty, and the Sarbanes-Oxley Act," *St. John's Law Review* 76 (2004):875, 896; David L. Hudson Jr., "No Place to Blow the Whistle," ABA Journal eReport, February 1, 2005.
222. Government Accountability Office (GAO), *Whistleblower Protection Program* (Washington, DC: GAO, January 2009), 18, 35. *See also* GAO, Department of Energy, Whistleblower Protections Need Strengthening (Washington, DC: GAO, July 2016).

223. Matt Apuzzo and Ben Protess, "Justice Department Sets Sights on Wall Street Executives," *New York Times*, September 9, 2015, and Samuel W. Buell, "Is the White Collar Offender Privileged?," *Duke Law Journal* 63 (2014):823, 833.
224. Soltes, *Why They Do It*, 43.
225. Soltes, *Why They Do It*, 42–43.
226. For mixed findings, see Rosoff et al., *Profit without Honor*, 407. For suggestions that white-collar offenders no longer receive lenient treatment, see Buell, "Is the White Collar Offender Privileged?" For increasing government pressure on organizations to identify white-collar offenders, see Aputzzo and Protess, "Justice Department Sets Sights on Wall Street Executives." For data documenting shorter sentences for white-collar offenders, see Katie A. Fredericks, Rima E. McComas, and Georgie Ann Weatherby, "White Collar Crime: Recidivism, Deterrence, and Social Impact," *Forensic Research and Criminology International Journal* 2 (2016):00039; Peter Gottschalk and Torbjorn Rundmo, "Crime: The Amount and Disparity of Sentencing—A Comparison of Corporate and Occupational White Collar Criminals," *International Journal of Law, Crime, and Justice* 42 (2014):175, 177; Sean Madden, Richard D. Hartley, Jeffrey T. Walker, and J. Mitchell Miller, "Sympathy for the Devil: An Exploration of Federal Judicial Discretion in the Processing of White Collar Offenders," *American Journal of Criminal Justice* 37 (2012):4.
227. Buell, "Is the White Collar Offender Privileged?," 836–837.
228. Maddan et al., "Sympathy for the Devil," 4, 15.
229. Robert Tillman and Henry Pontell, "Is Justice 'Collar-Blind?': Punishing Medicaid Provider Fraud," *Criminology* 53 (1988):294.
230. Gretchen Morgenson, "Legal Fees Mount at Fannie and Freddie," *New York Times*, February 22, 2012, B1.
231. For examples of campaigns involving at least a hundred letters, see Peter J. Henning, "The Challenge of Sentencing White-Collar Defendants," *New York Times*, February 25, 2013.
232. Rosoff et al., *Profit without Honor*, 406.
233. Henning, "Challenge of Sentencing White-Collar Defendants."
234. Adam Brandolph, "White-Collar Criminals Often Avoid Prison Terms," *Trib Live*, January 19, 2014, http://triblive.com/news/allegheny/5431279-74/collar-jail-criminals.
235. Brandolph, "White Collar Criminals."
236. Fredericks et al., "White Collar Crime."
237. Dyan Machan and Graham Button, "Beyond the Slammer," *Forbes*, November 26, 1990.
238. Rosoff et al., *Profit without Honor*, 408.
239. Ewing, "Inside VW's Campaign of Trickery," B5; Nathan Bomey, "VW Pleads Guilty to Conspiracy, Obstruction of Justice: 6 Execs Charged," *USA Today*, January 11, 2017. *See also* Adam Goldman, Hiroko Tabuchi, and Jack Ewing, "F.B.I. Arrests Volkswagen Executive on Conspiracy Charge in Emissions Scandal," *New York Times*, January 9, 2017.
240. Calabresi, "Wells Fargo Customer Fraud" (quoting Warren).
241. Gandel, "Wells Fargo Exec."
242. Fredericks et al., "White Collar Crime."
243. Gottschalk and Rundmo, "Crime," 177; Nicole Leeper Piquero, Stephanie Carmichael, and Alex R. Piquero, "Assessing the Perceived Seriousness of White-Collar and Street Crimes," *Crime and Delinquency* 54 (2008):291, 306.
244. For examples, see Rena Steinzor and Sidney Shapiro, *The People's Agents and the Battle to Protect the American Future* (Chicago: University of Chicago Press, 2010), 67.
245. Mary Jo White, Testimony on the Fiscal Year 2017 Budget Request of the U.S. Securities and Exchange Commission Before the Subcommittee on Financial Services and General Government, Committee on Appropriations, United States House of Representatives, March 22, 2016, https://www.sec.gov/news/testimony/testimony-white-sec-fy-2017-budget-request.html.
246. White, Testimony.

247. John Braithwaite, *Shame and Reintegration* (New York: Cambridge University Press, 1989); John Coffee, "No Soul to Damn, No Body to Kick: An Unscandalized Inquiry into the Problem of Corporate Punishment," *Michigan Law Review* 79 (1981):424.
248. Michael Corkery, "Wells Fargo John Stumpf Has His Wall Street Comeuppance," *New York Times*, September 19, 2016.
249. Treviño et al., "Behavioral Ethics in Organizations," 970; Treviño et al., "(Un)Ethical Behavior in Organizations," 641; Greenberg, "Cognitive Geometry of Employee Theft," 187.
250. Miceli et al., *Whistleblowing in Organizations*, 99, 135.
251. Deborah L. Rhode, "Where Is the Leadership in Moral Leadership?," in Deborah L. Rhode, *Moral Leadership: The Theory and Practice of Power, Judgment, and Policy* (San Francisco: Jossey-Bass, 2006), 52–53.
252. Jim Collins, *Good to Great: Why Some Companies Make the Leap and Others Don't* (New York: HarperCollins, 2001), 21, 38.
253. Collins, *Good to Great*, 215
254. Collins, *Good to Great*, 215.
255. Mukul Pandya, Robbie Shell, and Susan Warner, *Lasting Leadership: What You Can Learn from the Top 25 Business People of Our Times* (Upper Saddle River, NJ: Wharton School, 2005), xv.
256. The discussions of Lee Iacocca are silent on his devaluation of safety concerns. Pandya et al., *Lasting Leadership*.

## Chapter 4

1. Tax Gap for Tax Year 2006, Internal Revenue Service (2006), https://www.irs.gov/pub/newsroom/overview_tax_gap_2006.pdf. For higher estimates, see Edgar L. Feige and Richard Cebula, *America's Underground Economy: Measuring the Size, Growth and Determinants of Income Tax Evasion in the U.S.* (Madison: University of Wisconsin-Madison, January 2011).
2. Alex Raskolnikov, "Crime and Punishment in Taxation: Deceit, Deterrence, and the Self-Adjusting Penalty," *Columbia Law Review* 106 (2006):569, 574.
3. Daniel S. Goldberg, *The Death of the Income Tax: A Progressive Consumption Tax and the Path to Fiscal Reform* (New York: Oxford University Press, 2013), 112.
4. Tax Gap, State of California Franchise Tax Board, (2006), https://www.ftb.ca.gov/Tax_Gap/index.shtml.
5. Stuart P. Green, *Lying, Cheating and Stealing: A Moral Theory of White-Collar Crime* (New York: Oxford University Press, 2007).
6. Joshua D. Rosenberg, "The Psychology of Taxes: Why They Drive Us Crazy and How We Can Make Them Sane," *Virginia Tax Review* 16 (1996):157, 191.
7. Green, *Lying, Cheating and Stealing*, 245.
8. Amy Feldman and Joan Caplin, "Should You Cheat on Your Taxes?," *Money*, April 2001.
9. Donald L. Barlett and James B. Steele, *The Great American Tax Dodge: How Spiraling Fraud and Avoidance Are Killing Fairness, Destroying the Income Tax, and Costing You* (Boston: Little, Brown, 2000), 21.
10. Feldman and Caplin, "Should You Cheat on Your Taxes?."
11. Barlett and Steele, *Great American Tax Dodge*, 47–48.
12. James Fanelli, "Manhattan Strip Club Claimed Dancers are Like Sex Therapists to Dodge $3.1M in State Taxes," *New York Daily News*, May 12, 2017.
13. Nick Penzenstadler and David McKay Wilson, "More Than 100 Lawsuits, Disputes Over Taxes Tied to Trump and His Companies," *USA Today*, May 19, 2016.
14. Penzenstadler and Wilson, "More Than 100 Lawsuits." For one of those cases imposing a 35 percent penalty, see David Cay Johnston, *The Making of Donald Trump* (Brooklyn, NY: Melville House, 2016), 103.

15. Jon Swaine, "How Trump's $50m Golf Club Became $1.4m When It Came Time to Pay Tax," *The Guardian,* March 12, 2016; Penzenstadler and Wilson, "More Than 100 Lawsuits." For a similar case involving a Los Angeles club that Trump claimed was worth $50 million in his federal disclosure forms and $10 million in his property tax dispute, see Johnston, *The Making of Donald Trump,* 99.
16. Susan Cleary Morse, Stewart Karlinsky, and Joseph Bankman, "Cash Businesses and Tax Evasion," *Stanford Law and Policy Review* 20 (2009):37, 59, 62.
17. T.R. Reid, *A Fine Mess: A Global Quest for a Simpler, Fairer, and More Efficient Tax System* (New York: Penguin, 2017),198–201; Steven Erlander, Stephen Castle and Rick Gladstone, "Airing of Hidden Wealth, Stirs Inquiries and Rage," *New York Times,* April 6, 2016.
18. Barlett and Steele, *Great American Tax Dodge,* 83.
19. Laura Saunders, "Inside Swiss Banks' Tax Cheating Machinery," *Wall Street Journal,* October 22, 2015.
20. Joel Slemrod and Jon Bakija, *Taxing Ourselves: A Citizen's Guide to the Debate over Taxes* (Cambridge, MA: MIT Press, 2006), 175.
21. David Barstow, Mike McIntire, Patricia Cohen, Susanne Craig, and Russ Buettner, "Donald Trump Used Legally Dubious Method to Avoid Paying Taxes," *New York Times,* October 31, 2016; Max Ehrenfreund, "A Big Dirty Secret from Donald Trump's Tax Returns Has Been Exposed," *Washington Post,* November 1, 2016.
22. Ehrenfreund, "Big Dirty Secret" (quoting Donald Trump); Chris Kahn, "Trump Calls Tax Avoidance 'Smart,' Most Americans Call It 'Unpatriotic,' " Poll, Reuters, October 4, 2016, http://www.reuters.com/article/us-usa-election-poll-idUSKCN1242FH.
23. Kahn, "Trump Calls Tax Avoidance 'Smart.' "
24. David A. Fahrenthold, "Trump Foundation Admits to Violating Ban on 'Self-Dealing,' New Filing to IRS Shows," *Washington Post,* November 22, 2016; David Graham, "The Many Scandals of Donald Trump: A Cheat Sheet," *Atlantic,* November 22, 2016.
25. David A. Fahrenthold, "Trump Used $258,000 from His Charity to Settle Legal Problems," *Washington Post,* September 20, 2016; Graham, "Many Scandals;" Tim Mak and Andrew Desiderio, "Donald Trump Accused of Using His Charity as a Political Slush Fund," *The Daily Beast,* June 16, 2016, http://www.thedailybeast.com/articles/2016/06/16/donald-trump-accused-of-using-his-charity-as-a-political-slush-fund.
26. Graham, "Many Scandals," Mak and Desiderio, "Donald Trump Accused of Using His Charity."
27. David Johnston, "The New Presidency: Justice Dept. Designee; Clinton Not Fazed by Nominee's Hires," *New York Times,* January 15, 1993.
28. Clifford Krauss, "The New Presidency: Attorney-General Designate; A Top G.O.P. Senator Backs Nominee in a Storm," *New York Times,* January 16, 1993, A7.
29. Barlett and Steele, *Great American Tax Dodge,* 227 (quoting Senate Judiciary Committee Hearing).
30. Barlett and Steele, *Great American Tax Dodge,* 3.
31. Barlett and Steele, *Great American Tax Dodge,* 13.
32. Slemrod and Bakija, *Taxing Ourselves,* 178.
33. John S. Carroll, "How Taxpayers Think about Their Taxes: Frames and Values," in Joel Slemrod, ed., *Why People Pay Taxes: Tax Compliance and Enforcement* (Ann Arbor: University of Michigan Press, 1992), 43, 50.
34. Carroll, "How Taxpayers Think," 55.
35. Steven M. Sheffrin and Robert K. Triest, "Can Brute Deterrence Backfire? Perceptions and Attitudes in Taxpayer Compliance," in Slemrod, *Why People Pay Taxes,* 196.
36. Goldberg, *Death of the Income Tax,* 113.
37. Goldberg, *Death of the Income Tax,* 113.
38. Goldberg, *Death of the Income Tax,* 113.
39. Goldberg, *Death of the Income Tax,* 113.

40. Internal Revenue Service, IRS Releases New Tax Gap Estimates; Compliance Rates Remain Statistically Unchanged from Previous Study (January 6, 2012).
41. Goldberg, *Death of the Income Tax*, 117.
42. Goldberg, *Death of the Income Tax*, 117.
43. Goldberg, *Death of the Income Tax*, 116–117.
44. Goldberg, *Death of the Income Tax*, 117.
45. Tax Reform: A Century Foundation Guide to the Issues (New York: Century Foundation Press, 1999).
46. Internal Revenue Service, Federal Tax Compliance Research: Individual Income Tax Gap Estimates for 1985, 1988, and 1992 (April 1996), https://www.irs.gov/pub/irs-soi/p141596.pdf.
47. Internal Revenue Service, Reducing the Federal Tax Gap: A Report on Improving Voluntary Compliance (August 2, 2007), 11.
48. Slemrod and Bakija, *Taxing Ourselves*, 179.
49. Joel Slemrod, "Small Business and the Tax System," in Henry J. Aaron and Joel Slemrod, eds., *The Crisis in Tax Administration* (Washington, DC: Brookings, 2004), S69, 71–72.
50. Slemrod and Bakija, *Taxing Ourselves*, 178.
51. Michael Doran, "Tax Penalties and Tax Compliance," *Harvard Journal on Legislation* 46 (2009):111–112.
52. Doran, "Tax Penalties," 111–112.
53. Carroll, "How Taxpayers Think," 46.
54. Raskolnikov, "Crime and Punishment," 571.
55. Slemrod and Bajika, *Taxing Ourselves*, 180; Raskolnikov, "Crime and Punishment," 584.
56. Goldberg, *Death of the Income Tax*, 117.
57. Slemrod and Bakija, *Taxing Ourselves*, 185.
58. Doran, "Tax Penalties," 127.
59. Barlett and Steele, *Great American Tax Dodge*, 47.
60. Eugene Soltes, *Why They Do It: Inside the Mind of the White-Collar Criminal* (New York: Public Affairs, 2016), 90.
61. Soltes, *Why They Do It*, 361
62. Doran, "Tax Penalties," 117.
63. Doran, "Tax Penalties," 117.
64. Suzanne Woolley, "2015 Is the Best Year Yet to Cheat on Your Taxes: Budget Cuts at the IRS Mean Longer Phone Waits—and Fewer Audits," *Bloomberg Business*, January 15, 2015.
65. Gary S. Becker, "Crime and Punishment: An Economic Approach," *Journal of Political Economy* 76 (1968):169.
66. Doran, "Tax Penalties," 112.
67. Michael Wenzel, "Motivation or Rationalization? Causal Relations between Ethics, Norms, and Tax Compliance," *Journal of Economic Psychology* 46 (2005):491, 504–505.
68. Doran, "Tax Penalties," 112; Eric A. Posner, "The Legal Construction of Norms: Law and Social Norms: The Case of Tax Compliance," *Virginia Law Review* 86 (2000):1791.
69. Slemrod and Bakija, *Taxing Ourselves*, 3.
70. Reid, *A Fine Mess*, 6, 215; Slemrod and Bakija, *Taxing Ourselves*, 3.
71. Slemrod and Bakija, *Taxing Ourselves*, 4; Reid, *A Fine Mess*, 6.
72. IRS Form 1041, quoted in Reid, *A Fine Mess, 216.*
73. Reid, *A Fine Mess*, 217.
74. Slemrod and Bakija, *Taxing Ourselves*, 159.
75. Slemrod and Bakija, *Taxing Ourselves*, 159.
76. Slemrod and Bakija, *Taxing Ourselves*, 187.
77. Reid, *A Fine Mess*, 218; Joel Slemrod, "Cheating Ourselves: The Economics of Tax Evasion," *Journal of Economic Perspectives* 21 (2007):25, 40.
78. Barlett and Steele, *Great American Tax Dodge*, 24.
79. Chris Isidore, "Buffett Says He's Still Paying Lower Tax Rate than His Secretary," *CNN Money*, March 4, 2013, http://money.cnn.com/2013/03/04/news/economy/buffett-secretary-taxes/.

80. Kent W. Smith, "Reciprocity and Fairness: Positive Incentives for Tax Compliance," in Slemrod, *Why People Pay Taxes*, 226–227; Tom R. Tyler, *Why People Obey the Law* (Princeton, NJ: Princeton University Press, 1990).
81. Carroll, "How Taxpayers Think," 47.
82. Karyl Kinsey, "Deterrence and Alienation Effects of IRS Enforcement: An Analysis of Survey Data," in Slemrod, *Why People Pay Taxes*, 281.
83. Carroll, "How Taxpayers Think," 47; Posner, "Law and Social Norms," 1783.
84. Alan Wolfe, *Moral Freedom: The Impossible Idea That Defines the Way We Live Now* (New York: W.W. Norton, 2001), 107.
85. Sheffrin and Triest, "Can Brute Deterrence Backfire?," 203; Posner, "Law and Social Norms," 1784.
86. Smith, "Reciprocity and Fairness," 233–235; Posner, "Law and Social Norms," 1784.
87. http://i2.cdn.turner.com/cnn/2014/images/01/06/cnn.orc.poll.marijuana.pdf.
88. American Enterprise Institute for Public Policy Research, Public Opinion on Taxes: 1937 to Today (April 2014), 124; http://www.pewsocialtrends.org/2006/03/28/a-barometer-of-modern-morals/. According to the General Social Survey, over 80 percent said that it was wrong to cheat on taxes. IRA Oversight Board Annual Report (Washington, DC: Internal Revenue Service, 2002), 13.
89. American Enterprise Institute, Public Opinion on Taxes, 127.
90. National Public Radio/Kaiser Family Foundation, Kennedy School of Government, National Survey of Americans' Views on Taxes (April 2003), 7.
91. Reid, *A Fine Mess*, 13; CBS News Poll, April 14, 2017, http:www.cbsnews.com/news/poll-do-americans-think-their-tax-system-is-fair/. See also Pew Research Center, *Beyond Distrust: How Americans View Their Government* (Pew Research Center, November 2015), 116 (finding that 40 percent of Americans think that they pay more than their fair share).
92. American Enterprise Institute, Public Opinion on Taxes, 8.
93. American Enterprise Institute, Public Opinion on Taxes, 26–27.
94. American Enterprise Institute, Public Opinion on Taxes, 28.
95. American Enterprise Institute, Public Opinion on Taxes, 127.
96. American Enterprise Institute, Public Opinion on Taxes, 128.
97. David Callahan, *The Cheating Culture: Why More Americans Are Doing Wrong to Get Ahead* (New York: Mariner, 2004), 176–177.
98. Callahan, *Cheating Culture*, 177.
99. Callahan, *Cheating Culture*, 177.
100. Callahan, *Cheating Culture*, 252.
101. James Alm, Betty R. Jackson, and Michael McKee, "Deterrence and Beyond: Toward a Kinder, Gentler IRS," in Slemrod, *Why People Pay Taxes*, 325.
102. Joel Slemrod, Marsha Blumenthal, and Charles Christian, "Taxpayer Response to an Increased Probability of Audit: Evidence from a Controlled Experiment in Minnesota," *Journal of Public Economics* 79 (2001):455.
103. Jeffrey A. Dubin, "Criminal Investigation Enforcement Activities and Taxpayer Noncompliance," *Public Finance Review* 35 (2007):500, 523.
104. Reid, *A Fine Mess*, 214.
105. Joseph Bankman, "Eight Truths about Collecting Taxes from the Cash Economy," *Tax Notes* 117 (2007):506.
106. Slemrod and Bakija, *Taxing Ourselves*, 187.
107. Sheffrin and Triest, "Can Brute Deterrence Backfire?," 214.
108. Doran, "Tax Penalties," 133. However, experimental research suggests that such efforts may have only a minor effect on tax compliance. Marsha Blumenthal, Charles Christian, and Joel Slemrod, "Do Normative Appeals Affect Tax Compliance? Evidence from a Controlled Experiment in Minnesota," *National Tax Journal* 54 (2001):125.
109. Morse et al., "Cash Businesses and Tax Evasion," 62.
110. 22 U.S.C. § 2694(a)(2)(A) (2005). *See* J. Timothy J. Philipps et al., "What Part of RPOS Don't You Understand? An Update and Survey of Standards for Tax Return Positions,"

*Washington and Lee Law Review* 51 (1994):1163–1164. For shelters and reportable transactions, a transaction is subject to penalties unless "it is reasonable to believe that the position would be more likely than not be sustained on its merits." 26 U.S.C. § 6694 (a)(2)(B) (2015). No violation occurs if the position is disclosed and is not frivolous.

111. Doran, "Tax Penalties," 154.
112. Doran, "Tax Penalties," 154.
113. Doran, "Tax Penalties," 158.
114. Morse et al., "Cash Businesses and Tax Evasion," 56; Dennis J. Ventry Jr., "Whistleblowers and Qui Tam for Tax," *Tax Lawyer* 61 (2008):357.
115. Rosenberg, "Psychology of Taxes," 208.
116. United States Department of Justice, Fraud Statistics—Overview, October 1. 1987–September 30, 2015, https://www.justice.gov/opa/file/796866/download.
117. Raskolnikov, "Crime and Punishment," 571.
118. Raskolnikov, "Crime and Punishment," 571.
119. Doran, "Tax Penalties," 126.
120. Kevin McCoy, "Bank Leumi to Pay $400M in Tax Evasion Cases," *USA Today*, December 23, 2014.
121. McCoy, "Bank Leumi to Pay $400M."
122. Joel Slemrod, "Why People Pay Taxes," Introduction, in Slemrod, *Why People Pay Taxes*, 7.
123. Slemrod, "Why People Pay Taxes," 7.
124. Benno Torgler, "What Do We Know about Tax Fraud?: An Overview of Recent Developments," *Social Research* 75 (2008):1239, 1253.
125. Rosenberg, "Psychology of Taxes," 182.
126. Reid, *A Fine Mess*, 30.
127. Blumenthal et al., "Do Normative Appeals Affect Tax Compliance?," 131.
128. Ricardo Perez-Truglia and Ugo Troiana, "Shaming Those Who Skip Out on Taxes," *New York Times*, April 15, 2015.
129. Perez-Truglia and Troiana, "Shaming."
130. Perez-Truglia and Troiana, "Shaming."
131. Alex Raskolnikov, "Revealing Choices: Using Taxpayer Choice to Target Tax Enforcement," *Columbia Law Review* 1009 (2009):689, 691.
132. Raskolnikov, "Revealing Choices," 691.
133. Raskolnikov, "Revealing Choices," 691.
134. Raskolnikov, "Revealing Choices," 691.
135. Raskolnikov, "Revealing Choices," 691.
136. Joseph Bankman, Clifford Nass, and Joel Slemrod, Using the "Smart Return" to Reduce Tax Evasion, Stanford Public Law Working Paper No. 2578432 (March 14, 2015).
137. Bankman et al., Using the "Smart Return," 5.
138. Bankman et al., Using the "Smart Return," 5.
139. Bankman et al., Using the "Smart Return," 9.
140. Bankman et al., Using the "Smart Return," 6.
141. Bankman et al., Using the "Smart Return," 7.
142. *See* Chapter 1 and Lisa L. Shu et al., Signing at the Beginning Makes Ethics Salient and Decreases Dishonest Self-Reports in Comparison to Signing at the End, Proceedings of the National Academy of Sciences of the USA (August 27, 2012), http://www.pnas.org/content/early/2012/08/22/1209746109.full.pdf.
143. Christopher J. Bryan, Gabrielle S. Adams, and Benoît Monin, "When Cheating Would Make You a Cheater: Implicating the Self Prevents Unethical Behavior," *Journal of Experimental Psychology* (2013):1001.
144. Bankman, Nass, and Slemrod, Using the "Smart Return," 13.
145. Slemrod and Bakija, *Taxing Ourselves*, 308.
146. Slemrod and Bakija, *Taxing Ourselves*, 294.
147. Reid, *A Fine Mess*, 89; Steven Inskeep, "'Fine Mess': You Can Learn a Lot About a Country By Its Taxes," NPR, April 3, 2017, http://www.npr.org/templates/transcript/transcript.

php?storyId=522424621. When mortgage interest deductions are combined with property tax exemptions, four-fifths of the benefits go to households earning over $100,000. Matthew Desmond, “House Rules,” *New York Times Magazine*, May 14, 2017, 53.

148. Reid, *A Fine Mess*, 89-90; Inskeep, “ ‘Fine Mess.’ ”
149. Reid, *A Fine Mess*, 86.
150. Barlett and Steele, *Great American Tax Dodge*, 262–263.
151. Bankman, “Eight Truths.”
152. Reid, *A Fine Mess*, 221.
153. Reid, *A Fine Mess*, 220.
154. Reid, *A Fine Mess*, 223.
155. Reid, *A Fine Mess*, 251 (quoting Bill Bradley).
156. Barlett and Steele, *Great American Tax Dodge*, 262–263.
157. Slemrod and Bakija, *Taxing Ourselves*, 8.
158. Slemrod and Bakija, *Taxing Ourselves*, 9–10.
159. Slemrod and Bakija, *Taxing Ourselves*, 9; Reid, *A Fine Mess*, 97–100, 253.
160. Lane Kenworthy, “Taxes, The Good Society,” July 2016, https://lanekenworthy.net/taxes/.
161. Kenworthy, “Taxes; ” Reid, *A Fine Mess*, 237.
162. Goldberg, *Death of the Income Tax*, 199–255.
163. Alex Morash, “Media Response to Latest Analysis of Trump Tax Plan: It ‘Screws the Middle Class,’ ” *Media Matters*, September 21, 2016, https://www.mediamatters.org/research/2016/09/21/media-response-latest-analysis-trump-s-tax-plan-it-screws-middle-class/213233; Neil Irwin, “Winners and Losers in the Trump Tax Plan,” *New York Times*, April 26, 2017.
164. Katy O’Donnell, “Republicans Face Headwinds among Trump Voters over Corporate Tax Cuts,” *Politico*, January 16, 2017, http://www.politico.com/story/2017/01/trump-taxes-poll-republicans-233656.
165. Gallup, “Americans Say Upper Income Pay Too Little in Taxes,” March 17, 2016, http://www.gallup.com/poll/190775/americans-say-upper-income-pay-little-taxes.aspx.
166. Irwin, “Winners and Losers.”
167. Irwin, “Winners and Losers;” Neil Irwin, "Under the Trump Tax Plan, We Might All Want to Become Corporations," *New York Times*, April 28, 2017.
168. Gil B. Manzon, Jr. and Tim Gray, “How Trump’s Tax Proposal Could Weaken Faith in the System’s Fairness,” *Business Insider*, May 1, 2017; Irwin, “Under the Trump Plan.”
169. NPR/Kaiser Family Foundation/Kennedy School of Government, National Survey of Americans’ Views on Taxes (April 2003), 2; American Enterprise Institute, Public Opinion on Taxes, 117.
170. American Enterprise Institute, Public Opinion on Taxes, 119.
171. Slemrod and Bakija, *Taxing Ourselves*, 3.

## *Chapter 5*

1. Susan D. Blum, *My Word!: Plagiarism and the College Culture* (Ithaca, NY: Cornell University Press, 2009), 22; Hoi K. Suen and Lan Yu, “Chronic Consequences of High Stakes Testing? Lessons from the Chinese Civil Service Exam,” *Comparative Education Review* 50 (2006):46, 50.
2. Blum, *My Word!*, 22; Ichisada Miyazaki, *China’s Examination Hell: The Civil Service Examinations of Imperial China*, translated by Conrad Schirokaauer (New Haven, CT: Yale University Press, 1981).
3. Scott McLemee, “What Is Plagiarism,” *The Chronicle of Higher Education*, December 17, 2004; Richard A. Posner, *The Little Book of Plagiarism* (New York: Pantheon, 2007), 50. For an account of the evolution of Western attitudes toward plagiarism, see Thomas Mallon, *Stolen Words: Forays into the Origins and Ravages of Plagiarism* (New York: Ticknor and Fields, 1989), 1–40.
4. Posner, *Little Book of Plagiarism*, 51.

5. "For War on Yale Cheating. Daily News Charges Faculty with Lack of Vigilance," *New York Times*, January 24, 1931, 2.
6. Robert Cooley Angell, *The Campus, a Study of Contemporary Undergraduate Life in the American University* (New York: D. Appleton & Company, 1928), 44.
7. Tricia Bertram Gallant, *Academic Integrity in the 21st Century: A Teaching and Learning Imperative*, ASHE Higher Education Report 33 (San Francisco: Jossey-Bass, 2008), 21.
8. Gregory J. Cizek, *Cheating on Tests: How to Do It, Detect It, and Prevent It* (Mahwah NJ: Lawrence Erlbaum, 1999), 44–46.
9. James M. Lang, *Cheating Lessons: Learning from Academic Dishonesty* (Cambridge, MA: Harvard University Press, 2013), 29. For examples, see Dale Mezzacappa, "Cheating Case Implicates Phila. Educators," *Education Week*, January 28, 2014; Richard Fausset, "Trial Opens in Atlanta School Cheating Scandal," *New York Times*, September 29, 2014.
10. Sharon L. Nichols and David C. Berliner, "The Pressure to Cheat in a High-Stakes Testing Environment," in Eric Anderman and Tamera B. Murdock, eds., *Psychology of Academic Cheating* (Burlington, MA: Elsevier Academic Press, 2007), 296–297.
11. Alan Blinder, "Atlanta Educators Convicted in School Cheating Scandal," *New York Times*, April 1, 2015.
12. Dan Berrett, "Harvard Cheating Scandal Points Out the Ambiguities of Collaboration," *The Chronicle of Higher Education*, September 5, 2012, 7.
13. Al Baker, "At Top School, Cheating Voids 70 Pupils' Tests," *New York Times*, July 9, 2012.
14. Jenny Anderson and Winnie Hu, "20 Students Now Accused in L.I. Case on Cheating," *New York Times*, November 22, 2011.
15. Dorothy L.R. Jones, "Academic Dishonesty: Are More Students Cheating?," *Business Communication Quarterly* 74 (2011):141–142.
16. Charlie Osborne, "How Do Students Use Tech to Cheat?," *ZDNet*, February 17, 2012, http://www.zdnet.com/article/how-do-students-use-tech-to-cheat/.
17. Gallant, *Academic Integrity*, 26.
18. Ed Dante, "The Shadow Scholar," *The Chronicle of Higher Education*, November 12, 2010. *See* Dave Tomar, *The Shadow Scholar: How I Made a Living Helping College Kids Cheat* (New York: Bloomsbury, 2012).
19. Tomar, *Shadow Scholar*, 199.
20. Charles McGrath, "Term Paper Project, Part II," *New York Times*, September 17, 2006; Dan Ariely, *The (Honest) Truth about Dishonesty: How We Lie to Everyone, Especially Ourselves* (New York: HarperCollins, 2012), 211–213.
21. Ariely, *(Honest) Truth about Dishonesty*, 211–213.
22. Ariely, *(Honest) Truth about Dishonesty*, 211–213.
23. Donald L. McCabe, Kenneth D. Butterfield, and Linda K. Treviño, *Cheating in College: Why Students Do It and What Educators Can Do about It* (Baltimore, MD: Johns Hopkins University Press, 2012), 3.
24. Daniel Hart and Gustavo Carlo, "Moral Development in Adolescence," *Journal of Research on Adolescence* 15 (2005):223.
25. Gallant, *Academic Integrity*, 3; Donald L. McCabe and Linda Klebe Treviño, "Individual and Contextual Influences on Academic Dishonesty: A Multicampus Investigation," *Research in Higher Education* 38 (1997):379.
26. Bernard E. Whitley Jr., "Factors Associated with Cheating among College Students: A Review," *Research in Higher Education* 39 (1998):235, 238.
27. Vivian Yee, "Stuyvesant Students Describe the How and the Why of Cheating," *New York Times*, September 25, 2012.
28. Jennifer Yardley, Melanie M. Domenech Rodríguez, Scott C. Bates, and Jonathan Nelson, "True Confessions?: Alumni's Retrospective Reports on Undergraduate Cheating Behaviors," *Ethics & Behavior* 19 (2009):1.

29. McCabe et al., *Cheating in College*, 149–150 (39 percent graduate students and 30 percent law students); Katherine Mangan, "Survey Finds Widespread Cheating in M.B.A. Programs," *Chronicle of Higher Education*, September 19, 2006 (47 percent graduate students and 56 percent business school students).
30. Daniel E. Martin, Asha Rao, and Lloyd R. Sloan, "Plagiarism, Integrity and Workplace Deviance: A Criterion Study," *Ethics & Behavior* 19 (2009):36.
31. Jeffrey L. Seglin, "The Right Thing; Lies Can Have a (Long) Life of Their Own," *New York Times*, June 16, 2002, 3.
32. William M. Chace, "A Question of Honor," *American Scholar*, March 1, 2012, 20, 24.
33. Margaret P. Jendrek, "Faculty Reactions to Academic Dishonesty," *Journal of College Student Development* 30 (1989):401, 404–405.
34. McCabe et al., *Cheating in College*, 60.
35. Robert T. Burns, Kim Marie McGoldrick, and Peter W. Schuhmann, "Self-Reports of Student Cheating: Does a Definition of Cheating Matter?," *Journal of Economic Education* 38 (2007):3.
36. Anderman and Murdock, *Psychology of Academic Cheating*, 13.
37. Josephson Institute of Ethics, *The Ethics of American Youth* (Los Angeles: Josephson Institute of Ethics, 2012), 11, 24–25.
38. McCabe et al., *Cheating in College*, 24–25.
39. McCabe et al., *Cheating in College*, 24–25.
40. Patricia A. Hutton, "Understanding Student Cheating and What Educators Can Do about It," *College Teaching* 54 (2006):171.
41. Leonard Pitts Jr., "Cheating Is Almost Not Wrong," *Southern Illinoisan*, December 15, 2004.
42. Maria Fátima Rocha and Aurora A.C. Teixeira, A Cross-Country Evaluation of Cheating in Academia: Is It Related to 'Real World' Business Ethics? (Working Paper 112, Faculdade de Economia: Universidade do Porto, 2006).
43. Stephen F. Davis, Patrick F. Drinan, and Tricia Bertram Gallant, *Cheating in School: What We Know and What We Can Do* (Malden, MA: Wiley-Blackwell, 2009), 45.
44. Richard A. Bernardi, Caitlin A. Banzhoff, Abigail M. Martino, and Katelyn J. Svasta, "Challenges to Academic Integrity: Identifying the Factors Associated with the Cheating Chain," *Accounting Education: An International Journal* 21 (2012):247, 249.
45. Rama Lakshmi, "These Indian Parents Climbed a School Wall to Help Their Kids Cheat on an Exam," *Washington Post*, March 19, 2015.
46. Gallant, *Academic Integrity* 51; Davis et al., *Cheating in School*, 78. Angela D. Miller, Tamera B. Murcock, Eric M. Anderman, and Amy L. Poindexter, "Who Are All These Cheaters? Characteristics of Academically Dishonest Students," in Anderman and Murdoch, *Psychology of Academic Cheating*, 17; Tamera B. Murdock and Jason M. Stephens, "Is Cheating Wrong? Students Reasoning about Academic Dishonesty," in Anderman and Murdock, *Psychology of Academic Cheating*, 230; Chris Park, "In Other (People's) Words: Plagiarism by University Students—Literature and Lessons," *Assessment & Evaluation in Higher Education* 28 (2003):471.
47. Pamela Burton, Honesty and Dishonesty, in Tom Lickona, ed., *Moral Development and Behavior: Theory, Research and Social Issues* (Dumfries, NC: Holt McDougal, 1976), 173, 176. Walter Mischel, *Personality and Assessment* (Mahwah, NJ: Lawrence Erlbaum, 1968); Walter Mischel and Yuichi Shoda, "A Cognitive-Affective System Theory of Personality: Reconceptualizing Situations, Dispositions, Dynamics, and Invariance in Personality Structure," *Psychological Review* 102 (1995):246.
48. Murdock and Stephens, "Is Cheating Wrong?," 232.
49. Cizek, *Cheating on Tests*, 100, 103.
50. Donald L. McCabe, Linda Klebe Treviño, and Kenneth D. Butterfield, "Cheating in Academic Institutions: A Decade of Research," *Ethics & Behavior* 11 (2001):219, 227–228. Anderman and Murdock, *Psychology of Academic Cheating*, 11.

51. Bernard E. Whitley Jr., Amanda B. Nelson, and Curtis J. Jones, "Gender Differences in Cheating Attitudes and Classroom Cheating Behavior: A Meta-analysis," *Sex Roles* 41 (1999):657.
52. McCabe et al., *Cheating in College*, 74.
53. Cizek, *Cheating on Tests*, 94–95; McCabe et al., *Cheating in College*, 83–84. *See* Hutton, "Understanding Student Cheating," 172 (summarizing studies); Deborah F. Crown and M. Shane Spiller, "Learning from the Literature on Collegiate Cheating: A Review of Empirical Research," *Journal of Business Ethics* 17 (1998):683; Joe Kerkvliet and Charles L. Sigmund, "Can We Control Cheating in the Classroom?," *Journal of Economic Education* 30 (1999):331–343; Kelly Honz, Kenneth A. Kiewra, and Ya-Shu Yang, "Cheating Perceptions and Prevalence across Academic Settings," *Mid-Western Educational Researcher* 23 (2010):10.
54. Richard Pérez Peña, "Studies Find More Students Cheating, With High Achievers No Exception," *New York Times*, September 7, 2012 (quoting Donald McCabe).
55. McCabe et al., *Cheating in College*, 84–86; Anderman and Murdock, *Psychology of Cheating*, 17, 211.
56. Tamera B. Murdock and Eric M. Anderman, "Motivational Perspectives on Student Cheating: Toward an Integrated Model of Academic Dishonesty," *Educational Psychologist* 41 (2006):129, 131; Whitely, "Factors Associated with Cheating," 235, 244; Alfie Kohn, "Who's Cheating Whom?," *Education Digest*, 73 (2008):6; Jeanette A. Davy, Joel F. Kincaid, Kenneth J. Smith, and Michelle A. Trawick, "An Examination of the Role of Attitudinal Characteristics and Motivation on the Cheating Behavior of Business Students," *Ethics and Behavior* 17 (2007):281, 298; Lang, *Cheating Lessons*, 39–41; Breanna Carey Ferolla, "Motivation and Its Effects on Cheating," *Applied Social Psychology*, October 30, 2012.
57. Whitely, "Factors Associated with Cheating," 250.
58. McCabe and Treviño, "Individual and Contextual Influences on Academic Dishonesty, 379;" Murdock and Anderman, "Motivational Perspectives on Student Cheating," 137; McCabe et al., "Cheating in Academic Institutions," 223; David A. Rettinger and Yair Kramer, "Situational and Personal Causes of Student Cheating," *Research on Higher Education* 50 (2009):293, 295–296; Lang, *Cheating Lessons*, 51.
59. Cizek, *Cheating on Tests*, 123.
60. Mollie K. Galloway, "Cheating in Advantaged High Schools: Prevalence, Justifications, and Possibilities for Change," *Ethics & Behavior* 22 (2012):378, 393.
61. Alejandro Zambra, "Reading Comprehension: Text No. 1," *New Yorker*, July 6, 2015.
62. Murdock and Anderman, "Motivational Perspectives on Student Cheating," 135, 137; Lynley H. Anderman, Tierra M. Freeman, and Christian E. Mueller, "The 'Social' Side of Social Context: Interpersonal and Affiliative Dimensions of Students' Experiences and Academic Dishonesty," in Anderman and Murdock, *Psychology of Academic Cheating*, 206–207.
63. Hutton, "Understanding Student Cheating," 172. *See also* Kohn, "Who's Cheating Whom?," 5; Lang, *Cheating Lessons*, 46; Jonathan Zimmerman, "Harvard Cheating Scandal? It Could Be Bad Teaching," *Christian Science Monitor*, September 13, 2012.
64. Carolyn Kleiner and Mary Lord, "The Cheating Game," *U.S. News and World Report*, November 22, 1999.
65. Davis et al., *Cheating in School*, 69; Whitely, "Factors Associated with Cheating," 253.
66. Carol M. Megehee and Deborah F. Spake, "The Impact of Perceived Peer Behavior, Probable Detection and Punishment Severity on Student Cheating Behavior," *Marketing Education Review* 18 (2008):5.
67. Galloway, "Cheating in Advantaged High Schools," 378; Arthur Levine and Diane R. Dean, *Generation on a Tightrope: A Portrait of Today's College Student* (San Francisco, Jossey-Bass, 2012); Karen E. Ablard and Wayne D. Parker, "Parents' Achievement Goals and Perfectionism in Their Academically Talented Children," *Journal of Youth and Adolescence* 26 (2007):651; Denise Clark Pope, *Doing School: How We Are Creating a Generation of*

*Stressed-Out, Materialistic, and Miseducated Students* (New Haven, CT: Yale University Press, 2001).

68. Murdock and Anderman, "Motivational Perspectives on Student Cheating," 137; Whitely, "Factors Associated with Cheating," 245; Rettinger and Kramer, "Situational and Personal Causes of Student Cheating," 295; Donald L. McCabe, "The Influence of Situational Ethics on Cheating among College Students," *Sociological Inquiry* 62 (1992):365; Murdock and Stephens, "Is Cheating Wrong?," in Anderman and Murdock, *Psychology of Academic Cheating*, 234–235.
69. Whitley, "Factors Associated With Cheating," 253; David Rettinger, "Applying Decision Theory to Academic Integrity Decisions," in Anderman and Murdock, *Psychology of Academic Cheating*, 165; Robert T. Burrus Jr., Adam T. Jones, Bill Sackley, and Mike Walker, "It's the Students, Stupid: How Perceptions of Student Reporting Impact Cheating," *American Economist* 58 (2013):51–52; Randall E. LaSalle, "The Perception of Detection, Severity of Punishment and the Probability of Cheating," *Journal of Forensic Studies in Accounting and Business* 1 (2009):93.
70. Davis et al., *Cheating in School*, 115. For an estimate of 2 percent, see Hutton, "Understanding Student Cheating," 171.
71. Murdock and Anderman, "Motivational Perspectives on Student Cheating," 136; Megehee and Spake, "Impact of Perceived Peer Behavior," 5; Stephanie Etter, Jackie J. Cramer, and Seth Finn, "Origins of Academic Dishonesty: Ethical Orientations and Personality Factors Associated with Attitudes about Cheating with Information Technology," *Journal of Research on Technology in Education* (2006):133–134; Whitely, "Factors Associated with Cheating," 251.
72. McCabe et al., "Cheating in Academic Institutions," 224.
73. For perceptions of risk, see Murdock and Anderman, "Motivational Perspectives on Student Cheating," 136. For the reminder, see Ariely, *(Honest) Truth about Dishonesty*.
74. Whitely, "Factors Associated with Cheating," 261.
75. Cizek, *Cheating on Tests*, 188.
76. Davis et al., *Cheating in School*, 65, 195.
77. Craig L. Scanlan, "Strategies to Promote a Climate of Academic Integrity and Minimize Student Cheating and Plagiarism," *Journal of Allied Health* 35 (2006):179–185.
78. Donald L. McCabe and Linda Klebe Treviño, "Academic Dishonesty: Honor Codes and Other Contextual Influences," *Journal of Higher Education* 64 (1993):522, 530.
79. James Bowman, *Honor: A History* (New York: Encounter Books, 2006), 5.
80. Lang, *Cheating Lessons*, 169; Donald L. McCabe, Linda Klebe Treviño, and Kenneth D. Butterfield, "Academic Integrity in Honor Code and Non-honor Code Environments: A Qualitative Investigation," *Journal of Higher Education* 70 (1999):223, 228.
81. Margaret P. Jendrek, "Students' Reactions to Academic Dishonesty," *Journal of College Student Development* 33 (1992):260, 262, 264.
82. Blum, *My Word!*, 154.
83. Blum, *My Word!*, 156.
84. Blum, *My Word!*, 157.
85. Donald L. McCabe and Gary Pavela, "Some Good News about Academic Integrity," *Change* (September/October, 2000):38.
86. McCabe et al., *Cheating in College*, 180.
87. Cizek, *Cheating on Tests*, 173.
88. Margaret P. Jendrek, "Faculty Reactions to Academic Dishonesty," *Journal of College Student Development* 30 (1989):401, 404–405.
89. McCabe et al., *Cheating in College*, 134–135; Donald L. McCabe, "Cheating among College and University Students: A North American Perspective," *International Journal for Educational Integrity* 1 (2005).
90. McCabe et al., *Cheating in College*, 134–35.
91. McCabe, "Cheating among College and University Students."
92. McCabe et al., *Cheating in College*, 138.

93. McCabe et al., *Cheating in College*, 138–139.
94. McCabe et al., *Cheating in College*, 141.
95. Rettinger and Kramer, "Situational and Personal Causes of Student Cheating," 293.
96. Gallant, *Academic Integrity*, 6.
97. Whitely, "Factors Associated with Cheating," 262; McCabe et al., "Cheating in Academic Institutions," 229.
98. Anderman et al., The "Social" Side of Social Context, in Anderman and Murdock, *Psychology of Academic Cheating*, 209; Hutton, "Understanding Student Cheating," 175; Davis et al., *Cheating in School*, 197.
99. Delores Craig and Ellis D. Evans, "Teacher and Student Perceptions of Academic Cheating in Middle and Senior High Schools," *Journal of Educational Research* 834 (September/October 1990):22, 50.
100. R.M. Aaron, "Student Academic Dishonesty: Are Collegiate Institutions Addressing the Issue?," *NASPA Journal* 29 (1992):107.
101. Davis et al., *Cheating in School*, 201.
102. Davis et al., *Cheating in School*, 165–166.
103. Hutton, "Understanding Student Cheating," 175.
104. "Stanford Investigating Cheating Claims," March 28, 2015, *The Daily Beast*, http://www.thedailybeast.com/cheats/2015/03/28/stanford-investigates-cheating-claims.html.
105. Sally Cole and Donald L. McCabe, "Issues in Academic Integrity," in Wanda L. Mercer, ed., *Critical Issues in Judicial Affairs: Current Trends in Practice* (San Francisco: Jossey-Bass, 1996), 66–67.
106. Galloway, "Cheating in Advantaged High Schools," 389.
107. Julia Lawrence, "71 Stuyvesant Students Retake Regents after Cheating Scandal," *Education News*, July 12, 2012.
108. Murdock and Anderman, "Motivational Perspectives on Student Cheating," 142. For the need for harsh penalties, see McCabe et al., "Cheating in Academic Institutions," 229.
109. Lang, *Cheating Lessons*, 223 (quoting Dan Ariely).
110. Cizek, *Cheating on Tests*, 165.
111. Megehee and Spake, "Impact of Perceived Peer Behavior," 17.
112. Charlie Osborne, "Anti-plagiarism Software Used by US Universities on the Rise," *Zdnet*, February 3, 2012, http://www.zdnet.com/article/anti-plagiarism-software-used-by-us-universities-on-the-rise/.
113. John M. Braxton, Eve M. Proper, and Alan E. Bayer, *Professors Behaving Badly: Faculty Misconduct in Graduate Education* (Baltimore, MD: Johns Hopkins University Press, 2011), 12.
114. Daniel Engber, "Ask Us Anything: How Common Is Scientific Fraud?," *Popular Science*, March 30, 2015.
115. Sharon Begley, "Science Journal Retracts Gay-Marriage Study after Evidence of Fraud," *Reuters*, May 28, 2015.
116. Gallant, *Academic Integrity*.
117. Stacey Stowe, "Research Lab Falsified Tests on Toxins," Reports Say, *New York Times*, September 6, 2003.
118. Karen Thomas, "Rise in Cheating Called Response to Fall in Values," *USA Today*, August 2, 1995, 1A.
119. Lawrence J. Rhoades, "New Institutional Research Misconduct Activity: 1992–2001" (2004), 11, https://ori.hhs.gov/images/ddblock/NewInstitutionalResearchMisconductActivity.pdf.
120. Adam Marcus and Ivan Oransky, "What's Behind Big Science Frauds?," *New York Times*, May 22, 2015.
121. Justin E. Bekelman et al., "Scope and Impact of Financial Conflicts of Interest in Biomedical Research: A Systematic Review," *Journal of American Medical Association* 289 (2003):454, 456.
122. Eric Lipton, "Food Industry Enlisted Academics in G.M.O. Lobbying War, Emails Show," *New York Times*, September 5, 2015.

123. For discussion of the need for such policies for legal academics, see Robin Feldman, Mark A. Lemley, Jonathan S. Masur, and Arti K. Rai, "Open Letter on Ethical Norms in Intellectual Property Scholarship," *Harvard Journal of Law & Technology* 29 (2016):339.
124. Posner, *Little Book of Plagiarism*, 9.
125. *See Oxford Dictionary of English* (Oxford: Oxford University Press, 2010); Stuart P. Green, "Plagiarism, Norms and the Limits of Theft Law: Some Observations on the Use of Criminal Sanctions in Enforcing Intellectual Property Rights," *Hastings Law Review* 54 (2002):167, 173.
126. Green, "Plagiarism, Norms, and the Limits of Theft Law," 173, 181.
127. Anthony Grafton, *The Footnote: A Curious History* (Cambridge, MA: Harvard University Press, 1997).
128. Stacey Patton, "My Advisor Stole My Research," *Chronicle of Higher Education*, November 11, 2012; Braxton et al., *Professors Behaving Badly*, 17–18.
129. Posner, *Little Book of Plagiarism*, 24–26.
130. Paul Basken, "U. of Pennsylvania Absolves Psychiatry Chairman of Ghostwriting Complaint," *Chronicle of Higher Education*, February 29, 2012.
131. *See* Green, "Plagiarism, Norms and the Limits of Theft Law," 190.
132. Lisa G. Lerman, "Misattribution in Legal Scholarship: Plagiarism, Ghostwriting, and Authorship," *South Texas Law Review* 42 (2001):467, 471.
133. Lerman, "Missattribution in Legal Scholarship," 475 (quoting MLA standard).
134. Lerman, "Missattribution in Legal Scholarship," 476.
135. Association of American Law Schools, Statement of Good Practices by Law Professors in the Discharge of Their Ethical and Professional Responsibilities, in 199 *Handbook* (1989):92.
136. Posner, *Little Book of Plagiarism*, 101–102.
137. Posner, *Little Book of Plagiarism*, 14–15.
138. Green, "Plagiarism, Norms, and the Limits of Theft Law," 196.
139. Sara Rimer, "When Plagiarism's Shadow Falls on Admired Scholars," *New York Times*, November 24, 2004; Noah Peters, "Punishing Plagiarizing Professors," *Cavalier Daily*, October 1, 2004; Joseph Bottum, "Laurence Tribe and the Problem of Borrowed Scholarship," *The Weekly Standard*, October 4, 2004.
140. Rimer, "When Plagiarism's Shadow Falls" (quoting Laurence Tribe).
141. Thomas Bartlett, "Harvard U. Says Law Professor's Borrowing of Sentences Was an 'Unintentional Lapse,' " *The Chronicle of Higher Education*, April 15, 2005.
142. Rimer, "When Plagiarism's Shadow Falls;" Peters, "Punishing Plagiarizing Professors."
143. Posner, *Little Book of Plagiarism*, 7.
144. Blum, *My Word!*, 16.
145. Posner, *Little Book of Plagiarism*, 93–94.
146. David Levering Lewis, "Failing to Know Martin Luther King, Jr.," *Journal of American History* 78 (1991):81; Clayborne Carson, "Editing Martin Luther King, Jr.: Political and Scholarly Issues," in George Bornstein and Ralph G. Williams, eds., *Palimpsest: Editorial Theory in the Humanities* (Ann Arbor: University of Michigan Press, 1993):305–316.
147. David Plotz, "The Plagiarist: Why Stephen Ambrose Is a Vampire," *Slate.com*, January 11, 2002, http://www.slate.com/id/2060618/.
148. Ron Grossman, "Petty Plagiarism Is Stain on U. of C.," *Chicago Tribune*, June 16, 1996, D3.
149. David D. Kirkpatrick, "As Historian's Fame Grows, So Do Questions on Methods," *New York Times*, January 11, 2002, (quoting Stephen Ambrose).
150. Kirkpatrick, "As Historian's Fame Grows" http://www.nytimes.com/2002/01/11/us/as-historian-s-fame-grows-so-do-questions-on-methods.html (quoting Stephen Ambrose).
151. "How the Ambrose Story Developed," *History News Network*, April, 2010, http://historynewsnetwork.org/article/504 (quoting Ambrose).
152. "The Top 6 Trump Administration Plagiarism Scandals (so Far)," *Plagiarism Today*, January 24, 2017, https://www.plagiarismtoday.com/2017/01/24/the-top-6-trump-administration-plagiarism-scandals.

153. Maggie Haberman, "After Plagiarism Reports, Monica Crowley Won't Take White House Job," *New York Times*, January 16, 2017; John Wagner, "Trump National Security Spokeswoman Monica Crowley to Forgo Post amid Plagiarism Charges," *Washington Post*, January 16, 2017.
154. Mike DeBonis and Emma Brown, "DeVos Questionnaire Appears to Include Passages from Uncited Sources," *Washington Post*, January 31, 2017.
155. "The Betsy Devos Plagiarism Scandal," *Plagiarism Today*, February 2, 2017, https://www.plagiarismtoday.com/2017/02/02/the-betsy-davos-plagiarism-scandal/.
156. Chris Geidner, "A Short Section in Neil Gorsuch's 2006 Book Appears To Be Copied From a Law Review Article," *BuzzFeed*, April 4, 2017, https://www.buzzfeed.com/chrisgeidner/a-short-section-in-neil-gorsuchs-2006-book-appears-to-be?utm_term=.ayqQjgoDv#.dnl7A21z9; John Bresnahan and Burgess Everett, "Gorsuch's Writings Borrow from Other Authors," *Politico*, April 4, 2017, http://www.politico.com/story/2017/04/gorsuch-writings-supreme-court-236891. *See also* Margaret Hartmann, Neil Gorsuch Accused of Plagiarism Days Before Confirmation Vote, *New York Magazine*, April 5, 2017, http://nymag.com/daily/intelligencer/2017/04/neil-gorsuch-accused-of-plagiarizing-parts-of-his-book.html.
157. Bresnahan and Everett, "Gorsuch's Writings;" Geidner, "A Short Section."
158. Bresnahan and Everett, "Gorsuch's Writings."
159. Bresnahan and Everett, "Gorsuch's Writings (quoting Christopher Sprigman).
160. Thomas Bartlett and Scott Smallwood, "Mentor vs Protégé," *Chronicle of Higher Education*, December 17, 2004; David Glenn, "Judge or Judge Not?," *Chronicle of Higher Education*, December 17, 2004, A16.
161. Glenn, "Judge or Judge Not?"
162. Thomas Bartlett and Scott Smallwood, "Four Academic Plagiarists You've Never Heard Of: How Many More Are out There?," *Chronicle of Higher Education*, December 17, 2004, http://www.chronicle.com/article/Four-Academic-Plagiarists/31890.
163. Bartlett and Smallwood, "Four Academic Plagiarists" (quoting Peter Charles Hoffer).
164. Peter Schmidt, "UNLV Fires Professor for Repeated Plagiarism," *Chronicle of Higher Education*, December 2, 2014.
165. Bartlett and Smallwood, "Four Academic Plagiarists" (quoting George Carney).
166. Bartlett and Smallwood, "Four Academic Plagiarists" (quoting George Carney).
167. Bartlett and Smallwood, "Mentor vs. Protégé" (quoting Charles Arnntzen).
168. Scott Smallwood, "The Fallout," *The Chronicle of Higher Education*, December 17, 2004; Thomas Bartlett and Scott Smallwood, "Just Deserts? (Plagiarizing)," *Chronicle of Higher Education*, April 1, 2005.
169. Thomas Bartlett, "Missouri Dean Appears to Have Plagiarized a Speech by Cornel West," *Chronicle of Higher Education*, June 24, 2005.
170. Plotz, "The Plagiarist;" the phrase comes from Harold Bloom, *The Anxiety of Influence: A Theory of Poetry* (Oxford University Press, 1997).
171. Alan S. Brown and Hildy E. Halliday, "Crytomnesia and Source Memory Difficulties," *American Journal of Psychology* 104 (1991):475; Patricia L. Tenpenny, "Can Plagiarism Occur Inadvertently?," *Bulletin of the Psychonomic Society* (1992):456; Green, "Plagiarism, Norms and the Limits of Theft Law," 186.
172. Posner, *Little Book of Plagiarism*, 100. *See also* Green, "Plagiarism, Norms, and the Limits of Theft Law," 180.
173. Glenn, "Judge or Judge Not?"
174. Posner, *Little Book of Plagiarism*, 7.
175. Thomas Bartlett, "Theology Professor Is Accused of Plagiarism in His Book on Ethics," *Chronicle of Higher Education*, January 21, 2005.
176. Jonathan Pitts, "A Twice Told Tale: Joe Balkoski Heard the Story First Hand, From an Eyewitness to History," *Baltimore Sun*, March 10, 2002, E7.
177. J. Michael Keyes, "On Cribbing Mrs. Trump's RNC Speech," *National Law Journal*, July 25, 2016, 26.

178. The occasion was the 2016 Al Smith dinner. *See* http://time.com/4539981/read-the-transcipt-donald-trump-speech-al-smith-dinner.
179. Michael Hayne, "Trump Plagiarized His Best Joke at Al Smith Dinner and Rachel Maddow Caught Him Red Handed," *ifyouonlynews*, October 22, 2016, http://www.ifyouonlynews.com/politics/trump-plagiarized-his-best-joke-at-al-smith-dinner-and-rachel-maddow-caught-him-red-handed-video/; Maddow Blog(@MaddowBlog) October 22, 2016, https://twitter.com/MaddowBlog/status/789642868684009472.
180. Posner, *Little Book of Plagiarism*, 37.

## *Chapter 6*

1. Alex Sayf Cummings, *Democracy of Sound: Music Piracy and the Remaking of American Copyright in the Twentieth Century* (New York: Oxford University Press, 2013).
2. John Tehranian, *Infringement Nation: Copyright 2.0 and You* (New York: Oxford University Press, 2011), xx.
3. Tehranian, *Infringement Nation*, 2–4.
4. Gregory N. Mandel, Anne A. Fast, and Kristina R. Olson, Intellectual Property Law's Plagiarism Fallacy (unpublished paper, 2015), 43.
5. Mandel et al., Intellectual Property Law's Plagiarism Fallacy, 25.
6. Mandel et al., Intellectual Property Law's Plagiarism Fallacy, 30, 35.
7. Adam Poltrack, "Pirated TV: How It Works and Why It Can't Be Stopped," *Digital Trends*, March 9, 2013, http://www.digitaltrends.com/home-theater/pirated-tv-can-and-should-it-be-stopped/.
8. David Callahan, *The Cheating Culture: Why More Americans Are Doing Wrong to Get Ahead* (New York: Harcourt, 2004), 188.
9. Callahan, *Cheating Culture*, 185; Edna Gundersen, "Piracy Has Its Hooks In," *USA Today*, May 6, 2003; D.C. Denison, "The Legacy of Napster: Shutdown for Service Looms, But File-Sharing Approach Very Much Alive and Thriving," *Boston Globe*, May 16, 2002.
10. Jenna Wortham, "The Unrepentant Bootlegger," *New York Times*, September 27, 2014.
11. Fred Von Lohmann, "Is Suing Your Customers a Good Idea?," *Law.com*, Sept. 29, 2004.
12. Nick Bilton, "Internet Pirates Will Always Win," *New York Times*, August 4, 2012.
13. Todd Spangler, '"Game of Thrones' Breaks All-Time TV Piracy Record," *Variety*, May 11, 2015, http://variety.com/2015/digital/news/game-of-thrones-piracy-record-1201492163/.
14. Robert G. Hammond, "Profit Leak? Pre-Release File Sharing and the Music Industry," *Southern Economic Journal* 81 (2014):387.
15. Susan Jennings, "Online Piracy Is Bad: Here's How to Make Sure Your Kids Understand That," Institute for Policy Innovation, April 10, 2014.
16. Mark Lemley, IP in a World without Scarcity (unpublished draft, 2014), 27. Online music piracy led to a 31 percent decline in the value of the global recorded music industry between 2004 and 2010. International Federation of Phonographic Industry, "Digital Music Report: Music at the Touch of a Button" (2011), http://www.ifpi.org/content/library/DMR2011 pdf.
17. Poltrack, "Pirated TV."
18. United States Department of Justice, "Prosecuting Intellectual Property Crimes" (2006), http://www.justice.gov/sites/default/files/criminal-ccips/legacy/2015/03/26/prosecuting_ip_crimes_manual_2013.pdf.
19. Bert Weijters, Frank Goedertier, and Sofie Verstreken, "Online Music Consumption in Today's Technological Context: Putting the Influence of Ethics in Perspective," *Journal of Business Ethics* 124 (2014):537, 546.
20. Mohsen Manesh, "The Immorality of Theft, the Amorality of Infringement," *Stanford Technology Law Review* 5 (2006).
21. Wortham, "The Unrepentant Bootlegger."

22. Amanda Lenhart and Susannah Fox, “Downloading Free Music: Internet Music Lovers Don’t Think It’s Stealing,” Pew Internet & American Life Project’s Online Music Report (2000), 2.
23. Stacey M. Lantagne, “The Morality of MP3s: The Failure of the Recording Industry’s Plan of Attack,” *Harvard Journal of Law and Technology* 18 (2004):269, 278.
24. Weijters et al., “Online Music Consumption,” 546.
25. Callahan, *Cheating Culture*, 187.
26. Susan D. Blum, *My Word!: Plagiarism and College Culture* (Ithaca, NY: Cornell University Press, 2009), 162.
27. Stephen Witt, *How Music Got Free: The End of an Industry, the Turn of the Century, and the Patient Zero of Piracy* (New York: Viking, 2015).
28. Cummings, *Democracy of Sound*, 203.
29. For a discussion of the problems with the legislation, see Mark Lemley, David S. Levine, and David G. Post, “Don’t Break the Internet,” *Stanford Law Review Online* 64 (2011):34; David Moon, Patrick Ruffini, and David Segal, *Hacking Politics: How Geeks, Progressives, the Tea Party, Gamers, Anarchists and Suits Teamed Up to Defeat SOPA and Save the Internet* (New York: OR Books, 2013).
30. Jennings, “Online Piracy Is Bad.”
31. Tehranian, *Infringement Nation*, xxi.
32. Wortham, “Unrepentant Bootlegger.”
33. Victor Li, Manhattan, “Federal Judge Kimba Wood Calls Record Companies’ Request for $75 Trillion in Damages ‘Absurd’ in Lime Wire Copyright Case,” *American Lawyer*, March 15, 2011; Cummings, *Democracy of Sound*, 200.
34. Cummings, *Democracy of Sound*, 201.
35. Lemley, IP in a World without Scarcity, 28.
36. Mark F. Schultz, “Reconciling Social Norms and Copyright Law: Strategies for Persuading People to Pay for Recorded Music,” *Journal of Intellectual Property Law* 17 (2009):59, 73.
37. Bilton, “Internet Pirates Will Always Win.”
38. Tom R. Tyler, “Compliance with Intellectual Property Laws: A Psychological Perspective,” *New York University Journal of International Law and Politics* 29 (1997):219, 221.
39. Tyler, “Compliance with Intellectual Property Laws,” 224–226.
40. Tyler, “Compliance with Intellectual Property Laws,” 233.
41. Tyler, “Compliance with Intellectual Property;” Donald P. Harris, “The New Prohibition: A Look at the Copyright Wars through the Lens of Alcohol Prohibition,” *Tennessee Law Review* 80 (2012):101, 123.
42. Higher Education Opportunity Act of 2008, 123 Stat. 1384 §§ 485, 487 (2009).
43. Higher Education Opportunity Act of 2008, § 487(a)(29).
44. Morgan Baskin, “Think Twice before Illegally Downloading—Intellectual Property Companies Are Watching You,” *USA Today*, March 5, 2015, http://college.usatoday.com/2015/03/05/think-twice-before-illegally-downloading-intellectual-property-companies-are-watching-you/.
45. Schultz, “Reconciling Social Norms and Copyright Law,” 78.
46. Wortham, “Unrepentant Bootlegger.”
47. Schultz, “Reconciling Social Norms and Copyright Law,” 80.
48. John Seabrook, “Revenue Streams: Is Spotify the Music Industry’s Friend or Its Foe?,” *New Yorker*, November 24, 2014.
49. Michael Driscoll, “Selling Songs for a Song? Scrutinizing the Streaming Model,” *Wall Street Journal*, March 27, 2015.
50. Matt Vella, “Apple’s Next Trick: Upending Streaming Music,” *Time*, June 11 2015, 22.
51. James Cook, “Norway Has Figured Out How to Solve the Problem of Music Piracy,” *Business Insider*, January 27, 2015.
52. Paul Tassi, “Whatever Happened to the War on Piracy?,” *Forbes*, January 24, 2014, http://www.forbes.com/sites/insertcoin/2014/01/24/whatever-happened-to-the-war-on-piracy/.

53. Tassi, "Whatever Happened to the War on Piracy?."
54. Tassi, "Whatever Happened to the War on Piracy?."
55. Schultz, "Reconciling Social Norms and Copyright Law," 88.
56. Tyler, "Compliance with Intellectual Property Laws," 229.
57. Wortham, "Unrepentant Bootlegger."
58. Wortham, "Unrepentant Bootlegger" (quoting Michael D. Robinson, chief of operations and content protection for the Motion Picture Association of America).
59. Tehranian, *Infringement Nation*, xxii.
60. Tobias Regner, "Why Consumers Pay Voluntarily: Evidence from Online Music," Jena Economic Research Papers, No. 2010-081 (2010).
61. Paul Thompson, "Radiohead's *In Rainbows* Successes Revealed," *Pitchfork*, October 15, 2008, http://pitchfork.com/news/33749-radioheads-in-rainbows-successes-revealed/; Schultz, "Reconciling Social Norms and Copyright Law," 84.
62. Chris Welch, "UK Police Try to Spook Piracy Website Users with Banner Ads," *The Verge*, July 29, 2014, http://www.theverge.com/2014/7/29/5949043/police-try-to-spook-pirates-with-banner-ads.
63. Harris, "New Prohibition," 154.
64. William W. Fisher III, *Promises to Keep: Technology, Law, and the Future of Entertainment* (Stanford, CA: Stanford University Press, 2004), 199–203; Neil Weinstock Netanel, "Impose a Noncommercial Use Levy to Allow Free Peer-to-Peer File Sharing," *Harvard Journal of Law and Technology* 17 (2003):1.
65. Wortham, "Unrepentant Bootlegger."
66. Wortham, "Unrepentant Bootlegger."
67. Fred von Lohmann, "A Better Way Forward: Voluntary Collective Licensing of Music File Sharing," Electronic Frontier Foundation, April 30, 2008, https://www.eff.org/files/eff-a-better-way-forward.pdf.
68. Tehranian, *Infringement Nation*, 147–151.
69. Roberta Rosenthal Kwall, "Inspiration and Innovation: The Intrinsic Dimension of the Artistic Soul," *Notre Dame Law Review*, 81 (2006):1945, 1950.
70. Lemley, IP in a World without Scarcity, 29.
71. Cummings, *Democracy of Sound*, 214.
72. Lemley, IP in a World without Scarcity, 32.

## *Chapter 7*

1. Dwane Hal Dean, "Perceptions of the Ethicality of Consumer Insurance Claim Fraud," *Journal of Business Ethics* 54 (2004):67.
2. Insurance Information Institute, Insurance Fraud (March 2015); Federal Bureau of Investigation, "Insurance Fraud" (2015), http://www.fbi.gov/stats-services/publications; Laura Mazzuca Toops, "Seeing Red: Insurance Fraud," *American Agent and Broker*, December 2013, 29.
3. Toops, "Seeing Red," 29.
4. FBI, "Insurance Fraud."
5. Utah Insurance Department Fraud Division FY 2014 Annual Report (Utah Insurance Department, 2014), 5.
6. Coalition Against Insurance Fraud, "Four Faces Study: Why Some Americans Do—and Don't—Tolerate Insurance Fraud" (Coalition Against Insurance Fraud, 2007), http://www.insurancefraud.org/four-faces-study.htm#.VmCWPnarRhF.
7. Financial Crimes Intelligence Unit, 2010 Mortgage Fraud Report, 6; Corelogic, 2013 Mortgage Fraud Report (Corelogic, September 2013), 3.
8. Insurance Information Institute, Insurance Fraud.
9. Kenneth Reich, "People Defend Lies to Insurer, Survey Finds," *Los Angeles Times*, November 14, 1991, A15.

10. Sharon Tennyson, "Moral, Social, and Economic Dimensions of Insurance Claims Fraud," *Social Research* 75 (2008):1181, 1191.
11. Toops, "Seeing Red," 29.
12. Insurance Information Institute, Insurance Fraud.
13. James Quiggle, "Disability Cons Set Up Workers for Taxpayer-Funded Retirement," *Journal of Insurance Fraud in America* 3 (Winter 2012–2013):22.
14. "Payments to Disabled Cop Suspended after Sun-Times Reports," *Chicago Sun-Times*, August 30, 2012.
15. Quiggle, "Disability Cons," 23.
16. Laura Trueman, "Able-Bodied People Defrauding Social Security Disability Program," *Daily Signal*, October 12, 2012, http://dailysignal.com/2012/10/12/able-bodied-people-defrauding-social-security-disability-program/.
17. Coalition Against Insurance Fraud, "By the Numbers: Fraud Statistics," (May 19, 2017, 11:00 AM), http://www.insurancefraud.org/statistics.htm.
18. Press Release, Accenture, One-Fourth of Americans Say It's Acceptable to Defraud Insurance Companies, Accenture Survey Finds, February 12, 2003; Insurance Research Council, "Insurance Fraud: A Public View, 2013 Edition" (Insurance Research Council, 2013); Dennis Jay and James Quiggle, Coalition Against Insurance Fraud, "By the Numbers; Fraud Statistics," (May 19, 2017, 11:00 AM), http://www.insurancefraud.org/statistics.htm.
19. Insurance Research Council, Insurance Fraud; Coalition Against Insurance Fraud, "By the Numbers."
20. Coalition Against Insurance Fraud, "Four Faces of Insurance Fraud," 2008.
21. William C. Lesch and Bruce W. Byars, "See No Evil, Speak No Evil: Why Consumers Don't Report Fraud," *Journal of Insurance Fraud in America* (Winter 2012–2013):19.
22. Lesch and Byars, "See No Evil, Speak No Evil," 20.
23. Lesch and Byars, "See No Evil, Speak No Evil," 15; Tennyson, "Moral, Social, and Economic Dimensions of Insurance Claims Fraud," 1181.
24. Coalition Against Insurance Fraud, "Four Faces of Insurance Fraud."
25. Alan Wolfe, *Moral Freedom: The Impossible Idea That Defines the Way We Live Now* (New York: W.W. Norton, 2001), 109.
26. Dean, "Perceptions of the Ethicality of Consumer Insurance Claim Fraud," 76–77.
27. Dean, "Perceptions of the Ethicality of Consumer Insurance Claim Fraud," 78.
28. Insurance Research Council, "Fraud and Buildup in Auto Insurance Claims 2008 Edition" (Insurance Research Council, 2008).
29. Coalition Against Insurance Fraud, "By the Numbers."
30. Insurance Information Institute, Insurance Fraud.
31. Insurance Information Institute, Insurance Fraud.
32. David Callahan, *The Cheating Culture: Why More Americans Are Doing Wrong to Get Ahead* (New York: Harcourt, 2004), 191–92.
33. Coalition Against Insurance Fraud, "Fraud Statistics."
34. Stephen Carroll and Allan Abrahamse, "The Frequency of Excess Auto Personal Injury Claims," *American Law and Economics Review* 3 (2001):228, 248.
35. Insurance Research Council, "Fraud and Buildup in Auto Injury Insurance Claims," 2.
36. Insurance Information Institute, "Insurance Fraud."
37. Martha Neil, "Top PA Court Disbars Ex-Judge Convicted in Auto Insurance Fraud: Civil Suit Says Judge Is Victim," *ABA Journal*, June 18, 2012.
38. Coalition Against Insurance Fraud, "The Power of Partnering: Bridging the Divides" (Coalition Against Insurance Fraud, 2013), 19.
39. Coalition Against Insurance Fraud, "Power of Partnering," 21.
40. Coalition Against Insurance Fraud, "Power of Partnering," 20.
41. Coalition Against Insurance Fraud, "Victim Impact Statements," (May 19, 2017, 11:06 AM), http://www.insurancefraud.org/the-impact-of-insurance-fraud.htm.

42. Francis E. McGovern, "Looking to the Future of Mass Torts: A Comment on Schuck and Siliciano," *Cornell Law Review* 80 (1995):1022, 1024. *See* Nora Freeman Engstrom, "Civil Litigation, Retaliatory RICO, and the Ineradicable Problem of Fraud" (working paper, 2015).
43. Coalition Against Insurance Fraud, "By the Numbers."
44. Coalition Against Insurance Fraud, "Workers Compensation Scams," (May 19, 2017, 11:55 AM), http://www.insurancefraud.org/scam-alerts-workers-compensation.htm#.VmHd5L-rVBA.
45. FBI, "Insurance Fraud."
46. Dan Fastenberg, "Postal Carrier Caught in Workers' Comp Fraud on 'Price is Right,'" *AOL.com*, June 5, 2013.
47. "California Woman Arrested for Workers' Comp Fraud after Competing in Beauty Pageants," *Fox News*, August 13, 2014.
48. Katie Nelson, "Employee of Santa Clara Company Charged with Felony Workers' Comp Fraud after Caught Skydiving," *San Jose Mercury News*, April 16, 2015.
49. Coalition Against Insurance Fraud, "Workers Compensation Scams."
50. Coalition Against Insurance Fraud, "Workers Compensation Scams."
51. Coalition Against Insurance Fraud, "Workers Compensation Scams."
52. Coalition Against Insurance Fraud, "Workers Compensation Scams."
53. Coalition Against Insurance Fraud, "Workers Compensation Scams."
54. Eric Lichtblau, "U.S. Says Florida Network Defrauded Medicare and Medicaid of Over $1 Billion," *New York Times*, July 22, 2016; Kelli Kennedy, "Authorities: $1B Medicare Fraud Nursing Home Scam, 3 Charged," *Washington Post*, July 22, 2016; U.S. Department of Justice, Office of Public Affairs, "Three Individuals Charged in $1 Billion Medicare Fraud and Money Laundering Scheme," July 22, 2016, https://www.justice.gov/opa/pr/three-individuals-charged-1-billion-medicare-fraud-and-money-laundering-scheme; Insurance Information Institute, Insurance Fraud (summarizing FBI Financial Crimes Report).
55. Robert Lenzner and Michael Maiello, "The $22 Billion Gold Rush," *Forbes*, March 24, 2006 (quoting class counsel Michael Fishbein). Other plaintiffs' lawyers disagreed. *See* Engstrom, "Civil Litigation."
56. In re Diet Drugs Products Liability Litigation v. American Home Products Corporation, 2002 WL 32154242, 12 (E.D. Pa. November 14, 2002).
57. Insurance Information Institute, Insurance Fraud (summarizing FBI Financial Crimes Report). *See also* Utah Insurance Department, 2014 Annual Report, 15
58. Insurance Information Institute, Insurance Fraud.
59. Utah Department of Insurance, 2014 Annual Report, 20–23.
60. Coalition Against Insurance Fraud, "By the Numbers."
61. Toops, "Seeing Red," 31.
62. United States Department of Justice, Office of Public Affairs, "Justice Department Recovers Nearly $6 Billion from False Claims Act Cases in Fiscal Year 2014," November 20, 2014, https://www.justice.gov/opa/pr/justice-department-recovers-nearly-6-billion-false-claims-act-cases-fiscal-year-2014.
63. U.S. Justice Department, "Justice Department Recovers Nearly $6 Billion."
64. U.S. Justice Department, "Justice Department Recovers Nearly $6 Billion."
65. Los Angeles District Attorney, "15 Indicted in $150 Million Insurance Fraud, Patient Scam Conspiracy," September 15, 2015, http://da.co.la.ca.us/media/news/15-indicted-in-150-million-insurance-fraud-patient-scam-conspiracy.
66. Stephen M. Rosoff, Henry N. Pontell, and Robert Tillman, *Profit without Honor: White Collar Crime and the Looting of America* (Upper Saddle River NJ.: Prentice Hall, 1998), 333–334.
67. Coalition Against Insurance Fraud, "Power of Partnering," 20.
68. Rosoff et al., *Profit without Honor*, 201.

69. Toops, "Seeing Red," 31 (quoting Jim Quiggle).
70. Douglas Kennedy, "Healthy Spoils from a Very Sick System," *New York Post*, April 18, 1995.
71. "The $272 Billion Swindle: Why Thieves Love America's Health-Care System," *Economist*, May 31, 2014.
72. "$272 Billion Swindle."
73. Financial Crimes Intelligence Unit, Directorate of Intelligence, Federal Bureau of Investigation, "2010 Mortgage Fraud Report: Year in Review" (August 2011), 5.
74. James Charles Smith, "The Structural Causes of Mortgage Fraud," *Syracuse Law Review* 60 (2010):473.
75. Smith, "Structural Causes of Mortgage Fraud," 473.
76. Atif R. Mian and Amir Sufi, "Fraudulent Income Overstatement on Mortgage Applications during the Credit Expansion of 2002 to 2005" (Chicago: University of Chicago Law School, Kreisman Working Paper on Housing Law and Policy No. 21, February 2015).
77. Federal Financial Institutions Examination Council, "The Detection and Deterrence of Mortgage Fraud against Financial Institutions: A White Paper" (Arlington, VA, July 13, 2009).
78. Rich Lord, "Court Documents Raise Questions about Role of Former DEA Agent in Mortgage Fraud Case," *Pittsburgh Post-Gazette*, May 24, 2015, A-1.
79. Michael Hudson, *The Monster: How a Gang of Predatory Lenders and Wall Street Bankers Fleeced America—and Spawned a Global Crisis* (New York: St. Martin's Press, 2010), discussed in David Leonhardt, "How Mortgage Fraud Made the Financial Crisis Worse," *New York Times*, February 12, 2015.
80. Department of Insurance, Securities and Banking, District of Columbia, Things to Know about Mortgage Fraud and Straw Buying (2015).
81. Financial Crimes Intelligence Unit, 2010 Mortgage Fraud Report: Year in Review, 17.
82. Fred Schulte, "Lawyers Use Loopholes in Key Mortgage Program to Cheat Homeowners," *Huffington Post*, January 12, 2017, http://www.huffingtonpost.com/entry/lawyers-use-loopholes-in-key-mortgage-program-to-cheat-homeowners_us_579ffc83e4b0693164c2687a.
83. Schulte, "Lawyers Use Loopholes."
84. Darwin BondGraham, Trial Begins for East Bay Landlord Accused of Rigging Foreclosure Auctions, East Bay Express, May 15, 2017, http://www.eastbayexpress.com/SevenDays/archives/2017/05/15/trial-begins-for-east-bay-landlord-accused-of-rigging-foreclosure-auctions.
85. Planet Money, Episode 363: "Why People Do Bad Things," http://www.npr.org/sections/money/2015/07/03/419543470/episode-363-why-people-do-bad-things.
86. Planet Money, "Why People Do Bad Things" (quoting Chana Joffe-Walt).
87. George Avalos, "Task Force Targets Home Buyers, Brokers Who Lied on Mortgage Applications," *San Jose Mercury News*, October 31, 2008.
88. Avalos, "Task Force" (quoting Don Morton).
89. Avalos, "Task Force" (quoting Robert Gnaizda, of the Greenlining Institute).
90. U.S. Department of Justice, Audit of the Department of Justice's Efforts to Address Mortgage Fraud, March 2014, https://oig.justice.gov/reports/2014/a1412.pdf.
91. Jay and Quiggle, "Fraud Statistics."
92. Insurance Research Council, Insurance Fraud: A Public View (Insurance Research Council, 2013).
93. Insurance Information Institute, Insurance Fraud.
94. Quiggle, "Disability Cons," 25. For the amounts returned by Medicare fraud enforcement efforts, see Coalition Against Insurance Fraud, "By the Numbers."
95. U.S. Department of Justice, Three Individuals Charged in $1 Billion Medicare Fraud and Money Laundering Scheme.
96. Automobile Insurers Bureau of Massachusetts and Insurance Fraud Bureau of Massachusetts, Community Fraud Initiative: A Five-Year Retrospective (2009); Coalition Against Insurance Fraud, "By the Numbers."

97. John Beshears and Francesca Gino, "Leaders as Decision Architects," *Harvard Business Review*, May 2015, 60.
98. Coalition Against Insurance Fraud, "Workers Compensation Scams."
99. Jay and Quiggle, "Fraud Statistics."
100. Schulte, "Lawyers Use Loopholes."
101. Greg Hunter, "Workers Comp Scams That Push the Limits," *ABC News*, http://abcnews.go.com/GMA/story?id=127996&page=1&singlePage=true.
102. Coalition Against Insurance Fraud, "By the Numbers."

## *Chapter 8*

1. Nathan Tabor, "Adultery Is Killing the American Family," *RenewAmerica*, September 22, 2005, http://www.renewamerica.com/columns/tabor/050922 (quoting J. Lindsay Short). This chapter is based on Deborah L. Rhode, *Adultery: Infidelity and the Law* (Cambridge, MA: Harvard University Press, 2016).
2. Kate Figes, *Our Cheating Hearts: Love and Loyalty, Lust & Lies* (London: Virago, 2013), 26.
3. Figes, *Our Cheating Hearts*, 22.
4. Rhode, *Adultery*.
5. Bernard Gert, *Morality: Its Nature and Justification* (New York: Oxford University Press, 1998), 198.
6. "Cheating in a Wired World," *Contemporary Sexuality* (October 2010):1; Katherine Hertlein and Fred Piercy, "Internet Infidelity: A Critical Review of the Literature," *The Family Journal: Counseling and Therapy for Couples and Families* 14 (2010):366.
7. Peggy Drexler, "The New Face of Infidelity: Research Shows Women May Be Cheating Now Almost as Much as Men; The Toll of New Temptations," *Wall Street Journal*, October 19, 2012.
8. Drexler, "New Face of Infidelity;" Edward O. Laumann, John H. Gagnon, Robert T. Michael, and Stuart Michaels, *The Social Organization of Sexuality: Sexual Practices in the United States* (Chicago: University of Chicago Press, 1994), 216 (22 percent of husbands and 13 percent of wives admitted to at least one extramarital affair). For other studies, see Helen E. Fisher, "Serial Monogamy and Clandestine Adultery: Evolution and Consequences of the Dual Human Reproductive Strategy" (Oxford Scholarship Online, 2011).
9. Laura Kipnis, "Adultery," *Critical Inquiry* 24 (1998):289, 293, n.4; Mark A. Whisman and Douglas K. Snyder, "Sexual Infidelity in a National Survey of American Women: Differences in Prevalence and Correlates as a Function of Method of Assessment," *Journal of Family Psychology* 21 (2007):147 (noting that lower prevalence rates are found in face-to-face interviews than on anonymous questionnaires).
10. Michael Norman, "Getting Serious about Adultery; Who Does It and Why They Risk It," *New York Times*, July 4, 1998; Lauren Rosewarne, *Cheating on the Sisterhood: Infidelity and Feminism* (Santa Barbara, CA: Praeger, 2009); Louise Desalvo, *Adultery* (Boston: Beacon Press, 1999), 26.
11. Norman, "Getting Serious about Adultery." *See also* Drexler, "New Face of Infidelity."
12. Andrew Greeley, "Marital Infidelity," *Society*, May/June 1994, 10. For religion, see Irene Tsapelas, Helen E. Fisher, and Arthur Aron, "Infidelity: When, Where, Why," in William R. Cupach and Brian H. Spitzberg, eds., *The Dark Side of Close Relationships II*, (New York, Routledge, 2010); and Judith Treas and Deirdre Giesen, "Sexual Infidelity among Married and Cohabiting Americans," *Journal of Marriage and the Family* 62 (February 2000):48, 59.
13. Richard Johnson, "The Demography of Adultery: Graphic," *National Post*, November 16, 2012, http://news.nationalpost.com/news/canada/graphic-the-demography-of-adultery. *See also* Adrian J. Blow and Kelley Hartnett, "Infidelity in Committed Relationships II: A Substantive Review," *Journal of Marital and Family Therapy* 31 (2005):217, 225.
14. Tom W. Smith, *American Sexual Behavior: Trends, Socio-Demographic Differences, and Risk Behavior* (Chicago: National Opinion Research Center, 2006).
15. Joris Lammers, Janka I. Soker, Jennifer Jordan, Monique Pollmann, and Diederik A. Stapel, "Power Increases Infidelity among Men and Women," *Psychological Science* 20 (2011):l.

16. Treas and Giesen, "Sexual Infidelity among Married and Cohabiting Americans," 49; Anita L. Vangelisti and Mandi Gerstenberger, "Communication and Marital Infidelity," in Graham Allan, Jean Duncombe, Karen Harrison, and Dennis Marsden eds., *The State of Affairs* (New York: Routledge, 2004), 60; Bram P. Buunk and Pieternel Dijkstra, "Men, Women, and Infidelity: Sex Differences in Extradyadic Sex and Jealousy," in Duncombe et al., *State of Affairs*, 104; Anthony Peter Thompson, "Emotional and Sexual Components of Extramarital Relations," *Journal of Marriage and Family* 46 (1984):35–36.
17. Drexler, "New Face of Infidelity;" Kristen P. Mark, Erick Janssen, and Robin R. Milhausen, "Infidelity in Heterosexual Couples: Demographic, Interpersonal, and Personality-Related Predictors of Extradyadic Sex," *Archives of Sexual Behavior* 40 (2011):971–982.
18. Annette Lawson, *Adultery: An Analysis of Love and Betrayal* (New York: Basic Books, 1988), 28.
19. Pamela Druckerman, *Lust in Translation* (New York, Penguin, 2007), 51. For recent evidence, see Tara Parker-Pope, "Love, Sex and the Changing Landscape of Infidelity," *New York Times*, October 27, 2008.
20. Frank Pittman, *Private Lies: Infidelity and the Betrayal of Intimacy* (New York: W.W. Norton, 1989), 174.
21. David P. Barash and Judith Eve Lipton, *The Myth of Monogamy* (New York, NY: W.H. Freeman, 2001), 10.
22. David M. Buss, *The Dangerous Passion: Why Jealousy Is as Necessary as Love and Sex* (New York: Free Press, 2000), 35; Barash and Lipton, *Myth of Monogamy*, 19, 59; Helen E. Fisher, *Anatomy of Love: The Natural History of Monogamy, Adultery, and Divorce* (New York: W.W. Norton, 1992); Norman, "Getting Serious about Adultery."
23. Richard A. Friedman, "Infidelity Lurks in Your Genes," *New York Times*, May 22, 2015.
24. Treas and Giesen, "Sexual Infidelity among Married and Cohabiting Americans," 48, 59.
25. Figes, *Our Cheating Hearts*, 4–5; Albert Ellis, "Healthy and Disturbed Reasons for Having Extramarital Relations," in Gerhard Neubeck, ed., *Extramarital Relations* (Englewood Cliffs, NJ: Prentice Hall, 1969), 153, 155–158.
26. Lise VanderVoort and Steve Duck, "Sex, Lies, and . . . Transformation," in Duncombe et al., *State of Affairs*, 59; Figes, *Our Cheating Hearts*, 4–5; Kate Figes, "The Infidelity Epidemic," *Daily Mail* (United Kingdom), April 19, 2013.
27. VanderVoort and Duck, "Sex, Lies, and . . . Transformation," 59.
28. Lynn Atwater, "Getting Involved: Women's Transition to First Extramarital Sex," *Alternative Lifestyles* 2 (February 1979):33, 51.
29. Atwater, "Getting Involved," 57.
30. Michael Baisden, *Never Satisfied: How & Why Men Cheat* (Katy, TX: Legacy Publishing, 1995), 115.
31. Druckerman, *Lust in Translation*, 78; Steven M. Ortiz, "Traveling with the Ball Club: A Code of Conduct for Wives Only," *Symbolic Interaction* 20 (1997):225.
32. Trish Hall, "Infidelity and Women, Shifting Patterns," *New York Times*, June 1, 1987, B8.
33. Treas and Giesen, "Sexual Infidelity among Married and Cohabiting Americans," 59; Anthony P. Thompson, "Extramarital Sex: A Review of the Research Literature," *Journal of Sex Research* 19 (1983):1, 10. For studies finding a correlation between marital dissatisfaction and extramarital affairs, and those finding no relationship, see Mark et al., "Infidelity in Heterosexual Couples," 971.
34. David C. Atkins, Donald H. Baucom, and Neil S. Jacobson, "Understanding Infidelity: Correlates in a National Random Sample," *Journal of Family Psychology* 15 (2001):735, 745–746.
35. Chien Liu, "A Theory of Marital Sexual Life," *Journal of Marriage and Family* 62 (2000):363.
36. Hall, "Infidelity and Women," B8.
37. Treas and Giesen, "Sexual Infidelity among Married and Cohabiting Americans," 59 (studies inconsistent on whether poor relationships lead to extramarital sex); Joseph Hooper, "Infidelity Comes Out of the Closet," *New York Times*, April 29, 1999 (citing study finding that

men's infidelity was more often the cause for troubled marriages than the effect); Blow and Hartnett, "Infidelity in Committed Relationships II," 217, 222 (citing studies finding little correlation between relationship satisfaction and fidelity); Elizabeth S. Allen and David C. Atkins, "The Association of Divorce and Extramarital Sex in a Representative U.S. Sample," *Journal of Family Issues* 33 (2012):1477, 1489 (citing study finding that individuals reported that their partner's infidelity was more frequently the cause rather than the result of marital problems).

38. Tsapelas et al., "Infidelity."
39. Druckerman, *Lust in Translation*, 99.
40. Blow and Hartnett, "Infidelity in Committed Relationships II," 227.
41. Blow and Hartnett, "Infidelity in Committed Relationships II," 222.
42. Rosewarne, *Cheating on the Sisterhood*, 78.
43. Drukerman, *Lust in Translation*, 274.
44. Hooper, "Infidelity Comes Out of the Closet."
45. Graham Allan, "Being Unfaithful: His and Her Affairs," in Duncombe et al., *State of Affairs*, 134.
46. Hooper, "Infidelity Comes Out of the Closet."
47. Shirley P. Glass and Thomas L. Wright, "Justifications for Extramarital Relationships: The Association between Attitudes, Behavior and Gender," *Journal of Sex Research* 29 (1992):361.
48. Rosewarne, *Cheating on the Sisterhood*, 139.
49. Shirley P. Glass and Thomas L. Wright, "Sex Differences in Type of Extramarital Involvement and Marital Dissatisfaction," *Sex Roles* 12 (1985):1101, 1113.
50. Hanna Rosin, "Why We Cheat: Spouses in Happy Marriages Have Affairs. What Are We All Looking For?," *Slate*, March 27, 2014, http://www.slate.com/articles/double_x/doublex/2014/03/esther_perel_on_affairs_spouses_in_happy_marriages_cheat_and_americans_don.html (quoting Esther Perel).
51. Lawson, *Adultery*, 200.
52. Lawson, *Adultery*, 200 (two-thirds of women and one-half of men reported a sense of being alive as the most important pleasure).
53. Allan, "Being Unfaithful," 129.
54. Figes, *Our Cheating Hearts*, 139.
55. John F. Cuber, "Adultery: Reality versus Stereotype," in Gerhard Neubeck ed., *Extramarital Relations* (New York: Prentice-Hall, 1969), 191. *See also* Chapter 8 in John F. Cuber and Peggy B. Harroff, *Sex and the Significant Americans, A Study of Sexual Behavior Among the Affluent* (New York: Penguin, 1966).
56. Neubeck, *Extramarital Relations*, 71.
57. Rosewarne, *Cheating on the Sisterhood*, 209, 116. *See also* Richard Tuch, *The Single Woman-Married Man Syndrome* (Northvale, NJ: Jason Aronson, 2000), 11–12, 16–17.
58. Rosewarne, *Cheating on the Sisterhood*, 209; Baisden, *Never Satisfied*.
59. Blow and Hartnett, "Infidelity in Committed Relationships II," 227.
60. Jennifer S. Hirsch et al., *The Secret: Love, Marriage, and HIV* (Nashville, TN: Vanderbilt University Press, 2009), 1 (quoting Henry Gauthier Villars).
61. Figes, *Our Cheating Hearts*, 194.
62. Figes, *Our Cheating Hearts*, 257.
63. Figes, *Our Cheating Hearts*, 257.
64. Hall, "Infidelity and Women," B8.
65. Blow and Hartnett, "Infidelity in Committed Relationships II," 227.
66. Figes, *Our Cheating Hearts*, 195–196.
67. Druckerman, *Lust in Translation*, 274.
68. Lawson, *Adultery*, 231.
69. Allan, "Being Unfaithful," 136.
70. Figes, *Our Cheating Hearts*, 162.
71. Kipnis, "Adultery," 293, 323.

72. Lawson, *Adultery*, 168.
73. Figes, *Our Cheating Hearts*, 155; Figes, "Infidelity Epidemic."
74. Druckerman, *Lust in Translation*, 12.
75. Figes, *Our Cheating Hearts*, 74; Glass and Wright, "Sex Differences in Type of Extramarital Involvement and Marital Dissatisfaction," 1101, 1103.
76. Alfred DeMaris, "Burning the Candle at Both Ends: Extramarital Sex as a Precursor of Marital Disruption," *Journal of Family Issues* 34 (2013):1475, 1478; Figes, *Our Cheating Hearts*, 133.
77. Allen and Atkins, "Association of Divorce and Extramarital Sex," 1477, 1488.
78. Allen and Atkins, "Association of Divorce and Extramarital Sex," 1488.
79. Martin Daly and Margo Wilson, "The Evolutionary Social Psychology and Family Homicide," *Science* 242 (1988), in Charles Crawford and Dennis L. Krebs, eds., *Handbook of Evolutionary Psychology: Ideas, Issues, and Applications* (1998), 431–456; Vangelisti and Gerstenberger, "Communication and Marital Infidelity," 59; Julianna M. Nemeth, Amy E. Bonomi, Meghan A. Lee, and Jennifer M. Ludwin, "Sexual Infidelity as Trigger for Intimate Partner Violence," *Journal of Women's Health* 21 (2012):942.
80. Buunk and Dijkstra, "Men, Women, and Infidelity," 108.
81. Figes, *Our Cheating Hearts*, 35.
82. Buunk and Dijkstra, "Men, Women and Infidelity," 115.
83. Buunk and Dijkstra, "Men, Women, and Infidelity," 111–112.
84. Jean Duncombe and Dennis Marsden, "'From Here to Epiphany . . .': Power and Identity in the Narrative of an Affair," in Duncombe et al., *State of Affairs*, 143.
85. Lawson, *Adultery*, 136.
86. Figes, *Our Cheating Hearts*, 207.
87. Figes, *Our Cheating Hearts*, 207.
88. FIges, *Our Cheating Hearts*, 190.
89. Figes, *Our Cheating Hearts*, 208–212.
90. Catherine Johnson, "The New Woman Infidelity Report," *New Woman*, November 1986, 74.
91. Laurel Richardson, *The New Other Woman: Contemporary Single Women in Affairs with Married Men* (New York: Free Press, 1985), 129.
92. Richardson, *New Other Woman*, 129.
93. Richardson, *New Other Woman*, 149.
94. Baisden, *Never Satisfied*, 181, 253.
95. U.S. Poll: Adultery Unacceptable to Most, UPI (June 25, 2009, 05:29 PM), http://www.upi.com/Top_News/2009/06/25/US-poll-Adultery-unacceptable-to-most/96431245965385/ (reporting that 92 percent of those surveyed said extramarital sex was wrong).
96. John Sides, "Americans Have Become More Opposed to Adultery. Why?," *The Monkey Cage* (July 27, 2011), http://themonkeycage.org/2011/07/americans-have-become-more-opposed-to-adultery-why/.
97. Lorraine Ali and Lisa Miller, "The Secret Lives of Wives," *Newsweek*, July 12, 2004, http://www.dearpeggy.com/5-media/announce28.html.
98. Sides, "Americans Have Become More Opposed to Adultery;" Andrew Sullivan, "The Growing Stigma against Adultery," *The Dish* (July 28, 2011).
99. Sides, "Americans Have Become More Opposed to Adultery." (Why? The logic goes something like this: "If you're in an unhappy marriage, don't cheat. Just get divorced.").
100. Treas and Giesen, "Sexual Infidelity among Married and Cohabiting Americans."
101. Roper Center for Public Opinion Research, iPOLL Databank, *CBS News Poll*, (September 18–20, 1997).
102. Pew Research, "A Barometer of Modern Morals: Sex, Drugs, and the 1040," Pew Research Center (March 28, 2006), http://www.pewsocialtrends.org/2006/03/28/a-barometer-of-modern-morals. In the poll, researchers read respondents a list of 10 behaviors, and respondents said whether the behavior was "morally acceptable, morally wrong, or not a moral issue."

103. "How Do Americans View Adultery?," *CNN.com* (August 20, 1998), http://www.cnn.com/ALLPOLITICS/1998/08/20/adultery.poll (86 percent viewed adultery as morally wrong compared with 79 percent who viewed prostitution as morally wrong).
104. "Political Allegiance Shaped by Stance on Moral Issues in U.S.," *Angus Reid Public Opinion* (October 11, 2010), http://angusreidglobal.com/wp-content/uploads/2010/10/2010.10.11_Morality_USA.pdf.
105. "How Do Americans View Adultery?."
106. Pamela Druckerman, "Our Ready Embrace of Those Cheating Pols," *Washington Post*, July 15, 2007; Eric D. Widmer, Judith Treas, and Robert Newcomb, "Attitudes toward Nonmarital Sex in 24 Countries," *Journal of Sex Research* 35 (1988):349, 351.
107. Women were more likely (77 percent) than men (69 percent) to think that an adulterous member of the clergy should be dismissed. Roper Center for Public Opinion Research, iPOLL Databank, *Gallup/CNN/USA Today Poll*, (June 10, 1997).
108. Gallup/CNN/USA Today Poll.
109. Mercure v. Van Buren Township, 81 F. Supp. 2d 814 (E.D. Mich. 2000).
110. Seegmiller v. Laverkin City, 528 F.3d 762 (10th Cir. 2008).
111. *Seegmiller*, 528 F.3d at 772.
112. Stevens v. Holder, 966 F. Supp. 2d 622, 638 (E.D. Va. 2013).
113. *See* Rhode, *Adultery*, 60–62.
114. Associated Press Poll, June 1997, iPOLL Databank (retrieved March 10, 2014); Roper Center for Public Opinion Research, iPOLL Databank, *Gallup/CNN/USA Today Poll*, May, 1997(retrieved March 10, 2014) (61 percent); 55 percent of those with high school education or less and 71 percent of those with a college education.
115. Alyssa Newcomb, "Police Investigating Woman for Violating Adultery Law," *ABC News*, January 13, 2012, http://abcnews.go.com/blogs/headlines/2012/01/police-investigating-woman-for-violating-adultery-law/.
116. Barry Leibowitz, "Ariz. Man Wants Wife Prosecuted for Adultery," CBS News, January 18, 2012, http://www.cbsnews.com/news/ariz-man-wants-wife-prosecuted-for-adultery/.
117. Michael Sheridan, "Woman Caught Having Sex in Park, Charged with Adultery—in New York," *New York Daily News*, June 9, 2010 (quoting Larry Friedman).
118. Rhode, *Adultery*, 97.
119. Manual for Courts-Martial in the United States, Paragraphs 62(b)(1)–(3), 59(c)(2) (2008 ed).
120. Nancy Gibbs and John F. Dickerson, "Wings of Desire," TIME International (South Pacific Edition) June 2, 1997; Rhode, *Adultery*, 89–91.
121. David Van Biema and Sally B. Donnelly, "The Rules of Engagement," *TIME International* (South Pacific Edition,) June 2, 1997. For examples, see Rhode, *Adultery*, 100.
122. For examples, see Rhode, *Adultery*, 100–102.
123. Michael D. Shear, "Petraeus Quits; Evidence of Affair Was Found by F.B.I.," *New York Times*, November 9, 2012.
124. Roger Simon, "Petraeus Is Dumb, She's Dumber," *Politico*, November 13, 2012, http://www.politico.com/story/2012/11/petraeus-dumb-shes-dumber-083733.
125. CNN/ORC International Poll, iPoll Databank, November 27, 2012.
126. Quince Hopkins, "Rank Matters but Should Marriage? Adultery, Fraternization and Honor in the Military," *UCLA Women's Law Journal* 9 (1999):248, 260; Rhode, *Adultery*, 104.
127. Sewell Chan, "Is Adultery a Crime In New York?," *New York Times*, March 21, 2008.
128. Chan, "Is Adultery a Crime?
129. Bill Dentzer, "Legislative Reckoning All but Assured for Idaho's Guthrie, Perry," *Idaho Statesman*, September 16, 2016; Ruth Brown and Lis Stewart, "Two Idaho Legislators Face Investigations after Alleged Affair," *East Idaho News*, August 19, 2016.
130. Note, "Constitutional Barriers to Civil and Criminal Restrictions on Pre- and Extramarital Sex," *Harvard Law Review* 104 (1991):1660, 1672; Matthew Butler, "Getting Divorced: Grounds for Divorce: A Survey," *Journal of Contemporary Legal Issues* 11 (2000):16,

166 (property and alimony); Ali and Miller, "Secret Lives of Wives" (custody and support); Kelly McClure and Chris Meuse, "Adultery and Its Impact on Divorce," *Dallas Bar Association*, September, 2011; Peter Nash Swisher, "Marriage and Some Troubling Issues with No-Fault Divorce," *Regent University Law Review* 17 (2004):243; Farris v. Farris, 532 So. 2d 1041, 1043 (1988) (custody). For statutes providing for relevance of adultery in determining spousal support, see Fla. Stat. § 61.08(1) (2010); Ga. Code Ann. § 19-6-1(b) (2010); S.C. Code Ann. § 20-3-130(A) (2009); Va. Code Ann. § 20-107.1(E) (2010); W. Va. Code Ann. § 48-8-104 (2010). For adultery as an entitlement to alimony, see Adams v. Adams, 374 S.E.2d 450 (1988); N.C. Gen. Stat. § 50-16.2(I) (1989). For adultery as a bar to alimony, see Doe v. Doe, 634 S.E.2d 51 (S.C. Ct. App. 2006).

131. *Compare* Brown v. Brown, 237 S.E.2d 89, 91 (Va. 1977) (citing relevance of moral values) *with* Brinkley v. Brinkley, 336 S.E.2d 901 (Va. Ct. App. 1985) (affirming award of custody to adulterous mother) *and* Monk v. Monk, 386 So.2d 753, 755 (Ala. Civ. App. 1980) (awarding custody to adulterous mother where no adverse effect on child).
132. Rhode, *Adultery*, 84.
133. Rhode, *Adultery*, 79–82; Joanna L. Grossman and Lawrence M. Friedman, "The Legal Price of Adultery Goes Down: North Carolina and West Virginia Abandon Heartbalm Actions," *Justia*, June 24, 2014, https://verdict.justia.com/2014/06/24/legal-price-adultery-goes.
134. Jacob M. Appel, "Hate the Husband? Sue the Mistress!," *Huffington Post*, March 18, 2010, citing awards of $1.4 million and $2 million.
135. Oddo v. Presser, 581 S.E.2d 123 (N.C. Ct. App. 2003); Joanna L. Grossman and Lawrence M. Friedman, *Inside the Castle: Law and the Family in 20th Century America* (Princeton, NJ: Princeton University Press, 2011), 102.
136. Misenheimer v. Burris, 637 S.E.2d 173, 176 (N.C. 2006).
137. Grossman and Friedman, *Inside the Castle*, 102; Alice Gomstyn and Lee Ferran, "Wife's $9M Message to Mistresses: 'Lay Off,'" Abcnews.com, March 23, 2010.
138. Norton v. Macfarlane, 818 P.2d 8, 17 (Utah 1981).
139. "Man Sues Neighbor after Wife Dumps Him," *Chicago Tribune*, November 16, 2004.
140. Michael Kranish and Marc Fisher, *Trump Revealed: An American Journey of Ambition, Ego, Money, and Power* (New York: Scribner, 2016), 153–158; Howard Kurtz, "Marla Has Her Say about Ivana," *Washington Post*, July 25, 1990.
141. Donald Trump with Kate Bohner, *Trump: The Art of the Comeback* (New York: Times Books, 1997), 116; *see* Deborah L. Rhode, "Why Is Adultery Still a Crime?," *Los Angeles Times*, May 2, 2016 (quoting Donald Trump).
142. Roper Center for Public Opinion Research, iPOLL Databank, *Gallup/CNN/USA Today Poll*, June 2009 (June 26–28, 2009).
143. Quinnipiac University Poll, U.S. Voters Dislike Politicians Who Cheat Less than Those Who Abuse Power, Quinnipiac University National Poll Finds, April 28, 2014.
144. Robert P. Jones and Daniel Cox, "Clinton Maintains Double Digit Lead (51% vs. 36%) over Trump," *Public Religion Research Institute (PRRI)*, October 19, 2016, https://www.prri.org/research/prri-brookings-oct-19-poll-politics-election-clinton-double-digit-lead-trump/.
145. Gerard Baker, "Sex Americana," *Wall Street Journal*, June 27–28, 2009, W1 (quoting William Bennett).
146. Hugh Hartshorne and Mark A. May, *Studies in Deceit, Book II* (New York: Columbia University Teacher's College, 1930), 211–221.
147. *See* Rhode, *Adultery*, and James Pfiffner, "Presidential Character: Multidimensional or Seamless?," in Mark J. Rozell and Clyde Wilcox, *The Clinton Scandal and the Future of American Government* (Washington, DC: Georgetown University Press, 2000), 228–229.
148. Rhode, *Adultery*, 156-157.
149. Rhode, *Adultery*, 156–157; Paul J. Quirk, "Scandal Time: The Clinton Impeachment and the Distraction of American Politics," in Rozell and Wilcox, *Clinton Scandal*, 119, 129.

150. For such concerns, see Rhode, *Adultery*, 157, and J. Patrick Dobel, "Judging the Private Lives of Public Officials, Administration and Society" 30 (1998):115, 129.
151. Jim McGee, Tom Fiedler, and James Savage, "The Gary Hart Story: How It Happened," *Miami Herald*, May 10, 1987.
152. Paul Taylor, "Playing with Fire; When Gary Hart Destroyed His Own Candidacy, He Also Destroyed the Hopes and Dreams of His Loyal Staff," *Washington Post*, July 12, 1987 (quoting aide to Hart).
153. E.J. Dionne, David Johnston, Wayne King, and Jon Norheimer, "Courting Danger, The Fall of Gary Hart," *New York Times*, May 9, 1987.
154. Matt Bai, "How Gary Hart's Downfall Forever Changed American Politics," *New York Times Magazine*, September 18, 2014.
155. McGee et al., "Gary Hart Story."
156. "Gary Hart's Judgment," *New York Times*, May 5, 1987, A34.
157. Bai, "Gary Hart's Downfall."
158. Matt Bai, *All the Truth Is Out: The Week Politics Went Tabloid* (New York: Knopf Doubleday, 2014), 154–155.
159. Bai, *All the Truth Is Out*, 7.
160. Bai, *All the Truth Is Out*, 12–13.
161. Andrew Young, *The Politician: An Insider's Account of John Edwards's Pursuit of the Presidency and the Scandal That Brought Him Down* (New York: St. Martin's Press, 2010), 167.
162. Young, *The Politician*, 221.
163. John Heilemann and Mark Halperin, "Saint Elizabeth and the Ego Monster," *New York Magazine*, January 9, 2010.
164. Howard Kurtz and Lois Romano, "Edwards Admits He Had an Affair; Ex-candidate Says He Didn't Father Baby with Campaign Worker," *Washington Post*, August 9, 2008.
165. Katherine Q. Seelye, "Edwards Admits to Affair in 2006," *New York Times*, August 8, 2008.
166. Maureen Dowd, "Keeping It Rielle," *New York Times*, August 9, 2008.
167. Gabriel Sherman, "After the Fall," *New Republic*, June 29, 2010.
168. Kim Severson, "No New Trial for John Edwards," *New York Times*, June 13, 2012.
169. Peter Lattman and Kim Severson, "John Edwards Revisits His Past, Hanging Out Law Shingle Again," *New York Times*, November 19, 2013.
170. Sherman, "After the Fall."
171. Nigel Cawthorne, *Sex Lives of the Presidents: An Irreverent Expose of the Chief Executive from George Washington to the Present Day* (New York: St. Martin's 1998), 257.
172. Ken Gormley, *The Death of American Virtue: Clinton vs. Starr* (New York: Scribner, 2012), 10.
173. Peter Baker, *The Breach: Inside the Impeachment and Trial of William Jefferson Clinton* (New York: Scribner, 2000), 34.
174. Robert Busby, *Defending the American Presidency: Clinton and the Lewinsky Scandal* (New York: Palgrave, 2001), 42.
175. Wesley O. Hagood, *Presidential Sex: From the Founding Fathers to Bill Clinton* (New York: Citadel, 1998), 216–217.
176. Busby, *Defending the American Presidency*, 43; Hagood, *Presidential Sex*, 209. David Brock, "His Cheating Heart," *American Spectator*, December 20, 1993, 21.
177. Dan Balz, "Clinton Concedes Marital 'Wrongdoing,'" *Washington Post*, January 27, 1992.
178. Andrew Morton, *Monica's Story* (New York: St. Martin's Press, 1999), 63.
179. Jeffrey Toobin, *A Vast Conspiracy* (New York: Random House, 1999), 85.
180. Toobin: *Vast Conspiracy*, 180.
181. Bill Clinton, *My Life* (New York: Knopf, 2009), 774.
182. Morton, *Monica's Story*, 151–152.
183. Joseph R. Blaney and William L. Benoit, *The Clinton Scandals and the Politics of Image Restoration* (Westport, CT: Praeger, 2001), 85.
184. Toobin, *Vast Conspiracy*, 244.

185. Elizabeth Drew, *The Corruption of American Politics: What Went Wrong and Why* (Woodstock, NY: Overlook Press, 1999), 323–325.
186. For excerpts, see James Bennet, "Testing of a President: The Overview: Clinton Admits Lewinsky Liaison to Jury; Tells Nation 'It Was Wrong' But Private,'" *New York Times*, August 18, 1998, A1.
187. Blaney and Benoit, *Clinton Scandals*, 99; Molly Andolina and Clyde Wilcox, "Public Opinion: The Paradox of Clinton's Popularity," in Rozell and Wilcox, eds., *Clinton Scandal*, 174; 188–189; CNN, Poll: More Americans Satisfied with Clinton's Explanation, August 17, 1998, http://www.cnn.com/ALLPOLITICS/1998/08/17/poll/.
188. "Poll: Clinton's Approval Rating Up in Wake of Impeachment," *allpolitics.com*, December 20, 1998, http://www.cnn.com/ALLPOLITICS/stories/1998/12/20/impeachment.poll/.
189. Maureen Dowd, "A Popular President," *New York Times*, July 19, 2014 (citing *Wall Street Journal*/NBC News/Annenberg Center poll).
190. Robbie Brown and Shaila Dewan, "Mysteries Remain after Governor Admits an Affair," *New York Times*, June 24, 2009.
191. Brown and Dewan, "Mysteries Remain;" Tamara Lush and Evan Berland, "S.C. Gov 'Crossed Lines' with Women," AP, July 28, 2009. *See* Alex Roth and Valerie Bauerlein, "Sanford Says He Had Extramarital Affair," *Wall Street Journal*, June 24, 2009. Cliff LeBlanc and John O'Connor, "Sanford Admits Affair: I've Let Down a Lot of People," *The State* (Columbia, South Carolina), June 25, 2009.
192. Brown and Dewan, "Mysteries Remain."
193. Roper Center for Public Opinion Research, iPOLL Databank, *Gallup/CNN/USA Today Poll*, June, 2009, (June 26–28, 2009).
194. "Leadership in South Carolina," *New York Times*, June 26, 2009.
195. Shaila Dewan, "S.C. Panel Kills Measure to Impeach Governor," *New York Times*, December 16, 2009.
196. Robbie Brown, "Sanford's Wife Files for Divorce," *New York Times*, December 11, 2009; Jenny Sanford, *Staying True* (New York: Ballantine Books, 2010).
197. The couple's plans to marry have been on hold while they focus on their children. Emily Heil, "Rep. Mark Sanford's Former Fiancee Clarifies: They're Still Together," *Washington Post*, December 10, 2015. *See also* Kate Bennett, " 'Luv Guv' Sanford Spotted with Argentine Girl Friend," *Politico*, June 18, 2015.
198. Ashley Parker, "On Capitol Hill, Sanford Picks Up Where He Left Off," *New York Times*, May 15, 2013.
199. Ross Douthat, "Mark Sanford's God," *NewYorkTimes.com*, May 9, 2013, http://douthat.blogs.nytimes.com/2013/05/09/mark-sanfords-god/?php=true&-type==blogs&_r=0 (quoting Jonah Goldberg).
200. Kim Severson, "Looking Past Sex Scandal, South Carolina Returns Ex-governor to Congress," *New York Times*, May 7, 2013.
201. Nate Silver, "Sanford and the Electoral Effect of Sex Scandals," *New York Times*, May 8, 2013.
202. Bai, *All the Truth Is Out*, 23.
203. Joanne B. Ciulla, "Dangerous Liaisons: Adultery and the Ethics of Presidential Leadership," in Georges Goethals and Douglas Bradburn, eds., *Politics, Ethics and Change: The Legacy of James MacGregor Burns* (Northampton, MA: Edward Elgar, 2016), 92.

## Chapter 9

1. Josephson Institute of Ethics, *2012 Report Card on the Ethics of American Youth* (Los Angeles: Josephson Institute, 2012).
2. Josephson Institute of Ethics, *2012 Report Card*.
3. Christian Smith, with Kari Christoffersen, Hillary Davidson, and Patricia Snell Herzog, *Lost in Transition* (New York: Oxford University Press, 2011), 21.
4. Smith, *Lost in Transition*, 21.
5. Smith, *Lost in Transition*, 23.

6. Smith, *Lost in Transition*, 47, 48.
7. William Damon and Anne Colby, *The Power of Ideals: The Real Story of Moral Choice* (New York: Oxford University Press, 2015), 120.
8. Alan Wolfe, *Moral Freedom: The Impossible Idea That Defines the Way We Live Now* (New York, W.W. Norton, 2001), 125.
9. Wolfe, *Moral Freedom*, 108.
10. Wolfe, *Moral Freedom*, 130.
11. Smith, *Lost in Transition*, 141.
12. Sue Shellenbarger, "How Could a Sweet Third-Grader Just Cheat on That School Exam?," *Wall Street Journal*, May 15, 2013.
13. Shellenbarger, "How Could a Sweet Third-Grader Just Cheat."
14. For the importance of modeling behavior, see Marvin W. Berkowitz and John H. Grych, "Fostering Goodness: Teaching Parents to Facilitate Children's Moral Development," *Journal of Moral Education* 27 (1998):371, 384–385.
15. Diane Baumrind, "Parenting Styles and Adolescent Development," in Richard M. Lerner, Ann C. Peterson, and Jeanne Brooks-Gunn, eds., *The Encyclopedia of Adolescence* (New York: Garland, 1989). *See also* Lawrence Steinberg, Nina S. Mounts, Susie D. Lamborn, and Sanford M. Dornbusch, "Authoritative Parenting and Adolescent Adjustment across Varied Ecological Niches," *Journal of Research on Adolescence* 1 (1991):19.
16. Berkowitz and Grych, "Fostering Goodness," 371, 382; Thomas Lickona, *Raising Good Children: From Birth through the Teenage Years* (New York: Bantam Books, 1983), 18–19; William Damon, *The Moral Child: Nurturing Children's Moral Growth* (New York: Free Press, 2008), 124.
17. Berkowitz and Grych, "Fostering Goodness," 384.
18. Berkowitz and Grych, "Fostering Goodness," 385. *See also* Lickona, *Raising Good Children*, 20.
19. Sonia L. Nazario, "Schoolteachers Say It's Wrongheaded to Try to Teach Students What's Right," *Wall Street Journal*, April 6, 1990; "A Study of Core Values and the Schools," *Phi Delta Kappan*, October 1996, discussed in Thomas Lickona, "The Case for Character Education," *Tikkun*, January/February 1997, 26.
20. Paul Tough, *How Children Succeed: Grit, Curiosity, and the Hidden Power of Character* (Boston: Houghton Mifflin Harcourt, 2012), 59. *See* Roger Rosenblatt, "Teaching Johnny to Be Good," *New York Times Magazine*, April 30, 1995; and Charles Helwig, Elliot Turiel, and Larry Nucci, "Character Education after the Bandwagon Has Gone," Paper presented at Developmental Perspectives and Approaches to Character Education Symposium at American Educational Research Association Meeting, Chicago, March 1997.
21. Esther Brown, "No Child Left Behind and the Teaching of Character Education," *ABNF Journal* (Summer 2013):77–78.
22. Sense of Congress regarding Good Character, Public Law No. 105–244 Section 863.
23. Anita L. Allen, *The New Ethics: A Tour of the Twenty-First Century Moral Landscape* (New York: Miramax Books, 2004), 74.
24. Brown, "No Child Left Behind," 79.
25. Social and Character Development Research Consortium, *Efficacy of Schoolwide Programs to Promote Social and Character Development and Reduce Problem Behavior in Elementary School Children* (Washington, DC: National Center for Education Research, Institute of Education Sciences, U.S. Department of Education, 2010); Sarah D. Sparks, "Character Education Found to Fall Short in Federal Study," *Education Week*, October 21, 2010.
26. Francis Schoonmaker Bolin and Robert L. Kennedy, *Growing Up Caring: Exploring Values and Decision Making* (Lake Forest, IL: Glencoe, Macmillan/McGraw Hill, 1990), 34.
27. Sparks, "Character Education Found to Fall Short in Federal Study."
28. Thomas Lickona, *Educating for Character: How Our Schools Can Teach Respect and Responsibility* (New York: Bantam, 1991), 13.
29. "Poll Shows Most Prefer Values Taught at School," *Fort Worth Star-Telegram*, October 9, 1994, 8. *See* William J. Bennett, *Book of Virtues: A Treasury of Great Moral Stories* (New York: Simon and Schuster, 1993).
30. Stephen L. Carter, *Integrity* (New York: Perseus Basic Books, 1996), 238.

31. Bennett, *Book of Virtues.*
32. Marvin W. Berkowitz, "Civics and Moral Education," in Bob Moon, Sally Brown, and Miriam Ben-Peretz, eds., *Routledge International Companion to Education* (New York: Routledge, 2000), 897, 905.
33. Berkowitz, "Civics and Moral Education," 907. *See also* Marvin W. Berkowitz, *The Education of the Compete Moral Person* (Aberdeen, Scotland: Gordon Cook Foundation, 1995); William Damon and Anne Colby, "Education and Moral Commitment," *Journal of Moral Education* 25 (1996), 31; and Edward F. DeRoche and Mary M. Williams, *Educating Hearts and Minds: A Comprehensive Character Education Framework* (Thousand Oaks, CA: Sage, 1998).
34. De Roche and Williams, *Educating Hearts and Minds*, 59.
35. De Roche and Williams, *Educating Hearts and Minds*, 73.
36. Christopher Peterson and Martin E.P. Seligman, *Character Strengths and Virtues* (New York: Oxford University Press, 2004), 27.
37. R.M. Aaron, "Student Academic Dishonesty: Are Collegiate Institutions Addressing the Issue?," *NASPA Journal* 29 (1992):107.
38. Jeffrey A. Dubin, "Criminal Investigation Enforcement Activities and Taxpayer Noncompliance," *Public Finance Review* 35 (2007):500, 523.
39. Insurance Information Institute, "Insurance Fraud" (March 2015).
40. Lisa L. Shu et al., "Signing at the Beginning Makes Ethics Salient and Decreases Dishonest Self-Reports in Comparison to Signing at the End," Proceedings of the National Academy of Sciences of the USA (August 27, 2012), http://www.pnas.org/content/early/2012/08/22/1209746109.full.pdf; John Beshears and Francesca Gino, "Leaders as Decision Architects," *Harvard Business Review* (May 2015):60.
41. Randy Cohen, *The Good, the Bad, & the Difference, How to Tell Right from Wrong in Everyday Situations* (New York: Broadway Books, 2002), 53–54.
42. Cohen, *The Good, The Bad, & the Difference*, 37.
43. Roy V. Baumeister and Julie Juola Exline, "Virtue, Personality, and Social Relations: Self Control as the Moral Muscle," *Journal of Personality* 67 (1999):1165, 1176–1177.
44. Mark Twain, *The Innocents Abroad* (New York: Oxford University Press, 1996 ed.) (original ed. 1896), 590.

# INDEX


ABC/*Washington Post* poll
  on tax evasion by the wealthy, 68
  on tax reform, 74
Academic cheating, 75–85. *See also* Plagiarism
  character education programs in schools, 136–137
  conditions facilitating, 80, 83
  contemporary situation of, 76, 137
  faculty's failure to enforce rules, 81–82, 139
  fairness as part of learning experience, 82
  file-sharing violations, 96–97
  fraternities and sororities assisting in, 79
  frequency of, 4–5, 77–78, 133, 175n29
  gender differences in, 79
  high-tech cheating, 76
  history of, 75
  honor codes, 16, 80–81
  instructor's quality and fairness as issues, 80, 82
  international comparison of frequency, 78
  Internet and, 76
  leniency, effect of, 83
  likelihood of detection for student cheating, 80, 83
  national initiatives to address, 84
  parental pressure and, 78, 80, 135
  prestigious institutions involved in, 76, 83
  prior cheating as predictive of, 80
  proctoring exams, 83
  profile of individual cheaters, 78–80
  punishment for, 80, 82, 83, 97, 137
  rationalizations for, 78–80
  reinforcement of ethical conduct, 15, 83, 137
  reporting procedures, 82, 83, 139
  research misconduct, 84–85
  responses to, 80–84, 136–137
  skills programs for students as part of response to, 83, 137
  student reluctance to inform another student, 81, 133
  student-run honor councils, 81
Accenture survey on padding insurance claims, 103
Adultery. *See* Marital infidelity
Affordable Care Act of 2010, 110
Airley, Dan, 76, 83
Alienation of affection, 123
Allen, Anita, 136–137
Almonte, Danny, 22
Amateur Athletic Union basketball coaches, 22
Ambrose, Stephen, 87–88, 90–91
American Academy of Matrimonial Lawyers, 113
American Assembly (Columbia University), 4, 94
American Historical Association, 87
Amphetamine, 25, 26, 154n104
Anabolic steroids, 25, 28
Angell, Robert, 75
Angus Reid survey on marital infidelity, 120
Apple Music, 97
Aramony, William, 39
Archer, Bill, 73
Ariely, Dan, 10, 11–12, 20
Armstrong, Lance, 27–28
Arson, 102
Arthur Anderson, 42, 44
*The Art of the Comeback* (Trump), 124
Ashley Madison (Internet site), 113
Association of American Law Schools, 86
Athletes. *See* Sports cheating
Atlanta educators guilty of racketeering for systemic cheating, 76

Atlanta Falcons, 22
Attestation statements of truthfulness, 16–17, 72, 111, 138
Attorneys. *See* Lawyers
Auburn University curriculum for athletes, 33
Auto body repair shops, 104
Auto insurance fraud, 104–105
Auto manufacturers, 41, 42, 49, 133, 160n65

Bai, Matt, 130
Baird, Zoe, 63
Baisden, Michael, 119
Bakija, Jon, 66, 73
Bamberger, George, 30
Bank Leumi, 70
Bankman, Joseph, 71–72
Bank of America, 37
Banks, Dave, 121
Barkley, Charles, 31
Barra, Mary, 49
Bay Area Laboratory Cooperative (BALCO), 28
Bazerman, Max, 7
Becker, Boris, 62
Belichick, Bill, 23
Benefits vs. harms analysis, 4, 11, 25, 61, 66, 70–71
Benevolent lies, 2
Bennett, William, 124
Best practices
  disclosure of research and writing contributions, 86
  moral education, 137
  whistle-blowing, 55
BF Goodrich, 49
Biden, Joseph, 63, 91
Blue Cross and Blue Shield on recovery from antifraud investigations, 110
"Boiled frog problem," 9
Bok, Sissela, 2, 142n21
Bonds, Barry, 28
Boston Marathon, 19
Boy Scouts' merit badge "Respect Copyrights," 98
Bradley, Bill, 73
Brady, Tom, 21–22
Bribery, 20–21, 23
Buffet, Warren, 66
Butterfield, Kenneth, 77

Cabrera, Melky, 30
California Department of Savings and Loans Commissioner, 43
Callahan, David, 68
Canseco, Jose, 28
Carter, Stephen, 23
CBS News on student cheating, 78
Center for Academic Integrity, 84
Center for Public Integrity, 109
Character Counts Coalition, 136
Character education programs, 136–137
"Cheater's high," 14
Cheating. *See also* Academic cheating; Insurance fraud; Marital infidelity; Mortgage fraud; Sports cheating; Tax evasion
  causes of, 5–6, 134–135
  costs of, 1, 4, 133, 138
  cultures and contexts, 15–16, 124
  decision-making processes, 6–9, 17
  definitions of, 2–4, 134
  ethical codes, effectiveness of, 16, 138
  ethical enforcement structures and, 17–18
  habituation and desensitization to, 8
  likelihood of getting caught as factor. *See* Likelihood of detection
  moral intent and, 14–15
  moral reminders, effectiveness of, 16–17, 72, 111, 138
  rationalizations, 1, 8, 10–14, 134–135
  scope of, 4–5
  situational variables and, 5, 11, 134, 139
  social influences, 5, 9–10
  strategies to address, 15–18, 135–139
*The Cheating Culture* (Callahan), 68
*Cheating the Spread* (Figone), 21
Children. *See also* Academic cheating; Sports cheating
  child athletes, 22
  child custody decisions, 123, 192n131
  effect of marital infidelity on, 119
  parental pressure resulting in cheating, 78, 80, 135
  parental role in encouraging ethical behavior of, 15, 80, 135
Chinese civil service exams, cheating on, 75
*Chronicle of Higher Education*, 89
Churchill, Winston, 51
Cialdini, Robert, 17
Ciulla, Joanne, 130
Class action suits, 14, 39, 106
Clemens, Roger, 28
Clinics engaged in workers' compensation fraud, 105–106
Clinton, Bill, 19, 63, 66, 125, 127–129, 136
Clinton, Hillary Rodham, 85, 127–129
Coalition Against Insurance Fraud, 107
Coburn, Tom, 102
Coffee, John, 40
Cognitive dissonance, 10
Cognitive moral development, 6
Cohen, Randy, 138–139
Colby, Ann, 134
College football games, 35
College sports. *See* Sports cheating
Collins, Jim, 58

Columbia University's American Assembly, 4, 94
Conflicts of interest, 7, 10
  rules for faculty, 85
Consumer fraud, 14. *See also* Copyright infringement; Insurance fraud
Consumer role in combatting insurance fraud, 111
Contractor fraud after natural disasters, 102
Copyright infringement, 85, 93–99
  adaptation strategies, 96–98
  causes of, 94–95
  costs of, 94, 181n16
  deterrence strategies, 95–96
  ease of detecting electronically, 93
  fair use, 85, 98
  flat-fee streaming and downloading services, 97–98, 139
  frequency of, 93, 94
  likelihood of detection, 93, 94
  peer-to-peer file-sharing, 93, 94, 97
  penalties and damages, 93, 95–96, 99
  persuasion strategies, 98
  rationalizations and excuses for, 95
  reforms needed to reconcile legal and social norms, 99, 139
  surrender approach, 98–99
Copyright Term Extension Act of 1998, 95
Cornell University, 35
Corporate fraud. *See* Organizations, cheating in
Costs associated with cheating, 1, 4, 133, 138
  copyright infringement, 94, 181n16
  health insurance fraud, 101
  insurance fraud, 4, 101, 104, 106, 138
  in organizational settings, 37–39
  tax evasion, 4, 61, 72
Credibility at issue, 3, 90, 124
Credit Suisse, 17
Criminal conversation, 123
Crowley, Monica, 88
Cryptomnesia, 90
Cultural contexts and cheating, 15–16, 124
  workplace culture, 40, 41–45
Cyberloafing, 13, 38, 44

Damon, William, 134
Dartmouth College, 7, 35
*The Death of the Income Tax* (Goldberg), 74
Deflategate, 21
Department of ____. *See name of specific department*
De Steno, David, 6
Detection. *See* Likelihood of detection
Deterrence strategies. *See also* Sanctions
  academic cheating, 80, 82
  copyright infringement, 95–96
  mortgage fraud, 111
  tax evasion, 65, 68, 69–70, 138
DeVos, Betsy, 88
Diekmann, Kristina A. , 7
*Digital Life*'s survey on downloading practices, 93
Disability fraud, 102, 110
Disaster-related insurance fraud, 102, 104–105
Dishonesty. *See* Cheating
Dismissal from job for adulterous relationships, 120–121
Divorce, 118, 120, 123, 133, 191–192n130
Doehring, Jim, 26
Domestic violence, 118, 133
Doping in athletic competitions, 24–29
  ban against, 24–25
  current challenges, 26–29
  historical background, 25–26
  likelihood of detection, 28
  penalties and enforcement, 29
  substances constituting, 24
  therapeutic use exemption, 28–29
Doran, Michael, 69
Dowd, Maureen, 127
Downloading, illegal, 4, 13. *See also* Copyright infringement
  peer-to-peer file-sharing, 93, 94, 97
Drier, Mark, 9, 12
Druckerman, Pamela, 117–118
Drug testing, 28, 30. *See also* Doping in athletic competitions

Ease of continuing to cheat, 3, 8–9, 22, 24, 78, 83, 109
Eastern Intercollegiate Athletic Association, 35
Ebbers, Bernard, 5
Education Department, U.S., study on character education programs, 136
Edwards, John and Elizabeth, 125, 126–127, 130
Ego strength, 15
Eisenhower, Dwight, 19
Electronic Frontier Foundation, 99
Employee theft, 4, 37–38
Employment-related cheating. *See* Organizations, cheating in
Enron, 5, 16, 42, 43, 44, 46, 53
Ephedrine, 25
Ephron, Nora, 115
Erythropoietin (EPO), 25, 26
Escalation of commitment, 9
Ethical codes, 16, 53–54, 138
Ethical dissonance, 10
Ethical enforcement structures, 17–18, 137. *See also* Honor codes; Sanctions
Ethical fading, 7–8, 41
Ethical numbing, 8
Ethical reasoning skills, 137
Ethics training, 54–55

Euphemisms, use of, 8, 41
European practice of scholars publishing material written by assistants, 85

Fairchild, Gary, 5
Fairness. *See* Unfairness
Fair use, 85, 98
False Claims Act, 70
Family role. *See* Children
Federal Bureau of Investigation (FBI)
on healthcare fraud, 106–107
on mortgage fraud, 108, 110
sanctions for adulterous relationships within, 121
Federal Reserve Bank, 48
Fen-phen litigation, 106
Festinger, Leon, 10
Feurstein, Donald, 47–48
FIFA (International Federation of Association Football), 23
Figone, Albert J., 21
Financial crisis of 2008, 101, 108
*The Fitzgeralds and the Kennedys* (Goodwin), 87
Flat tax, 73
Flowers, Gennifer, 127–128
Foreclosure, 109
Fortune 500 companies, 42
Fraud
consumer fraud. *See* Consumer fraud
disability fraud, 102, 110
insurance. *See* Insurance fraud; *specific type of insurance*
mortgage fraud, 108–110
pension fund fraud, 39
research misconduct, 84
resume fraud, 38, 84
*From Hire to Liar: The Role of Deception in the Workplace* (Shulman), 38
Fudge factor theory, 10, 13–14
Fundamental attribution error, 5

Gallup polls
on schools teaching moral values, 136
on tax evasion by the wealthy, 68
Galvin, Pud, 25
Gambling and college sports, 20–21, 22
*Game of Shadows* (Fainaru-Wada & Williams), 28
*Game of Thrones* (HBO show), illegal downloads of, 94
Gatekeepers, 52
Gender differences
in academic cheating, 79
in insurance fraud, 103
in marital infidelity, 114, 116, 118–119, 122, 123
General Motors, 41, 49
General Social Survey
on marital infidelity, 114
on tax evasion, 171n88
Gert, Bernard, 2, 3, 113–114
Goldberg, Daniel S., 64, 74
Goldman Sachs, 46, 54
*Good to Great* (Collins), 58
Goodwin, Doris Kearns, 87, 91
Gorsuch, Neil, 88
Group loyalty, 44
*Growing Up Caring* (school text), 136
Gruneisen, Aline, 76
Gutfreund, John, 46, 48

Habituation and desensitization, 8
Haley, Alex, 87
Harding, Tonya, 22–23
Harper Collins, 88
Harrington, Noreen, 54
Harris poll on tax evasion, 64
Hart, Gary, 125–126
Hartshorn, Hugh, 5, 78–79
Harvard University
conflict of interest rules for faculty, 85
faculty committing plagiarism, 87
student cheating scandal, 76
Hatch, Orrin, 63
Health and Human Services Department, U.S.
National Fraud Prevention Partnership, 110
sanctions on Medicare/Medicaid fraud perpetrators, 110
Healthcare providers
in health insurance scams, 106
in workers' compensation scams, 105–106
Health insurance fraud, 106–108
Blue Cross and Blue Shield's recovery from antifraud investigations, 110
costs of, 101
types of, 106–107
*Heartburn* (Ephron), 115
Helmsley, Leona, 64
Hicks, Thomas, 25
Higher Education Act amendment of 1998, 136
Higher Education Opportunity Act of 2008, 96
High-tech cheating, 76
Hoffer, Peter Charles, 89
Holmes, Oliver Wendell, Jr., 74
Home appraisals, 108, 109
*The (Honest) Truth about Dishonesty* (Ariely), 10
Honesty
academic expectations of, 82. *See also* Honor codes
affirmations of. *See* Attestation statements of truthfulness
of athletes, 20, 25, 34
claims of, as puffery, 46

ethical codes encouraging, 138
as moral absolute, 2
parental role in promoting, 80, 135
philosophical views on, 2
public opinion viewing as an ideal that is tempered by reality, 134
school role in promoting, 15
of taxpayers, 65, 69
Honesty tests, 5
Honor codes, 16, 80–81
Horseracing Integrity and Safety Act (proposed, but not enacted), 27
Hotlines, 51, 111, 137
Hubbell, Web, 13
Human growth hormones, 25–26, 28
Hunter, Rielle, 126–127
Hurricane Katrina insurance fraud, 102
Hypocrites, 11, 12, 53

Identity theft, 107
India, publication of tax evaders' names in, 71
Infringement. *See* Copyright infringement
"The Inner Ring" (Lewis), 45
Insurance fraud, 101–111
arson, 102
auto insurance fraud, 104–105
causes of, 103–104
contractor fraud after natural disasters, 102
costs of, 4, 101, 104, 106, 138
disability claims, 102, 103
disaster-related claims, 102, 104–105
frequency of, 101, 102
gender differences in, 103
hard vs. soft fraud, 101–102
health insurance fraud, 106–108
insurance industry's reimbursement policies, 103–104
likelihood of detection, 94, 103, 107, 111
low likelihood of detection, 103
monetary recovery from antifraud investigations, 110, 138
opportunistic fraud, 102
organized crime perpetrating, 102, 104
oversubscription, 104–105
padding claims, 102–104
public relations campaigns, 111
rationalizations, 103
reporting, predictors of, 103
retaliation as cause of, 103
staging accidents, 102, 104, 110, 133
state insurance fraud bureaus, 110
strategies to address, 110–111
swearing by claimants to truthfulness of statements, 111
types of, 101–103
whistle-blowers, 111
workers' compensation fraud, 105–106
Insurance Information Institute, 101
Insurance Research Council, 103, 104
Integrity
academic integrity, 76, 80–84, 88
academic integrity pledges, 81
of athletes, 20, 24
claims of, as puffery, 46
loss of, as self-harm, 3
national loss of, 23
organizational role to promote, 16, 51
parental role to promote, 135
plagiarism undermining, 90–91
of politicians, 124, 127
research integrity programs, 75
values education to promote, 136
Intermediaries used in committing fraud, 11
International Association of Athletics Federation, 25
International Federation of Association Football (FIFA), 23
International Olympic Committee (IOC), 26, 29
Internet
academic misconduct and, 76
downloading illegally. *See* Copyright infringement; Downloading, illegal
extramarital relationships and, 113
offshore tax evasion over, 62
Internet service providers (ISPs)
detecting copyright violations, 93
issuing warnings of copyright infringement, 97
Irdeto (security firm) on film and TV piracy, 94
*It Takes a Village* (H. Clinton), 85

Jackall, Robert, 37, 39, 45
Jackie Robinson West Little League team, 22
Japanese tax system, 72–73
Jensen, Knud, 26
Johnson, Samuel, 3
Johnson and Johnson, 107
Jones, Marion, 27
Jordan, R. H., 31–32
Josephson, Michael, 24
Josephson Institute of Ethics, 133
JP Heinz, 40
JPMorgan Chase, 37
*Juiced* (Canseco), 28
Justice Department
corporate violators of SEC regulations prosecuted by, 18
Inspector General report on mortgage fraud, 110
National Center for Disaster Fraud, 102
National Fraud Prevention Partnership, 110
recovery of tax monies due to whistle-blowing, 70

Kahnemann, Daniel, 7
Kant, Immanuel, 2
Kickbacks in insurance fraud schemes, 106, 107
Kimmel, Jimmy, 61
King, Martin Luther, Jr., 87
Kinsey Institute survey on marital infidelity, 114
Kirshner, Julius, 87
Kohlberg, Lawrence, 6
Kozlowski, Dennis, 13, 62
KPMG study on employee theft, 4
Krimmage, Paul, 27

*Lasting Leadership* (Pandya, Shell, & Warner), 59
Lawyers
  fraudulent billing practices (padding) of, 8–9, 13, 44
  mortgage fraud, punishment of lawyers involved in, 111
  Ponzi scheme of Marc Drier, 9, 12
  "rescue attorneys" and mortgage fraud, 109
  in workers' compensation scams, 106
Lay, Ken, 5, 50
Lemley, Mark, 96, 99
Lerman, Lisa, 86
Leslie Fay accountants, 43
Lewinsky, Monica, 128–129
Lewis, C.S., 45
Lewis, Michael, 39–40
*Liar's Poker* (Lewis), 39–40
Likelihood of detection
  academic cheating by students, 80, 83
  doping by athletes, 28
  downloading piracy, 93, 94
  effect of low likelihood, 18, 133–134
  insurance fraud, 94, 103, 107, 111
  plagiarism, 85, 86
  sports cheating, 21, 24, 30
  tax evasion, 64–65, 69, 70
Limewire (file-sharing site), 96
Little League World Series, 22
Luban, David and Daniel, 30

Maddow, Rachel, 91
Madoff, Bernie, 10, 12
Magnatune, 98
Major League Baseball, 28
Maples, Marla, 124
Mar-a-Lago Club (Trump's resort), 39
Marital infidelity, 113–131
  causes of, 115–116
  child custody decisions and, 123, 192n131
  children, effect on, 119
  clergy held to higher standard, 120, 191n107
  consequences of, 116–119
  criminal conversation cases, 123
  criminal prohibitions on, 121, 139
  definition of, 113–114
  demographics of, 114
  divorce due to, 118, 123, 191–192n130
  domestic violence due to, 118
  frequency of, 4, 113–114
  gender differences in, 114, 116, 118–119, 122, 123
  genetic predisposition toward, 115
  international comparison of views on, 120
  jealousy in response to, 118–119
  job sanctions for, 120–121
  legal sanctions for, 121–123, 139
  marital satisfaction correlated with, 113, 115–116, 188–189n37
  military sanctions for, 120, 121–122
  political sanctions for, 124–130
  predictors of, 116
  public opinion on, 120–121, 122, 131, 190n95, 190n102, 191n103
  sanctions for, 123–131
  shaming of individuals engaging in, 120
  spouse's discovery of, 117–118
Martial (Roman poet), 75
Matza, David, 12
May, Mark, 5, 78–79
McCabe, Donald, 77, 81
McCaffrey, Ed, 62
McCartney, Bill, 35
McGuire, Mark, 28
Media coverage of scandals
  deterrent effect of, 90
  turning into teachable moments, 138
Medicaid fraud, 56, 106, 107, 110
Medicare fraud, 42, 106, 107, 110, 186n94
Medicare Fraud Strike Task Force, 110
Meriwether, John, 47
Merrill Lynch, 10, 42
Messick, David, 7, 18
*Miami Herald* on Gary Hart's philandering, 125–126
Microsoft survey on Internet piracy, 94–95
Military sanctions for marital infidelity, 120, 121–122
Milken, Michael, 18
Minnesota study of taxpayers informed that their returns would be closely examined, 69
Mistrust, as cause of resentment, 17
Mitchell, George, 28
Modern Language Association's definition of plagiarism, 86
Montana, Joe, 21–22
Moral disengagement, 13
Moral intent, 14–15
*Moral Mazes* (Jackall), 39, 45
Moral reasoning and development, 6
Moral reminders, 16–17, 72, 111, 138

Morris, Dick, 128
Mortgage fraud, 101, 108–110
  application fraud, 101, 108
  appraisal fraud, 108, 109
  deterrence strategies, 111
  mortgage brokers' dishonesty, 101
  punishment of lawyers involved in, 111
  task force on San Francisco Bay Area home mortgage fraud, 109–110
Motion Picture Association of America, 98
Motivated blindness, 7, 28
Mozer, Paul, 47, 48
Mulvoy, Mark, 19–20
Murray, Patty, 88
Music piracy, 4, 13, 93, 181n16. *See also* Copyright infringement
Myers, Dee Dee, 63

Nass, Clifford, 72
National Association of Insurance Commissioners, 110
National Center for Disaster Fraud, 102
National Center for Education Statistics, 136
National Collegiate Athletic Association (NCAA), 22, 26, 32, 34
*National Enquirer* on John Edwards' philandering, 127
National Football League, 21
National Fraud Prevention Partnership, 110
National Health Care Fraud Association, 110
National Insurance Crime Bureau, 101, 110
National Science Foundation. *See* General Social Survey
Netflix, 98
Netherlands, tax auditing in, 69
NetNames on online copyright infringement, 94
Neuroscience, 7
*Never Satisfied: How and Why Men Cheat* (Baisden), 119
New England Patriots, 21, 23
New Orleans Saints, 22
New York Federal Reserve Bank, 48
*New York Times*
  on Gary Hart's philandering, 125–126
  on Mark Sanford's philandering, 129
*New York Times*/CBS poll on Internet file-sharing, 95
Nicklaus, Jack, 19
*Nightline* appearance of John Edwards, 127
Nike
  General Counsel, 52
  Oregon Project, 27
NinjaVideo (file-sharing site), 96
Nixon, Richard, 124
Noble lies, 2
No Child Left Behind Act, 76
Norway, norms governing Internet downloading, 97
NPR/Kaiser Family Foundation survey on tax reform, 74

Obama, Barack, 52
Occupy Wall Street, 56
Office of Research Integrity, 84
Offshore tax shelters, 62, 65
Ogletree, Charles, 87
Olympic games, 19, 23, 25–27, 29, 31
Ombudspersons, 51, 137
Opportunistic fraud, 102
Organizations, cheating in, 37–59
  American indifference to, 57
  conditions influencing, 41–50
  costs of, 37–39
  cyberloafing, 13, 38, 44
  diffusion and displacement of responsibility, 47–49
  ethical climate surveys, 138
  ethical cultures, need for, 16
  ethical leadership, 52–53, 137
  ethics codes, 53–54
  ethics training, 54–55
  financial sector, 37
  pilfering (employee theft), 4, 37–38
  rationalizations, 42, 44, 45, 54
  reluctance to air dirty laundry in public, 18
  research and reassessment, 58–59
  responses to cheating, 50–52, 137–139
  resume fraud, 38, 84
  sanctions, 56–58
  types of, 38
  Wall Street traders, 39, 40
  whistle-blowers, 17, 49–50, 55–56
  workplace culture, climate, and financial pressures, 40, 41–45
Organized crime and insurance fraud, 102, 104
Originality, 86
*Out of Character* (De Steno & Valdesolo), 6
Oversubscription in disaster insurance claims, 104–105

Palmer, Arnold, 20
Panama law firm, 62
Parent-child relationship. *See* Children
Paterson, David, 122
Peer-to-peer file-sharing, 93, 94, 97. *See also* Copyright infringement
Penalties for cheating. *See* Responses to cheating; Sanctions
Pennsylvania antifraud agency's public relations campaign against insurance fraud, 111
Pension fund fraud, 39
Perez-Truglia, Ricardo, 71
Perry, Gaylord, 21

Personality traits of cheaters, 5–6
Peterson, Christopher, 137
Petraeus, David, 122
Pew polls
  on Internet file sharing, 95
  on marital infidelity, 120, 190n102
  on tax reform, 74
Pfizer, 107
Philip Morris, 58
Plagiarism, 85–91
  celebrity vs. scholarly publications and, 85–86
  conditions that allow for persistence of, 89–90
  cryptomnesia and, 90
  defined, 85, 86
  detection services, availability of, 83
  excuses for, 89–90
  fear of retaliation for reporting, 89
  frequency of, 4–5, 85
  ghostwriting and, 85
  historical roots of, 75
  Internet and, 76
  likelihood of detection, 85, 86
  misleading readers as to authorship, 85–86
  sanctions and responses to, 87–88, 90
  secondary sources used instead of primary sources, 86–87
  by Trump nominees and appointees, 88
  Trump plagiarizing joke, 91, 181n178
  undermining core values of culture, 91
*Planet Money* (radio show) on mortgage fraud, 109
Plato, 2
Plotz, David, 89–90
Police departments, disciplining officers for adulterous relationships, 120–121
Politicians, punishment for marital infidelity, 124–130
Ponzi schemes, 9–12
Pop Warner football, 22
Pornography, 113
Positive Coaching Alliance, 35
Posner, Richard, 85, 86, 90
Pound, Dick, 27
Prescription fraud, 107
Price, David, 94
Princeton University, 7
Public opinion
  on Clinton's presidency, 129
  on copyright infringement, 93
  ethical attitudes, 133, 134, 138
  on insurance fraud, 103, 110
  on insurance industry's image, 103
  on marital infidelity, 114, 120–121, 122, 131, 190n95, 190n102, 191n103
  on politician's marital infidelity, 124–130
  on schools teaching moral values, 136
  on tax evasion, 64
  on tax system, 68
Public relations campaigns
  insurance fraud and, 111
  making scandals into teachable moments, 138
Punishment. *See* Responses to cheating; Sanctions

Radiohead, 98
Raskolnikov, Alex, 70, 71
Rationalizations, 1, 8, 10–14, 134–135
  for academic cheating, 78–80
  for copyright infringement, 95
  for insurance fraud, 103
  for marital infidelity, 115–116, 119
  for organizational cheating, 42, 44, 45, 54
  for plagiarism, 89–90
  for sports cheating, 20, 22
  for tax evasion, 13, 61, 66–68
Rawls, John, 2
Reid, T.R., 66, 69, 72
Reilly, Rick, 19
Reporting instances of cheating, 139. *See also* Whistle-blowers
  academic cheating, 82, 83
  plagiarism, 89
Reputation, damage to, 3, 21, 54
Rescue attorneys and mortgage fraud, 109
Research misconduct, 84–85
Respect, Integrity, Community, Excellence (RICE) as Enron ethics code, 16
Responses to cheating, 15–18, 135–139
  academic cheating, 80–84, 136–137
  insurance fraud, 110–111
  marital infidelity, 123–131
  organizations, 50–52, 137–139
  parental role, 135
  sanctions, 138. *See also specific types of cheating*
  sports cheating, 30–31, 138
  tax evasion, 68–74
Rest, James, 6, 14
Retaliation for reporting. *See* Whistle-blowers
Retaliatory cheating, 11, 16, 111
Retraction of scientific research findings, 84
Retributive justice, 44
Reward systems, 14
Rhode, Deborah, as legal aid intern, 2–3
Rice, Jerry, 21
Rightscorp, 97
Rogge, Jacques, 31
Role models
  athletes as, 20, 25, 27, 31, 35
  marital infidelity leading to job dismissal for, 120
  moral education best practices and, 137
  organizational leaders as, 16, 46, 52, 53
  parents as, 135, 195n14
  politicians as, 124
  scholars as, 77

teachers and school administrators as, 15, 23, 136–137
U.S. Department of Education head, 88
Roosevelt, Franklin Delano, 124
*Roots* (Haley), 87
Rosenberg , Joshua, 70–71
*Rough Ride* (Krimmage), 27
Runners who recruit workers to file workers' compensation claims, 106
Russia's Ministry of Sport and Federal Security Service, 29

Salomon Brothers, 40, 47
Sanctions, 17, 19, 167n226. *See also* Responses to cheating; Sentencing
academic cheating, 80, 82, 83, 97, 137
doping in athletic competitions, 29
lawyers involved in mortgage fraud, 111
marital infidelity, 123–131
organizations, cheating in, 56–58
plagiarism, 87–88, 90
sports cheating, 30–31
Sanford, Mark, 125, 129–130, 194n197
San Francisco Bay Area mortgage fraud, 109–110
Schools. *See* Academic cheating; Plagiarism
*Science* retracting article due to fabricated research, 84
Scurry, Briana, 24
Sears Roebuck, 14
Securities and Exchange Commission (SEC), 18, 40, 47, 57
Segraves, Donald, 102
Self-interest, 7, 16
Self-perception, distortion of, 3
Self-respect, loss of, 3, 14
Seligman, Martin, 137
Sentencing, 18, 23, 27, 56–57, 96, 107, 122, 167n226
Shackelford, Cynthia, 123
Shakespeare, William, 75
Shaming
of adulterers, 120
as effective social device, 138
of tax evaders, 71
Sharapova, Maria, 26–27
Shell companies, 62
Shell Oil, 54
Shockley, Jeremy, 30
"Should self" vs. "want self," 7, 15
Shulman, David, 38, 40
Siemen executives, 8
Silicon Valley entrepreneurs, 43
Silver, Nate, 130
Sinclair, Upton, 40–41
*60 Minutes* appearance of Bill and Hillary Clinton, 128
Slemrod, Joel, 66, 72, 73
Smith, Jay, 32
Snavely, Carl, 35
Social norms, 5, 9–10, 16, 97, 99, 134–135. *See also* Tax evasion
Southall, Richard, 32
Speeding, 11
Sponsorship of research, 84
Sports cheating, 19–35
baseball players, 21, 28, 30
child athletes, 22
college athletes, 20, 21, 32–34, 137
distance runners, 27
doping, 24–29
eliminating tolerance of, 35
equipment used to cheat, 21
faking injury, 23
figure skating, 22–23
football players, 21–22, 23, 29
golfers, 19–20
hockey players, 22
horse racing, 21
intentional assaults, 22
international soccer, 20–21, 22, 23–24, 30
likelihood of detection, 21, 24, 30
missed opportunities presented by, 34–35
officials engaging in cheating, 23
Olympic games, 19, 23
penalties and enforcement, 29, 30, 137
Pop Warner football teams, 22
professional athletes, 20
rationalizations, 20, 22
recruitment bribes, 22
reinforcement of ethical conduct, 15, 138
rigging matches and betting on outcomes, 20–21
strategies to address, 30–31, 138
techniques of, 20–24
Spotify, 97
Stanford University
on research misconduct, 84
student cheating scandal, 83
Starr, Kenneth, 128–129
State insurance fraud bureaus, 110
Sterne, Laurence, 90
Steroids as performance-enhancing drugs, 24, 26
Stop Online Piracy Act (SOPA, proposed but not enacted), 95
Strategies to address. *See* Responses to cheating
Strauss, Thomas, 48
Strychnine as performance-enhancing drug, 25
Student cheating. *See* Academic cheating
Stumpf, John, 46–47, 52–53, 58
Suarez, Luis, 30
Subprime lending market, 108
Suer, Oral, 5–6
Surveillance, 17, 51
Swift, Jonathan, 90
Sykes, Gresham, 12
Syracuse University curriculum for athletes, 33

System 1 thinking, 7
System 2 thinking, 7, 17

Tax evasion, 61–74
ancient Roman punishment for, 61
audit frequency as deterrent, 69, 138
benefits from tax revenues, need to emphasize, 70–71
by business taxpayers, 64
causes of, 65–68
characterized as victimless crime, 61
costs of, 4, 61, 72
deterrence combined with norm-based enforcement, 71–72
deterrence model and, 65, 68, 69–70
flat tax approach, 73
frequency of, 101
IRS ability to complete taxpayers' forms, 73
IRS detection of, likelihood of, 65
IRS expenditure to detect, 69
likelihood of detection, 64–65, 69, 70
loss of professional license as penalty for, 67
nature and frequency of, 61–64
norms model and, 65, 69, 70–71
penalties inadequate to curtail, 65, 70, 171n108, 171–172n110
perjury attestations as preventive, 72
publication of tax evaders' names, 71
public opinion on evasion, 64
public opinion on tax system, 68
radical simplification of tax code as remedy to, 72–73
rationalizations for, 13, 61, 66–68
sales tax, 72, 73
strategies to address, 68–74
tip income and, 64
underreporting of income, 64
value added tax (VAT), 73–74
wealthy favored by current tax system, 72, 173n147
whistle-blower programs, 70
Teachable moments, 15, 138
Tenbrunsel, Ann, 7, 18
Ten Commandments, 16
Tolstedt, Carrie, 52
Tour de France biking competition, 25, 27
Treviño, Linda, 54, 77
Tribe, Lawrence, 87
Troiana, Ugo, 71
Trudeau, Gary, 18
Trump, Donald
adultery of, 124, 130
Americans' indifference to his cheating, 1, 124
businesses of, failure to pay low-level workers, 39
golf cheating by, 19–20
plagiarism by nominees and appointees of, 88
plagiarism of joke by, 91, 181n178
public paying price for his indifference to ethics, 52
refusal to release tax returns, 63
tax evasion by, 62, 169n15
tax reform as campaign promise, 74
Trump, Melania, plagiarizing from Michelle Obama, 91
Trump Foundation, tax filings of, 63
Trump University, 1, 63
Tru Optik estimate of illegal downloading, 94, 97
Truthfulness. *See* Honesty
Twain, Mark, 139
Tyler, Tom, 96

Undocumented aliens, 39, 40, 63
Unfairness
as factor influencing behavior, 3, 11
in academia, 80, 82
copyright infringement, 96, 99
employee cheating, 44, 51
insurance fraud, 111
Prohibition's failure and, 96
regulatory unfairness, 42
tax evasion, 61, 66– 68
values education and, 135, 136
United Kingdom
"Operation Creative" (persuasive strategy to counter copyright infringement), 98
precision withholding in, 72–73
publication of tax evaders' names in, 71
United Way, 39
University of Dayton firing scientist for plagiarism, 89
University of Michigan curriculum for athletes, 33
University of Minnesota academic assistance for athletes, 33
University of Missouri professor accused of plagiarism, 89
University of North Carolina (UNC) curriculum for athletes, 32–33, 34
University of Oklahoma professor accused of plagiarism, 89
University of Oregon plagiarizing Stanford's teaching assistant handbook, 90
University of Tennessee whistle-blower on academic assistance for athletes, 33
University of Washington academic assistance for athletes, 33
U.S. Anti-Doping Agency, 27, 30
U.S. Figure Skating Association, 23
U.S. Olympic Committee, 26

Valdesolo, Piercarlo, 6
Value added tax (VAT), 73–74
Video downloading. *See* Copyright infringement
Villars, Henry Gauthier, 117
Vinson & Elkins, 50
Volkswagen, 41, 44–45, 47, 57, 160n65

Wade-Benzoni, Kimberly, 7
Wages, 39, 44
Wall Street traders, 39, 40
Walmart, 39, 49–50
"Want self" vs. "should self," 7, 15
Warren, Elizabeth, 57
Watkins, Sherron, 50
Weaver, Gary, 54
Wells Fargo, 17, 40, 43, 44, 46–47, 52–53, 58
West, Cornel, 89
Wharton School, 18
*When Harry Met Sally* (movie), 116
Whistle-blowers
  assessment of effectiveness of, 138
  insurance fraud, 111
  in organizations, 17, 49–50, 55–56
  tax evasion, 70
  University of Tennessee whistle-blower on academic assistance for athletes, 33
White, Mary Jo, 58
White-collar offenders, 8, 12, 13, 18, 37, 43, 56–57, 101, 167n226
White lies, 2
Willful ignorance, 7, 28, 139
Willingham, Mary, 32
Wolfe, Allen, 103, 134
Workers' compensation fraud, 105–106, 111
Workplace cheating. *See* Organizations, cheating in
World Anti-Doping Agency (WADA), 24, 29
WorldCom, 40
World Cup soccer players, 22
Wright, Betsy, 127

Yale University cheating scandals, 75
York Capital Management hedge fund, 52
Young, Andrew, 126, 127

Zambra, Alejandro, 79
Zero tolerance, 111